Learning
RED HAT
LINUX

THIRD EDITION

Bill McCarty

O'REILLY®

Beijing · Cambridge · Farnham · Köln · Paris · Sebastopol · Taipei · Tokyo

Learning Red Hat Linux, Third Edition
by Bill McCarty

Published by O'Reilly & Associates, Inc., 1005 Gravenstein Highway North, Sebastopol, CA 95472.

O'Reilly & Associates books may be purchased for educational, business, or sales promotional use. Online editions are also available for most titles (*safari.oreilly.com*). For more information, contact our corporate/institutional sales department: (800) 998-9938 or *corporate@oreilly.com*.

Editor:	Andy Oram
Production Editor:	Jane Ellin
Cover Designer:	Edie Freedman
Interior Designer:	Bret Kerr

Printing History:

September 1999:	First Edition.
January 2002:	Second Edition.
March 2003:	Third Edition.

ISBN: 0-596-00469-9

[M]

Table of Contents

Preface

You've probably heard about Linux from a magazine, radio or TV program, or a friend. You're wondering what Linux is about and whether you should give it a try. If so, particularly if you currently use Microsoft Windows, this book was written for you.

When the first edition of this book was being written, Linux was a much talked about novelty. Today, Linux has invaded corporate information technology departments, becoming a popular technology used by hobbyists and professionals alike.

As predicted in the first edition of this book, Linux is becoming easier to use. If you work with Microsoft Windows and have dabbled a bit in MS-DOS or are curious about what happens inside Windows, you already have the skills to install and configure Linux. Thousands of people from all walks of life have already done so.

This book is based on Red Hat Linux, the most popular Linux distribution. It includes two CDs that contain everything you need to install and configure your own Red Hat Linux system. This book will make your Linux journey easier by giving you the big picture, providing you with step-by-step procedures, and getting you started doing useful or fun activities such as word processing or games. This book focuses on the needs of the new Linux user and on desktop Linux applications. You'll learn about networks and servers, but the details of those topics are left for more advanced books.

Organization of This Book

Chapter 1, *Why Run Linux?*
>   This chapter is designed to introduce you to Linux and help you determine whether Linux is appropriate for you.

Chapter 2, *Preparing to Install Red Hat Linux*
>   This chapter helps you understand what's involved in installing Red Hat Linux and guides you through the process of gathering information about your system necessary to successfully install Linux.

Chapter 3, *Installing Red Hat Linux*

This chapter takes you step-by-step through the installation of Red Hat Linux.

Chapter 4, *How Linux Works*

Before you can effectively use a desktop environment, you need to know some Linux fundamentals. This chapter explains basic Linux concepts that underlie graphical and nongraphical system use.

Chapter 5, *Using the GNOME and KDE Desktops*

This chapter explains how to configure and use the GNOME and KDE desktop environments.

Chapter 6, *Using Linux Applications*

This chapter describes the OpenOffice.org application suite, the Evolution email client and scheduler, the Pilot/Handspring tool, and GnomeToaster.

Chapter 7, *Conquering the bash Shell*

This chapter digs deeper into the *bash* shell, the Linux command-line interface. You'll learn how to use the Linux command-line interface, which resembles MS-DOS but is much more powerful and sophisticated. Here you'll see firsthand just how powerful and easy to use Linux can be.

Chapter 8, *Installing Software Using the RPM Package Manager*

This chapter explains the RPM Package Manager, which helps you manage programs and applications.

Chapter 9, *Configuring and Administering Linux*

Administering a multiuser operating system such as Linux is somewhat more complicated than administering a single-user operating system, but Linux includes tools that simplify the work. This chapter shows you how to configure your Linux system, including how to configure sound and printers.

Chapter 10, *Connecting to the Internet*

This chapter shows you how to connect to the Internet via your Internet Service Provider (ISP). Once connected, you can use your Linux system to surf the Web and access other familiar Internet services.

Chapter 11, *Setting Up a Networked Workstation*

This chapter shows you how to connect your Linux system to other systems on your Local-Area Network.

Chapter 12, *Setting Up Internet Services*

This chapter shows you how to set up servers that users around the world can access via the Internet. For example, you'll learn how to install and configure Apache, the world's most popular web server.

Chapter 13, *Advanced Shell Usage and Shell Scripts*

This chapter shows how to use advanced shell features and how to create shell scripts that extend the capabilities of Linux.

Appendixes to the book help you locate important files and directories, manage the way your system boots, and use common Linux commands.

Sources of Information

If you are new to the world of Linux, there are a number of resources to explore and become familiar with. Having access to the Internet is helpful, but not essential.

Red Hat's Web Site

Your primary resource for information on Red Hat Linux is Red Hat's web site, *http://www.redhat.com*. Red Hat's web site includes more resources than can be mentioned here. Among the most important are:

The Red Hat Linux 8.0 support page
  http://www.redhat.com/support/resources/howto/rhl80.html

  There, you'll find:

  * The Official Red Hat Linux Installation Guide
  * Hardware Compatibility Lists
  * The Official Red Hat Linux Getting Started Guide
  * Red Hat Linux 8.0 All Errata
  * Red Hat Linux FAQ
  * Red Hat Linux 8.0 Reference Guide
  * Red Hat Linux 8.0 Customization Guide

The *redhat-install-list* mailing list
  https://listman.redhat.com/mailman/listinfo

  Here, you can obtain installation assistance from members of the Red Hat Linux community. Other mailing lists available via this page provide information and assistance useful after you've successfully installed Red Hat Linux.

Bugzilla
  http://bugzilla.redhat.com

  Bugzilla is a database that lists possible bugs affecting Red Hat Linux. The database often gives fixes or workarounds for bugs.

Linux Documentation Project Guides

The Linux Documentation Project (LDP) is a group of volunteers who have worked to produce books (guides), HOWTO documents, and manual pages on topics ranging from installation to kernel programming. More manuals are in development. For more information about the LDP, consult their web server at *http://www.tldp.org* or one of its many mirrors. The LDP works include:

Linux Installation and Getting Started
  By Matt Welsh et al. This book describes how to obtain, install, and use Linux. It includes an introductory Unix tutorial and information on systems administration, the X Window System, and networking.

Linux System Administrators Guide

By Lars Wirzenius and Joanna Oja. This book is a guide to general Linux system administration and covers topics such as creating and configuring users, performing system backups, configuring major software packages, and installing and upgrading software.

Linux System Adminstration Made Easy

By Steve Frampton. This book describes day-to-day administration and maintenance issues of relevance to Linux users.

Linux Programmers Guide

By B. Scott Burkett, Sven Goldt, John D. Harper, Sven van der Meer, and Matt Welsh. This book covers topics of interest to people who wish to develop application software for Linux.

The Linux Kernel

By David A. Rusling. This book provides an introduction to the Linux kernel, how it is constructed, and how it works. Take a tour of your kernel.

The Linux Kernel Module Programming Guide

By Ori Pomerantz. This guide explains how to write Linux kernel modules.

HOWTO documents

The Linux HOWTOs are a comprehensive series of papers detailing various aspects of the system—such as installation and configuration of the X Window System software or how to write in assembly language programming under Linux. These are generally located in the *HOWTO* subdirectory of the FTP sites listed later, or they are available on the Web at one of the many Linux Documentation Project mirror sites. See the file *HOWTO-INDEX* for a list of what's available.

You might want to obtain the *Installation HOWTO*, which describes how to install Linux on your system; the *Hardware Compatibility HOWTO*, which contains a list of hardware known to work with Linux; and the *Distribution HOWTO*, which lists software vendors selling Linux on diskette and CD-ROM.

Linux Frequently Asked Questions

The *Linux Frequently Asked Questions with Answers* (FAQ) contains a wide assortment of questions and answers about the system. It is a must-read for all newcomers.

Documentation Available via the Web

There are many Linux-based web sites available. The home site for the Linux Documentation Project can be accessed at *http://www.tldp.org*. You can find other useful Linux web sites by using a web search engine, such as Linux-powered Google (*http://www.google.com*).

Documentation Available Commercially

O'Reilly & Associates publishes a series of Linux books. They include:

Running Linux
> This installation and user guide to the system describes how to get the most out of personal computing with Linux.

Linux in a Nutshell
> Another in the successful "in a Nutshell" series, this book focuses on providing a broad reference text for Linux.

LPI Linux Certification in a Nutshell
> While this book is geared toward junior-level system administrators who want to take the Linux Professional Institute's exams for Level 1 Certification (LPIC-1), this book is also a great resource for new users, such as yourself.

Linux Journal and Linux Magazine

Linux Journal and *Linux Magazine* are monthly magazines for the Linux community, written and published by a number of Linux activists. They contain articles ranging from novice questions and answers to kernel programming internals. Even if you have Usenet access, these magazines are a good way to stay in touch with the Linux community.

Linux Journal is the older magazine and is published by SSC, Inc., for which details were listed previously. You can also find the magazine on the World Wide Web at *http://www.linuxjournal.com*.

Linux Magazine is a newer, independent publication. The home web site for the magazine is *http://www.linuxmagazine.com*.

Online Linux Support

There are many ways of obtaining help online, where volunteers from around the world offer expertise and services to assist users with questions and problems.

The Freenode is an IRC network devoted entirely to open projects—open source and open hardware alike. Some of its channels are designed to provide online Linux support services. IRC stands for Internet Relay Chat and is a network service that allows you to talk interactively on the Internet to other users. IRC networks support multiple channels on which groups of people talk. Whatever you type in a channel is seen by all other users of that channel.

There are a number of active channels on the OpenProjects IRC network where you will find users 24 hours a day, 7 days a week who are willing and able to help you solve any Linux problems you may have or just chat. You can use this service by installing an IRC client like *irc-II*, connecting to *servername irc.freenode.net:6667*, and joining the *#linpeople* channel.

Linux User Groups (LUGs)

Many Linux user groups around the world offer direct support to users, and many engage in activities such as installation days, talks and seminars, demonstration nights, and other completely social events. Linux user groups are a great way of meeting other Linux users in your area. There are a number of published lists of Linux user groups. Some of the better-known ones are:

Groups of Linux Users Everywhere
  http://www.ssc.com/glue/groups

LUG registry
  http://www.linux.org/users

Other Web Sites

The following are useful Linux-related web sites. Check them out to get the latest information about Linux. Perhaps the most useful is the home page of the Linux Documentation Project (LDP). There, you can find almost anything you want to know about Linux. The Linux Documentation Project web site includes a search engine that makes it easy to find what you need.

Linux Documentation Project
  http://www.tldp.org

Linux Gazette
  http://www.linuxgazette.com

Linux Today
  http://www.linuxtoday.com

Linux Web Ring
  http://nll.interl.net/lwr

  The Linux Web Ring offers a convenient way to explore a variety of Linux-related web sites. Participating web sites present links to one another; by following these links, you can circumnavigate the entire ring or you can use the Web Ring's home page to seek exactly the sort of page you're interested in.

Linux Weekly News
  http://www.lwn.net

O'Reilly & Associates Linux/Unix Center
  http://linux.oreilly.com

Slashdot
  http://www.slashdot.org

  The motto of the Slashdot web site is "News for nerds. Stuff that matters." You'll find a great deal of interesting news and information there, concerning not only Linux, but the open source community and computing generally.

Conventions Used in This Book

The following typographical conventions are used in this book:

Bold

> Used for commands, programs, and options. All terms shown in bold are typed literally.

Italic

> Used to show arguments and variables that should be replaced with user-supplied values. Italic is also used to indicate new terms and URLs, filenames and file extensions, and directories.

`Constant Width`

> Used to show the contents of files or the output from commands.

`Constant Width Bold`

> Used in examples and tables to show commands or other text that should be typed literally by the user.

`Constant Width Italic`

> Used in examples and tables to show text that should be replaced with user-supplied values.

#, $

> Used in some examples as the root shell prompt (#) and as the user prompt ($) under the Bourne or *bash* shells.

This signifies a tip, suggestion, or general note.

This indicates a warning or caution.

A final word about syntax: in many cases, the space between an option and its argument can be omitted. In other cases, the spacing (or lack of spacing) must be followed strictly. For example, **-wn** (no intervening space) might be interpreted differently from **-w** *n*. It's important to notice the spacing used in option syntax.

Path Notation

I use a shorthand notation to indicate paths. Instead of writing "From the Start menu, choose Find, then Files or Folders," I write: Start → Find → Files or Folders. I distinguish menus, dialog boxes, buttons, or other GUI elements only when the context would otherwise be unclear. Simply look for the GUI element whose label matches an element of the path.

Keyboard Accelerators

In a keyboard accelerator (such as **Ctrl-Alt-Del**), a dash indicates that the keys should be held down simultaneously, whereas a space means that the keys should be pressed sequentially. For example, **Ctrl-Esc** indicates that the Control and Escape keys should be held down simultaneously; **Ctrl Esc** means that the Control and Escape keys should be pressed sequentially.

Where a keyboard accelerator contains an uppercase letter, you should not type the Shift key unless it's given explicitly. For example, **Ctrl-C** indicates that you should press the Control and C keys; **Ctrl-Shift-C** indicates that you should press the Control, Shift, and C keys.

How to Contact Us

We have tested and verified the information in this book to the best of our ability, but you may find that features have changed (or even that we have made mistakes!). Please let us know about any errors you find, as well as your suggestions for future editions, by writing:

> O'Reilly & Associates, Inc.
> 1005 Gravenstein Highway North
> Sebastopol, CA 95472
> (800) 998-9938 (in the U.S. or Canada)
> (707) 829-0515 (international/local)
> (707) 829-0104 (fax)

You can also send us messages electronically. To be put on the mailing list or to request a catalog, send email to:

> *info@oreilly.com*

To ask technical questions or comment on the book, send email to:

> *bookquestions@oreilly.com*

We have a web site for the book, were we'll list examples, errata, and any plans for future editions. The site also includes a link to a forum where you can discuss the book with the author and other readers. You can access this site at:

> *http://www.oreilly.com/catalog/redhat3*

For more information about this book and others, see the O'Reilly web site:

> *http://www.oreilly.com*

Acknowledgments

Thanks to my editor, Andy Oram, who—beyond the usual editorial work and assistance—encouraged me to include more "cool stuff" in this book. As a result of

Andy's influence, this book is a great deal more fun to read. Andy also pointed out many errors, clarified many obscure sentences, and suggested many improvements. Thanks too to Margot Maley of Waterside Productions, Inc., who brought this authorship opportunity to my attention. And thanks to Stephanie Jordan of Red Hat for expediting our agreement to use Red Hat's trademark and CD-ROMs.

Several reviewers, some working for O'Reilly & Associates and some working elsewhere, commented on the manuscript and suggested helpful corrections and improvements. In particular, I'd like to thank Laurie Lynne Tucker, who diligently and promptly read the entire manuscript, found and corrected many errors, and suggested many clarifications and improvements. I greatly appreciate the reviewers' assistance and readily confess that any errors in the manuscript were added by me after their reviews and so are entirely my responsibility.

I also acknowledge the love, concern, and support of my savior, Jesus Christ. His perfect love is entirely undeserved.

## CHAPTER 1

Why Run Linux?

Welcome to Linux, the operating system everyone's talking about. Unlike the weather—which proverbial wisdom says you can't do anything about—you *can* do something about Linux. You can run it on your own PC, so that you can see firsthand what the talk is about and perhaps contribute suggestions to its future development.

This chapter is the first leg of your journey into the land of Linux. Here, you'll learn whether this particular journey is right for you and what you can expect down the road. If you're impatient to get started, you can jump ahead to the next chapter, which helps you prepare your PC for installing Linux. But, if you'd like to know more about the history and capabilities of Linux, read on.

What Is Linux?

Linux is an *operating system*, a software program that controls your computer. Most PC vendors load an operating system—generally, Microsoft Windows—onto the hard drive of a PC before delivering the PC; so, unless the hard drive of your PC has failed, you may not understand the function of an operating system.

An operating system handles user interaction with a system and provides a comfortable view of the system. In particular, it solves several problems arising from variation among hardware. As you're aware, no two PC models have identical hardware. For example, some PCs have an IDE hard drive, while others have a SCSI hard drive. Some PCs have one hard drive; others have two or more. Most PCs have a CD-ROM drive, but some do not. Some PCs have an Intel Pentium CPU, while others have an AMD Athlon, and so on.

Suppose that, in a world without operating systems, you're programming a new PC application—perhaps a new multimedia word processor. Your application must cope with all the possible variations of PC hardware. As a result, it becomes bulky and complex. Users don't like it because it consumes too much hard drive space, takes a long time to load, and—because of its size and complexity—has more bugs than it should. Operating systems solve this problem by providing a standard way for applications to access hardware devices. Thanks to the operating system, applications can be more compact, because they share the commonly used code for accessing the hardware. Applications can also be more reliable, because common code is written only once—and by expert programmers rather than by application programmers.

As you'll soon learn, operating systems do many other things as well; for example, they generally provide a filesystem so you can store and retrieve data and a user interface so you can control your computer. However, if you think of a computer's operating system as its subconscious mind, you won't be far off the mark. It's the computer's conscious mind—applications such as word processors and spreadsheets—that do useful work. But, without the subconscious—the operating system—the computer would cease breathing and applications would not function.

Pronouncing Linux

Internet newsgroup participants have long debated the proper pronunciation of Linux. Because Linus Torvalds originated the Linux kernel, it seems reasonable that his pronunciation of the word should reign as the standard. However, Linus is Finnish and his pronunciation of *Linux* is difficult for English speakers to approximate. Consequently, many variations in pronunciation have arisen. The most popular pronunciation sounds as though the word were spelled *Linnucks*, with the stress on the first syllable and a short *i*.

If your computer has a sound card, you can hear how Linus Torvalds pronounces Linux: *www.ssc.com/lj/linuxsay.html*. Linus's personal opinion is that how you pronounce *Linux* matters much less than whether you use it.

Desktop and Server Operating Systems

Now that you know what an operating system is, you may be wondering what operating systems other PC users are using. According to the market research firm IDC, Microsoft products account for about 92 percent of sales of desktop operating systems. Because Linux is a free operating system, Linux sales are a mere fraction of actual Linux installations. Unlike most commercial operating systems, Linux is not sold under terms of a per-seat license; a company is free to purchase a single Linux CD-ROM and install Linux on as many systems as they like. So, sales figures understate the popularity of Linux. Moreover, it's important to consider who uses a product and what they use it for, rather than merely the number of people using it. Linux is particularly popular among power users who run web sites and database and who do their own programming. Hence, though Linux *is* popular, its influence exceeds its popularity.

Later in this chapter you'll learn how Linux is distributed, but notice that Linux was termed a *free* operating system. If you have a high-speed Internet connection, you can download, install, and use Linux without paying anyone for anything (except perhaps your Internet Service Provider, who may impose a connection fee). It's anyone's guess how many people have downloaded Linux, but it appears that about 10 million computers now run Linux.

This book focuses on how Linux can be used on the desktop. However, if you plan to set up a Linux server and are unfamiliar with Linux and Unix, this book is also right for you

This book will take you through the basics of setting up and using Linux as a desktop system. After you've mastered what this book offers, you should consult *Running Linux*, by Matt Welsh, Matthias Kalle Dalheimer Terry Dawson, and Lar Kaufman (O'Reilly & Associates, Inc.), a more advanced book that focuses on setting up and using Linux servers. You might also enjoy *Linux in a Nutshell*, by Ellen Siever, Stephen Spainhour, Jessica P. Hekman, and Stephen Figgins (O'Reilly & Associates, Inc.); this book puts useful Linux reference information at your fingertips. *LPI Linux Certification in a Nutshell* by Jeffrey Dean (O'Reilly & Associates, Inc.) is a concise summary of Linux system administration information and procedures that's useful whether or not you're interested in seeking certification.

GNU/Linux

Properly speaking, the name *Linux* applies to the Linux kernel, the most basic and fundamental part of a computer operating system, rather than the entire operating system. Some people prefer to refer to the Linux operating system as GNU/Linux. Doing so emphasizes the contribution of the GNU project—which is described later in this chapter—to the development of the Linux operating system. However, Red Hat calls its operating system Red Hat Linux, not Red Hat GNU/Linux. Therefore, in this book we refer to both the kernel and operating system as Linux. Context will help you understand whether the entire operating system or only the kernel is meant.

How Linux Is Different

Linux is distinguished from other popular operating systems in three important ways:

- Linux is a cross-platform operating system that runs on many computer models. Only Unix, an ancestor of Linux, rivals Linux in this respect. In comparison, Windows 2000 and XP run only on CPUs having the Intel architecture.
- Linux is free, in two senses. First, as mentioned earlier, you can obtain and use Linux without paying anything to anybody. On the other hand, you may choose

to purchase Linux from a vendor who bundles Linux with special documentation or applications or who provides technical support. However, even in this case, the cost of Linux is likely to be a fraction of what you'd pay for another operating system. So, Linux is free or nearly free in an economic sense.

Second, and more important, Linux and many Linux applications are distributed in source form. This makes it possible for you and others to modify or improve them. You're *not* free to do this with most operating systems, which are distributed in binary form. For example, you can't make changes to Windows or Office—only Microsoft can do that. Because of this freedom, Linux is being constantly improved and updated, far outpacing the rate of progress of any other operating system. For example, Linux was the first operating system to support Intel's Itanium 64-bit CPU.

- Linux has more attractive features and performance. Free access to Linux source code lets programmers around the world implement new features and tweak Linux to improve its performance and reliability. The best of these features and tweaks are incorporated in the Linux kernel or made available as kernel patches or applications. Not even Microsoft can mobilize and support a software development team as large and dedicated as the volunteer Linux software development team, which numbers in the hundreds of thousands, including programmers, code reviewers, and testers.

The Origins of Linux

Linux traces its ancestry back to a mainframe operating system known as Multics (Multiplexed Information and Computing Service). Multics was one of the first multiuser computer systems and is still in use today. Participating in its development, which began in 1965, was Bell Telephone Labs, along with the Massachusetts Institute of Technology (MIT) and General Electric.

Two Bell Labs software engineers, Ken Thompson and Dennis Ritchie, worked on Multics until Bell Labs withdrew from the project in 1969. One of their favorite pastimes during the project was playing a multiuser game called Space Travel. Without access to a Multics computer, they found themselves unable to indulge their fantasies of flying around the galaxy. Resolving to remedy this, they decided to port the Space Travel game to run on an otherwise unused PDP-7 computer. Eventually, they implemented a rudimentary operating system they named *Unics*, as a pun on *Multics*. Somehow, the spelling of the name became *Unix*.

Their operating system was novel in several respects, most notably its portability. Most previous operating systems had been written for a specific target computer. Just as a tailor-made suit fits only its owner, such an operating system could not be easily adapted to run on an unfamiliar computer. In order to create a portable operating system, Ritchie and Thompson first created a programming language called C. Like assembly language, C let a programmer access low-level hardware facilities not available to programmers writing in a high-level language such as FORTRAN or COBOL. But, like FORTRAN and COBOL, a C program was not bound to a particular computer. Just as a ready-made suit can be altered here and there to fit a purchaser, writing Unix in C made it possible to easily adapt Unix to run on computers other than the PDP-7.

As word of their work spread and interest grew, Ritchie and Thompson made copies of Unix freely available to programmers around the world. These programmers revised and improved Unix, sending word of their changes back to Ritchie and Thompson, who incorporated the best improvements in their version of Unix. Eventually, several Unix variants arose. Prominent among these was BSD (Berkeley Systems Division) Unix, written at the University of California, Berkeley, in 1978. Bill Joy—one of the principals of the BSD project—later became a founder of Sun Microsystems, which sold another Unix variant (originally called SunOS and later called Solaris) to power its workstations. In 1984, AT&T, the parent company of Bell Labs, began selling its own version of Unix, known as System V.

Free Software

What Ritchie and Thompson began in a distinctly noncommercial fashion ended up spawning several legal squabbles. When AT&T grasped the commercial potential of Unix, it claimed Unix as its intellectual property and began charging a hefty licensing fee to those who wanted to use it. Soon, others who had implemented Unix-like operating systems were distributing licenses only for a fee. Understandably, those who had contributed improvements to Unix considered it unfair for AT&T and others to appropriate the fruits of their labors. This concern for profit was at odds with the democratic, share-and-share-alike spirit of the early days of Unix.

Some, including MIT scientist Richard M. Stallman, yearned for the return of those happier times and the mutual cooperation of programmers that had existed. So, in 1983, Stallman launched the GNU (*GNU's not Unix*) project, which aimed at creating a free Unix-like operating system. Like early Unix, the GNU operating system was to be distributed in source form so that programmers could read, modify, and redistribute it without restriction. Stallman's work at MIT had taught him that, by using the Internet as a means of communication, programmers could improve and adapt software at incredible speed, far outpacing the fastest rate possible using traditional software development models, in which few programmers actually see one another's source code.

As a means of organizing work on the GNU project, Stallman and others created the Free Software Foundation (FSF), a nonprofit corporation that seeks to promote free software and eliminate restrictions on the copying, redistribution, understanding, and modification of software. Among other activities, the FSF accepts tax-deductible charitable contributions and distributes copies of software and documentation for a small fee, using this revenue to fund its operations and support development activities.

If you find it peculiar that the FSF charges a fee—even a small fee—for "free" software, you should understand that the FSF intends the word *free* to refer primarily to freedom, not price. The FSF believes in three fundamental software freedoms:

- You can copy GNU software and give it away to anyone you choose.
- If you're a programmer, you can modify GNU software any way you like, because you have access to the source code. In return, your modified code should be available for others so they can enjoy the privileges of learning from and modifying it.
- You must provide a free copy of the source so that you cannot unfairly profit by changing the original.

Copyleft

Commercial software vendors protect their proprietary rights to software by copyrighting the software. In contrast, the FSF protects software freedom by *copylefting* its software under the GNU General Public License (GPL). To copyleft software, the FSF uses the same legal instrument used by proprietary software vendors—the copyright—but the FSF adds special license terms that guarantee freedom to users of the software. These terms give everyone the right to use, modify, and redistribute the software (or any software derived from it), but only if the distribution terms are unchanged. Thus, someone who attempts to transform FSF software into a proprietary product thereby loses the right to use, modify, or distribute the product.

If, rather than copyright its software, the FSF placed its software in the public domain, others would be free to transform it into a proprietary product, denying users the freedom intended by the original author of the software. For example, a company might distribute the software in binary rather than source form and require payment of a license fee for the privilege of making additional copies.

As the FSF puts it: "Proprietary software developers use copyright to take away the users' freedom; we use copyright to guarantee their freedom. That's why we reverse the name, changing *copyright* into *copyleft*."

The Linux Kernel

By the early 1990s, the FSF had obtained or written all the major components of the GNU operating system except for one: the kernel. About that time, Linus Torvalds, a Finnish computer science student, began work on a kernel for a Unix-like system. Linus had been working with Minix, a Unix-like operating system written by Andrew Tannenbaum primarily for pedagogical use. Linus was disappointed by the performance of the Minix kernel and believed that he could do better. He shared his preliminary work with others on Internet newsgroups. Soon, programmers around the world were working together to extend and improve his kernel, which became known as Linux (for *Linus's Minix*). As Table 1-1 shows, Linux grew rapidly. Linux was initially released on October 5, 1991, and as early as 1992, Linux had been integrated with GNU software and other open source software (*http://www.opensource. org*) to produce a fully functional operating system, which became known as Linux after the name of its kernel.

Table 1-1. The history of Linux

Version	Year	Estimated users	Kernel size (Kbytes)	Milestone(s)
0.01	1991	100	63	Linus Torvalds writes the Linux kernel.
0.99	1992	1000	431	GNU software is integrated with the Linux kernel, producing a fully functional operating system.
0.99	1993	20,000	938	High rate of code contributions prompts Linus to delegate code review responsibility.
1.0	1994	100,000	1,017	First production is released.
1.2	1995	500,000	1,850	Linux is ported to non-Intel processors.
2.0	1996	1,500,000	4,718	Linux supports multiple processors, IP masquerading, and Java.
2.2	1999	7,500,000	10,593	Linux growth rate exceeds that of Windows NT, according to market research firm Dataquest.
2.4	2001	10,000,000	19,789	Linux invades the enterprise as major companies begin using it.

Work on Linux has not ceased. Since the initial production release, the pace of development has accelerated as Linux has been adapted to include support for non-Intel processors and even multiple processors, sophisticated TCP/IP networking facilities such as firewalling, network address translation (NAT), and more. Versions of Linux are now available for such computer models and architectures as the PowerPC, the Compaq/DEC Alpha, the Motorola 68k, the Sun SPARC, the MIPS, and many others. Moreover, Linux does not implement an obscure Unix variant: it generally complies with the POSIX (Portable Operating System Interface) standard that forms the basis of the X/Open specifications of The Open Group.

The X Window System

Another important component of Linux is its *graphical user interface* (GUI; pronounced *gooey*), the *X Window System*. Unix was originally a mouse-less, text-based system that used noisy teletype machines rather than modern video monitors. The Unix command interface is very sophisticated and, even today, some power users prefer it to a point-and-click graphical environment, using their video monitors as though they are noiseless teletypes. Consequently, some remain unaware that Unix long ago outgrew its text-based childhood and now provides users a choice of graphical or command interfaces.

The X Window System (or simply *X*) was developed as part of MIT's Project Athena, which it began in 1984. By 1988, MIT released X to the public. MIT has since turned development of X over to the X Consortium. The XFree86 Project, Inc., in cooperation with the X Consortium, distributes a version of X that runs on Intel-architecture PCs.

X is a unique graphical user interface in three major respects:

- X integrates with a computer network, letting users access local and remote applications. For example, X lets you open a window that represents an application running on a remote host: the remote host does the heavy-duty computing; all your computer need do is pass the host your input and display the resulting output.

- X lets you configure its look and feel to an amazing degree. To do so, you run a special application—called a *window manager*—on top of X. A variety of window managers is available, including some that closely mimic the look and feel of Microsoft Windows. Desktop managers further extend X by providing common applications such as file browsers, menus, and control panels. GNOME and KDE are the most popular Linux desktop managers and are discussed in this book.

- X is optional. Systems used as servers are often configured without a GUI, saving resources to serve client requests.

Linux Distributions

Because Linux can be freely redistributed, you can obtain it in a variety of ways. Various individuals and organizations package Linux, often combining it with free or proprietary applications. Such a package that includes all the software you need to install and run Linux is called a *Linux distribution*. Table 1-2 shows some of the most popular Linux distributions.

Table 1-2. Popular Linux distributions and their home pages

Distribution	Home page
Debian GNU/Linux	*http://www.debian.org*
Linux-Mandrake	*http://www.linux-mandrake.com*
Red Hat Linux	*http://www.redhat.com*
Slackware Linux	*http://www.slackware.com*
SuSE Linux	*http://www.suse.com*

Red Hat, Linux-Mandrake, SuSE, and Slackware are packaged by commercial companies, which seek to profit by selling Linux-related products and services. However, because Linux is distributed under the GNU GPL, you can download these distributions from the respective companies' web sites or make additional copies of a

Linux distribution you purchase. (Note, however, that you cannot necessarily make additional copies of proprietary software that these companies may distribute with their Linux distribution.) Debian GNU/Linux is the product of volunteer effort conducted under the auspices of Software in the Public Interest, Inc. (*http://www.spi-inc. org*), a nonprofit corporation. This book is bundled with a copy of Red Hat Linux, which you can install and run on your PC and redistribute freely under the terms of the GPL and other applicable licenses. See installation CD-ROM 1 for details.

Linux Features and Performance

The origins of Linux and the availability of its source code set it apart from other operating systems. But most users choose an operating system based on features and performance—and Linux delivers these in spades.

Linux runs on a wider range of hardware platforms and runs adequately on less costly and powerful systems than other operating systems. Moreover, Linux systems are generally highly reliable.

But this impressive inventory of selling points doesn't end the matter. Let's consider some other technical characteristics of Linux that distinguish it from the pack.

Cost
> Foremost in the minds of many is the low cost of Linux. Comparable server operating systems can cost more than $100,000. On the other hand, the low cost of Linux makes it practical for use even as a desktop operating system. In that mode, it truly eclipses the competition.

Power
> Many desktop systems are employed as servers. Because of its design and heritage, the features and performance of Linux readily outshine those of desktop operating systems used as makeshift servers. For example, Microsoft's software license for Windows NT/2000 restricts the number of authenticated client connections; if you want your Windows NT/2000 server to be able to handle 100 authenticated clients, you must pay Microsoft a hefty license fee. However, Linux imposes no such restriction; your Linux desktop or server system is free to accept as many client connections as you think it can handle.

Reliability
> Again, because of its design and heritage, Linux provides more reliable data storage than competing desktop operating systems. Most Linux users store their disk data using the *ext3* filesystem, which is superior in performance and reliability to filesystems (partition types) provided by Microsoft operating systems, including FAT, FAT32, and NTFS. Of course, if you're worried about losing a whole disk to hardware failure, you can outfit Linux with the powerful standard known as Redundant Array of Independent Disks (RAID).

Microsoft claims that its NTFS filesystem is so reliable that you'll probably never need special software tools to recover lost data—truth is, Microsoft provides no such tools. Despite Microsoft's ambitious claims, some Windows NT users report that NTFS reliability is less than satisfactory. Here's a case in point:

> When my Windows NT workstation crashed a little over a year ago I discovered that its NTFS filesystem was damaged. I searched the Microsoft web site for recovery instructions and tools and found nothing that helped. So I went to my local software store and purchased a third-party disk recovery tool for Windows NT. When I opened the box, I was angered to discover that it supported recovery of FAT and FAT32 data, but not NTFS data.
>
> Eventually, I recovered 95 percent of my data by using a free Linux utility that was able to open the damaged NTFS partition and copy its files. If I'd been without Linux, I'd be without my data.

If you're an old computer dog who remembers the days of MS-DOS, you may have a fondness for what's now called the MS-DOS Prompt window or the Command Line Interface (CLI). However, if you've worked exclusively within the Windows point-and-click environment, you may not fully understand what the MS-DOS Prompt window is about. By typing commands in the MS-DOS Prompt window, you can direct the computer to perform a variety of tasks.

For most users, the MS-DOS Prompt is not as convenient as the GUI offered by Windows. That's because you must know the commands the operating system understands and must type them correctly if you expect the operating system to do your bidding.

However, the MS-DOS Prompt window lets you accomplish tasks that would be cumbersome and time-consuming if performed by pointing and clicking. Linux comes with a similar command interface, known as the *shell*. But, the word *similar* fails to do justice to the Linux shell's capabilities, because the MS-DOS Prompt provides only a fraction of the capabilities provided by the Linux shell.

You may have used the MS-DOS Prompt and, finding it distastefully cumbersome, forever rejected it in favor of pointing and clicking. If so, you'll be pleasantly surprised to see how easy it is to use the Linux shell. You'll certainly be pleased—perhaps amazed—by the enormous power it offers. Moreover, you can customize the operation of the Linux shell in an almost limitless number of ways and even choose from among a variety of shells, and automate your work by combining commands into files called *shell scripts*. You'll learn more about the Linux shell in Chapter 7.

If you're a programmer, you'll also admire the ease with which it's possible to develop portable, Unix-compliant software. Linux comes with a suite of software development tools, including an assembler, C/C++ compilers, a *make* application, and a source code librarian. All of these are freely distributable programs made available under the terms of the GNU GPL.

Reasons to Choose or Not Choose Linux

Notwithstanding its high points, Linux is not for everyone. You should approach your decision to use Linux as you'd approach any decision, by evaluating the pros and cons. Here are several reasons to run Linux:

You want a stable and reliable computing platform.
No popular operating system is more stable and reliable than Linux. If you're tired of crashes and hangs and the lost time and data they entail, you're a candidate for Linux.

You want a high-performance computing platform.
Linux can coax blazingly fast performance out of hardware below the minimum required to load and run other popular operating systems. And with ample memory and a fast CPU, Linux goes toe-to-toe with anything Microsoft or other vendors offer. If speed is your thing, Linux is your hot rod.

You need a low-cost or free operating system.
If you're on a budget or if you need to set up many systems, the low cost of Linux will let you reserve your hard-earned capital for hardware or other resources. Linux is the best operating system value on the planet.

You're a heavy network or Internet user.
If you use networks, especially the Internet, Linux's advanced support for TCP/IP may light up your life. Linux makes it easy to construct firewalls that protect your system against hackers or routers that let several computers share a single network connection.

You want to learn Unix or TCP/IP networking.
The best way—perhaps the only way—to learn more about Unix or TCP/IP networking (or computers generally) is through hands-on experience. Whether you're interested in such experience owing to personal curiosity or career ambition (system administrators are often handsomely paid), Linux affords you the opportunity to gain such experience at low cost, without leaving the comfort of your home.

You seek an alternative to Microsoft's vision of computing's future.
If you're tired of marching to the relentless drumbeat of the Redmond juggernaut, Linux offers a viable way to cut the umbilical cord and set about creating a new, open source computing destiny for yourself and others.

You want to have fun.
Hopefully, you've discovered that one of the best reasons for doing anything is that it's fun. Many Linux users report that they've never had so much fun with a computer. There's no better reason for running Linux than that.

To be frank, some folks shouldn't run Linux. If one or more of the following are true of you, you should run Linux *only* if you have a good friend who's knowledgeable about Linux, available by phone at odd hours, and works cheap:

You're scared of computers.
> If you're scared of computers, you should spend more time working with Windows 98/2000 before venturing into the Linux world. Linux may indeed be right for you, but it's not right just yet.

You don't like, or don't have the time and inclination, to tinker and learn.
> Setting up and running Linux will require you to learn new concepts and skills. None of these is especially difficult, but unless you're enthusiastic about learning and playing around, setting up and running Linux will stress you out. Instead, you should stick with the familiar.

You're married to certain Windows applications.
> You can run some Windows applications under Linux's WINE emulation, but this isn't true of every Windows application. Before putting your toe in the Linux waters, you should obtain up-to-date information on the status of WINE emulation of your favorite Windows applications (see *http://www.winehq.com*). Alternatively, you can purchase the commercial products VMware (see *http://www.vmware.com*) or Win4Lin (see *http://www.netraverse.com*) that enable you to run Windows applications or Windows itself under Linux.

> Rather than convert your desktop system to run Linux, you may prefer to install Linux on a second system or to set up your computer as a dual-boot system, running both Windows and Linux on separate partitions of a single hard drive. That way, you have your choice of running your favorite Windows applications or Linux whenever you desire.

> On the other hand, the quality of Linux applications continues to improve. Many Linux users are quite satisfied with Linux applications and desktop suites such as OpenOffice, which provides word processing, spreadsheet, and presentation programs. So, unless your marriage to Windows applications includes a formal vow, you may want to reconsider your marital status.

You're addicted to 3D gaming.
> 3D gaming is a resource-intensive form of computing. To provide the best possible gaming experience, designers of 3D games strive to take full benefit of advanced capabilities of sophisticated graphics adapters. However, manufacturers of graphic adapters do not always provide Linux-compatible drivers. And, even if a Linux-compatible driver is available for your graphics adapter, it may not fully support the adapter's capabilities. Moreover, relatively few game publishers release Linux versions of their games. So, if you're a 3D game aficionado, you'll likely prefer to keep one foot in the Windows world. But, that doesn't mean that you shouldn't run Linux; only that you probably shouldn't run *only* Linux.

Still game? Excellent! Please proceed to Chapter 2 and prepare to install Linux.

Preparing to Install Red Hat Linux

Before installing Linux, you must first gather some information about your system. This chapter presents information you need to know and tasks you need to perform before installing Linux. It helps you make certain that your IBM-compatible PC meets the minimum hardware requirements for Linux. It shows you how to document your Windows operating system configuration so that you can respond to questions presented by the Linux install procedure. It also describes the four types of Red Hat Linux installations. And, finally, it shows you how to prepare your hard disk for Linux.

Minimum Hardware Requirements

Linux supports a wide range of PC hardware, but not even Linux supports every known device and system. Your PC must meet certain minimum requirements in order to run Linux, which I describe in the following sections. For the latest and most complete information, you should check Red Hat's hardware compatibility web site, *http://hardware.redhat.com*. This site will also help you determine whether Linux supports the devices installed in your system. If you're not familiar with PC hardware, check out Robert and Barbara Thompson's *PC Hardware in a Nutshell: A Desktop Quick Reference* (O'Reilly), an excellent introduction and reference to PC hardware.

Central Processing Unit (CPU)

Red Hat Linux does not support the Intel i386 and earlier processors. However, it fully supports the Intel i486, Celeron, Pentium, Pentium Pro, Pentium II, Pentium III, and Pentium IV processors. Red Hat Linux also supports non-Intel processors such as the Cyrix 6x86 and the AMD K5, K6, and Athlon. However, a few problems are unique to non-Intel processors. For example, Red Hat reports that some AMD K6 systems freeze during the Linux install. Similarly, some users have also reported installation problems with AMD Athlons, which were solved by updating their system BIOS or replacing their system motherboard.*

Motherboard

The motherboard is the main part of a PC. It holds the CPU, RAM, and other internal computer components, linked by several buses. Red Hat Linux supports the standard ISA, EISA, PCI, and VESA (VLB) system buses used on most IBM-compatible PCs, as well as the AGP, USB, and IEEE 1394 (FireWire) auxiliary buses.

Your motherboard should include at least 64 MB of RAM for optimum Red Hat Linux performance. Some very determined and skilled users have managed to coax Linux into working on systems with as little as 4 MB of RAM. However, Red Hat does not recommend or support systems containing so little RAM. A handful of motherboards present special problems when installing Red Hat Linux. Generally, problems stem from a bad BIOS, for which a fix is often available. Check the Red Hat web site for details; the best way to do so is via the search page at *http://www.redhat.com/apps/support*.

Drives

An anonymous wag once quipped that one can never be too thin, be too rich, or have too much hard disk space. Fortunately, Linux is not extremely hungry for disk space. To install and use Red Hat Linux, you should have a minimum of 400 MB of free hard disk space. More realistically, you should have at least 2 GB.

For convenient installation using the CDs included with this book, your system needs a CD-ROM drive (both common types, IDE and SCSI, are acceptable). Most recently manufactured PCs can boot from a CD-ROM. If your PC can't do so, your system should include a 3.5-inch floppy drive. You'll use the floppy drive to boot your system from a special Linux diskette you create. Instructions for how to create the boot floppy can be found in Chapter 3.

 It's also possible to install Linux from a PCMCIA CD-ROM drive; an FTP, Web, or NFS server; or a hard drive. See the *Red Hat Linux 8.0 Installation Guide* and *Red Hat Linux 8.0 Reference Guide*, available at *http://www.redhat.com/docs/manuals/linux/*.

Collecting Information About Your System

Before you launch into the installation process, you should collect some basic information about your system. Generally, Red Hat's installer will successfully probe your

---

* Two of my Linux systems use AMD CPUs—a K6 and an Athlon; neither has presented special problems.

system and discover its configuration, but when it fails to do so, you must be prepared to supply the required information. Otherwise, you'll be forced to terminate the installation procedure, obtain the information, and then start all over again.

Information You Need

Table 2-1 specifies the configuration information you need and gives you space to conveniently record the information as you gather it. If your system currently runs Windows, you can obtain much of the needed information by using Windows utilities, as explained in the next section. To obtain the remaining information, you can consult your system documentation and the documentation for any devices installed by you. If your documentation is missing or incomplete, you may need to contact your hardware vendor or manufacturer. Alternatively, you may be able to find the needed information on the manufacturer's web site; use a search engine such as Google (which is powered by Linux) to discover the URL of the web site.

Sometimes, you'll need to examine your system's BIOS settings or open your system's case and examine the installed hardware; consult your system documentation to learn how to do so. Finally, if you're installing Linux in a large organization such as a business or a university, your system administrator might be a sympathetic (or not always sympathetic) source of the information you need.

Table 2-1. Configuration information needed to install Red Hat Linux

Device	Information needed
Hard drive(s)	The number, size, and model of each hard drive.
	Which hard drive is first, second, and so on.
	Which adapter type (IDE or SCSI) is used by each drive.
	For each IDE drive, whether or not the BIOS is set for LBA mode.
	The number and type of each existing partition and the amount of free disk space.
CD-ROM drive(s)	Which adapter type (IDE, SCSI, or other) is used by each drive.
	For each drive using a non-IDE, non-SCSI adapter, the make and model of the drive.
SCSI adapter (if any)	The make and model of the adapter.
RAM memory	The amount of installed RAM.
Video adapter	The make and model of the adapter and the amount of installed video RAM.
Video monitor	The make and model of the video monitor and the manufacturer's specifications, if available, especially the horizontal and vertical sync (refresh) rates.
Mouse	The type (serial, PS/2, or bus).
	The protocol (Microsoft, Logitech, MouseMan, etc.).
	The number of buttons.
	For a serial mouse, the serial port to which it's connected (COM1 or COM2).
Sound adapter (if any)	The make, chipset, and model of the adapter.
Network adapter (if any)	The make and model of the card.

Device	Information needed
IP address	The dotted-quad number, such as 10.1.2.7, that identifies your system to other Internet hosts. Many Internet Service Providers (ISPs) assign IP addresses dynamically, by using a DHCP server; in that case, you don't need to know the IP address of your system.
Netmask	A dotted-quad number that identifies the portion of your system's IP address that specifies its network address. The number typically contains one or more instances of the value 255. If your ISP is using DHCP, you don't need to know the netmask.
Gateway IP address	The IP address of the host that routes traffic between your system and the Internet. If your ISP is using DHCP, you don't need to know the gateway IP address.
DNS server	The IP address of one or more Internet hosts that provide domain name services (DNS) for your system. If your ISP is using DHCP, you don't need to know the DNS servers.
Domain name	The domain name of your system. This generally looks like *xxx*.net or *xxx*.com, with *xxx* identifying your Internet Service Provider. If your ISP is using DHCP, you don't need to know the domain name.
Hostname	The hostname of your system. You can generally find the hostname prefixed to the domain name. If your ISP is using DHCP, you don't need to know the hostname.

Collecting Configuration Information from Windows

If you run Windows 95/98, 2000, or XP, you can obtain much of the information needed to install Linux by using the Windows System Properties dialog box, which you can launch by using the Control Panel. Get the information as follows:

1. Click on the Start menu. A pop-up menu appears.

2. Select Settings on the pop-up menu and click on Control Panel in the submenu. The Control Panel appears.

3. Double-click on System. The System Properties dialog box appears. If necessary, click on the General tab, so that the dialog box resembles the one shown in Figure 2-1.

   The General tab of the System Properties dialog box shows the type of your system's processor and the amount of installed RAM.

4. Click on the Device Manager Tab (Windows 95/98) or Control Panel → Administrative Tools → Computer Management → Device Manager (Windows 2000/ XP) tab. The path you use to find the Device Manager may vary a bit, depending on your operating system and its configuration. The Device Manager appears, as shown in Figure 2-2.

   You can double-click on an icon (or single-click on the Plus key adjacent to an icon) to obtain additional information.

   You can gather the following information from the Device Manager tab:

   • The number and type (IDE or SCSI) of your system's hard drives

   • The make and model of CD-ROM drives

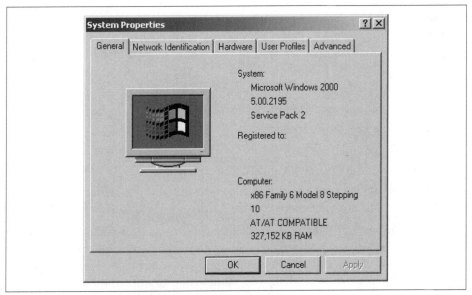

Figure 2-1. The General tab of the System Properties dialog box

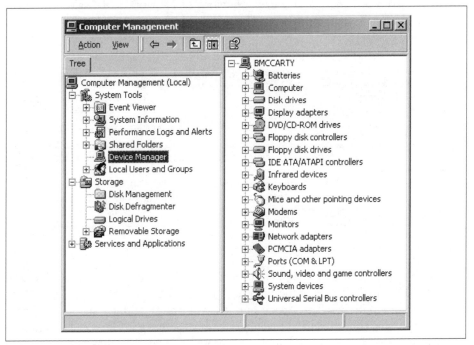

Figure 2-2. The Device Manager

Some installed CD-ROM drives do not appear in the Device Manager tab of the System Properties dialog box. Often the *C:\CONFIG.SYS* file will contain clues that help you learn more about such drives.

- The make and model of SCSI adapters, if any
- The make and model of the video adapter
- The type of mouse installed
- The make and model of multimedia adapters, such as sound cards, if any
- The make and model of network adapters, if any

When you've recorded the information provided by the Device Manager tab, click Cancel to exit the System Properties dialog box.

Red Hat Linux supports dial-up networking, as explained in Chapter 10. But the installation program doesn't configure dial-up networking, so you don't need to collect information about dial-up networking prior to installation. However, if your computer is attached to a network, you should collect information describing your network adapter:

1. In the Control Panel, double-click Network or Network and Dial-up Connections to launch the Network and Dial-up Connections dialog box, as shown in Figure 2-3.

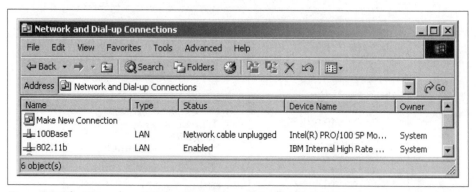

Figure 2-3. The Network and Dial-up Connections dialog box

2. Double-click your Ethernet adapter and then the associated Internet Protocol (TCP/IP) entry, launching the Internet Protocol (TCP/IP) Properties dialog box, shown in Figure 2-4. This dialog box tells you the IP address and subnet mask (netmask) of your system. If the "Obtain an IP address automatically" button is selected, the IP address and subnet mask will be blank. In that case, you don't need to be concerned about them because a DHCP server on your network supplies the network configuration automatically; Red Hat Linux can obtain its network configuration from this same server.

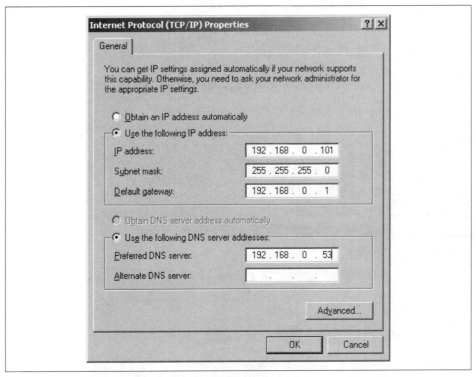

Figure 2-4. The Internet Protocol (TCP/IP) Properties dialog box

3. Click the Advanced button and then the DNS tab of the Advanced TCP/IP Settings dialog box. This tab, shown as Figure 2-5, provides the Host (hostname), Domain (domain name), and DNS Server information you'll need during installation.

4. Finally, click Cancel once to close the Advanced TCP/IP Settings dialog box and again to close the TCP/IP Properties dialog box. Clicking Cancel again closes the Network dialog box.

Installation Types

Red Hat Linux defines four installation types: *Personal Desktop*, *Workstation*, *Server*, and *Custom*. In addition, it is possible to upgrade an existing Red Hat Linux installation by selecting the Upgrade option.*

---

* Upgrading an existing Red Hat system is beyond the scope of this book, so we will not be covering the "Upgrade" installation option in Chapter 3.

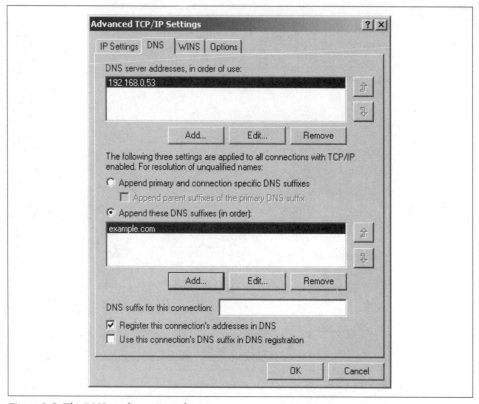

Figure 2-5. The DNS configuration tab

Personal Desktop Installation

If you're new to Linux, the Personal Desktop installation type is the easiest to perform, especially if you currently run Windows. In that case, the procedure will automatically configure your system to dual boot—in other words, whenever you start your system, a Linux utility known as GRUB will give you the choice of starting Windows or Linux. Both operating systems can reside on a single system as long as you have a large enough hard drive. A typical Personal Desktop installation requires at least 2 GB of free disk space. However, 4 GB or more is a better working figure, as optional applications and extra packages can consume significant space beyond the minimum.

 Even though the Personal Desktop installation type is generally the easiest, I recommend that you choose the Custom installation type, which is explained later. The Custom installation type is more flexible and therefore better able to help you cope with problems that may arise during installation.

Workstation Installation

The Workstation Installation type is based on the Personal Desktop installation type, to which it adds tools useful to software developers and system administrators. Like the Personal Desktop installation type, the Workstation Installation type requires 2–4 GB of free disk space.

Server Installation

The Server installation type is appropriate for systems that will host a web server or other services. It does not include a GUI, so it's not suitable for desktop use. You shouldn't set up a system using the Server installation type until you've had significant experience with Red Hat Linux. A typical Server installation requires from 1.3 to 2.3 GB or more of free disk space.

The Server installation type *destroys all data* on your hard drive, including any existing Windows and non-Windows partitions. Do not perform a Server installation if you want to preserve *any* data on your system.

Custom Installation

The Custom installation type gives you complete control over the installation process. You can specify whether to configure your system for dual booting, which software packages to install, and so on. The Custom install is covered in detail in Chapter 3.

To perform a Custom installation, you should have from 400 MB to 4.5 GB of free disk space available. However, 400 MB is an absolute minimum, and 4.5 GB is needed only if you're planning to install everything (including the kitchen sink). More realistically, you should have at least 2 GB of free space available. If you have the expertise and patience, you can omit certain packages that would otherwise be installed during a Custom installation so that your Linux system occupies less disk space. The Select Individual Packages option will be covered in Chapter 3.

Preparing Your Hard Disk

To prepare your hard disk for installing Linux, you must allocate the space in which Linux will reside. You'll learn how to do so in this section. First, I'll explain how hard disks are organized, followed by how to view the structure of a hard disk. Finally, I'll describe how to alter, or *partition*, the structure of your hard disk in preparation for installing Red Hat Linux.

How Hard Disks Are Organized

Let's start by reviewing facts you've probably learned by working with Windows. Most operating systems, including Windows 95/98, 2000, and XP, manage hard drives by dividing their storage space into units known as *partitions*. So that you can access a partition, Windows associates a drive letter (such as *C:* or *D:*) with it. Before you can store data on a partition, you must *format* it. Formatting a partition organizes the associated space into what is called a *filesystem*, which provides space for storing the names and attributes of files as well as the data they contain. Windows supports several types of filesystems, such as FAT, FAT32, and NTFS.

Partitions comprise the *logical structure* of a disk drive, the way humans and most computer programs understand the structure. However, disk drives have an underlying *physical structure* that more closely resembles the actual structure of the hardware. Figure 2-6 shows the logical and physical structure of a disk drive.

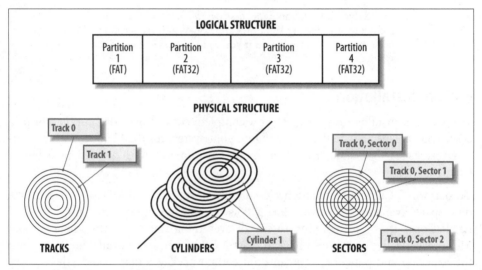

Figure 2-6. The structure of a hard disk

Mechanically, a hard disk is constructed of platters that resemble the phonograph records found in an old-fashioned jukebox. Each platter is associated with a read/write *head* that works much like the read/write head on a VCR, encoding data as a series of electromagnetic pulses. As the platter spins, the heads record data in concentric rings known as *tracks*, which are numbered beginning with zero. A hard disk may have hundreds or thousands of tracks.

All the tracks with the same radius are known as a *cylinder*. Like tracks, cylinders are numbered beginning with zero. The number of platters and cylinders of a drive determine the drive's *geometry*. Some PCs require you to specify the drive geometry in the BIOS setup. Most modern PCs autodetect the drive geometry but let you specify a custom value if you prefer.

Most operating systems prefer to read or write only part of a track, rather than an entire track. Consequently, tracks are divided into a series of *sectors*, each of which holds a fixed number of bytes, usually 512.

To correctly access a sector, a program needs to know the geometry of the drive. Because it's sometimes inconvenient to specify the geometry of a drive, some PC BIOS programs let you specify *logical byte addressing* (LBA). LBA sequentially numbers sectors, letting programs read or write a specified sector without the burden of specifying a cylinder or head number.

Viewing Disk Partitions

The first step in preparing your hard disk is viewing its partition information. Once you know how your hard disk is organized, you'll be able to determine how to reorganize it to accommodate Linux. To view the partitions that exist on your Windows 95/98 hard disk drives, you can use the **fdisk** utility. If your system runs Windows 2000 or XP, you must use the Disk Management tool, which resides within the Computer Management folder of the Administrative Tools control panel applet.

Using fdisk (Windows 95/98)

To use **fdisk**:

1. Click on the Windows Start menu. The Start pop-up menu appears.
2. Select Run. The Run dialog box appears.
3. Type "command" in the text box labelled Open. Then click OK or press Enter.
4. An MS-DOS Prompt window appears.
5. Type **fdisk** and press **Enter**. The **fdisk** menu appears, as shown in Figure 2-7.

> The **fdisk** menu may not appear immediately. Instead, Windows may ask if you want to enable large disk support; if this occurs, type **N** and press **Enter**. You don't need to enable large disk support to view partition information.

6. If your system has only one hard drive, you won't see option 5, titled "Change current fixed disk drive." If option 5 is available, type **5** and press **Enter**. This takes you to a screen resembling the one shown in Figure 2-8 that lets you specify the current fixed disk drive.

   If option 5 is not available, type the number associated with the "Display partition information" option and press **Enter**. The screen will resemble the one shown in Figure 2-8, though its arrangement will be somewhat different.

   The screen shows each hard drive and its size, numbering the drives beginning with 1. If a drive contains free space not allocated to a partition, the screen shows

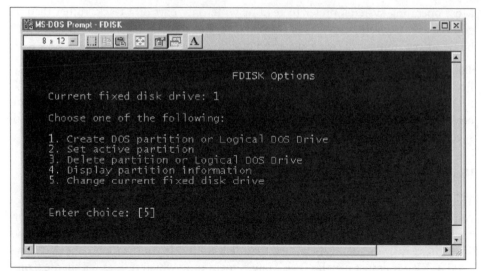

Figure 2-7. The fdisk Options screen

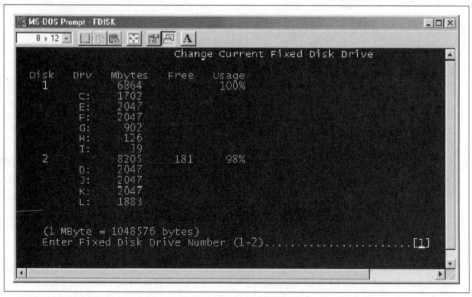

Figure 2-8. The fdisk "Change current fixed disk drive" screen

the amount of space available. The screen also shows how much of the drive's space has been allocated to partitions, as a percentage of the total drive space.

Under the information describing a drive, the screen shows the size of each partition that resides on the drive. The screen also shows the associated drive letter, if any.

7. When you're done viewing partition information, press **Esc** once or twice to exit **fdisk** and return to the MS-DOS prompt. You can then close the MS-DOS Prompt window by clicking on the Close icon in the upper-right corner of the window or by typing **exit** and pressing **Enter**.

Using the Disk Management tool (Windows 2000/XP)

To use the Disk Management tool, click Start → Control Panel → Administrative Tools → Disk Management. The tool graphically depicts your system's drives and the partitions and free space they contain, as shown in Figure 2-9.

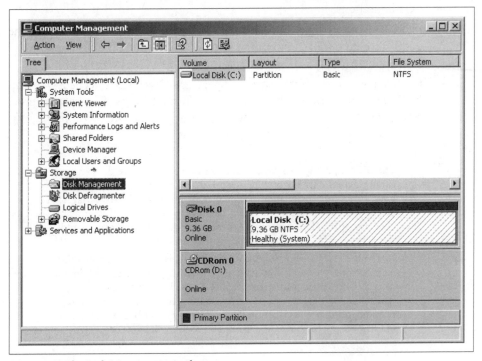

Figure 2-9. The Disk Management tool

Obtaining Sufficient Disk Space

Like Windows, Red Hat Linux requires special partitions on which to store its file-systems and swap data. You must devote two—or preferably three—partitions to Linux. By viewing the partitions on your hard drive, you can determine which of the following two cases best describes your system:

- Do you have enough free (unpartitioned) disk space to accommodate Linux? (You need 400 MB to 4.5 GB, depending on the type of installation you want and the number of packages you want to install.)

In this case, make a note of the drive that holds the free disk space. You can then begin the installation process described in Chapter 3. However, see the tip on PC BIOS limitations, later in this section.

- Do you lack enough free (unpartitioned) disk space to accommodate Linux?
- If you don't have sufficient disk space, you have several options:
  - If your system has room for an additional disk drive, you can install a new drive and use it to hold Linux. The upcoming section "Installing a new disk drive" offers some considerations and tips on installing a new drive. This is generally the best option, because it sidesteps problems arising due to PC BIOS limitations.
  - If you have one or more unused partitions, you can delete them and use the space you gain to hold Linux. The section "Identifying an unused partition" shows how to identify an unused partition.
  - If you have one or more partitions that are larger than needed, you can shrink them and use the space you gain to hold Linux. The section titled "Shrinking a partition" shows you how to determine whether a partition is larger than needed and how to free the excess space.

The BIOS of many PCs cannot access more than two hard drives and cannot access data beyond cylinder 1023 of a hard drive. In order to boot Linux, the installation program must create a 75-MB (or larger) boot partition (/boot) in an area accessible by the BIOS. If your available free space does not satisfy these criteria, you must obtain additional free space as described in the following sections.

Red Hat Linux supports LBA32, which can work around this problem. But many systems sold with advertised support for LBA32 do not actually support it. Moreover, enabling LBA32 support requires that you manually partition your system during installation. Therefore, I recommend that you partition your system as described in the following sections, to maximize the likelihood that it will work properly.

If you're unsure whether your free space satisfies these criteria, simply begin the installation; the installation program will notify you if it is unable to proceed. In that case, you can return to this chapter to learn how to gain or add additional disk space.

Installing a new disk drive

Often, the easiest way to install Linux is to install a new disk drive. If your system has only a single hard drive, you can probably install a second drive and place Linux on the new drive. Before purchasing a drive, you should make sure that the system provides room to mount the new drive and that you have the proper data and power cables. Be sure to install both disk drives on the primary disk controller so they can be booted; if you have an IDE CD-ROM drive, you should move it to the secondary controller.

If your system already has two disk drives, you probably can't simply add a third disk drive: the BIOS of most PCs lets you boot the system from only the first or second hard drive on the primary controller. In such a case, you can probably replace one of your existing drives with a larger drive adequate to support your existing needs and Linux.

Identifying an unused partition

You can use the drive letter information provided by **fdisk** to examine the contents of a partition in the Windows Explorer. If you can find a partition that holds no useful data but is large enough to accommodate the type of Linux installation you want, you can delete the partition and use the free space to hold Linux. At least 75 MB of the unused partition should reside within the first 1023 cylinders of the drive; otherwise, you will have to use a boot floppy to load Linux.*

The easiest way to delete a partition is to start installing Red Hat from the disks in this book, and then request deletion of the partition when the installation program gives you the opportunity. Make note in Table 2-1 of the partition you wish to delete and then begin the installation process described in Chapter 3.

Shrinking a partition

Even if all of your partitions contain useful data, one or more partitions may be larger than required. In that case, you can reduce the size of each such partition and reorganize the drive to include contiguous unused space to hold Linux. Again, at least 75 MB of the unused space should reside within the first 1023 cylinders of the disk drive; otherwise, you'll have to use a boot floppy to load Linux.

You can use the Windows Explorer to determine the amount of free disk space in a partition. Simply right-click on the drive icon and click on Properties in the pop-up menu. The Properties dialog box shows the amount of used and free disk space associated with the drive.

If you are able to find one or more FAT or FAT32 partitions that have sufficient free space for a Linux installation, you can use a special utility to split the used and unused portions of a partition into separate partitions. Disc 1 of Red Hat Linux includes the unsupported **fips** utility, which can split FAT and FAT32 partitions. For information on using **fips**, see the documentation in the *dosutils* directory of the CD-ROM.

 If you make a mistake while attempting to shrink a partition or if the software malfunctions, you may lose all data in one or more partitions. You should not attempt to shrink a partition until you've completely backed up your system and made sure that your backup is usable.

* Boot floppies, and how to create them, are discussed in Chapter 3.

Many Linux users find commercial partitioning tools—such as PowerQuest's *PartitionMagic* or VCOM's *Partition Commander*—helpful. Both tools are relatively inexpensive (approximately $40–$70) and support partition types and operations not supported by **fips**. For example, they can split NTFS and Linux *ext3* partitions. This is important, because you may not initially create Linux partitions of exactly the right size. Using **fips**, you'd be stuck; but, using PartitionMagic or Partition Commander, you can change your system's partition structure as many times as you like until you get it just right. For information on PartitionMagic, see the PowerQuest web site at *http://www.powerquest.com/partitionmagic*. For information on Partition Commander, see the VCOM web site at *http://www.v-com.com/product/pc_ind.html*.

Use of PartitionMagic or Partition Commander is beyond the scope of this book. I mention them here because I believe that, while they aren't free, they are valuable, timesaving tools for partitioning your hard drive. Instructions on how to install and use either tool are included with the product documentation.

## CHAPTER 3

Installing Red Hat Linux

This chapter shows you how to install Red Hat Linux by following a simple, step-by-step procedure. During the installation, you'll need to refer to the information you collected in Table 2-1 of Chapter 2. Most users will be able to complete the installation procedure without difficulty; however, this chapter includes a section that describes how you can obtain help if you encounter installation problems. Once you successfully complete the installation procedure, you'll have your own working Red Hat Linux system.

Installing the Operating System and Applications

To install Red Hat Linux, attach any optional devices you plan to use, such as a PCMCIA network card or external floppy drive, to your PC. Then, follow this simple step-by-step procedure:

1. Start the installation.
2. Select installation options.
3. Create partitions.
4. Configure the boot loader.
5. Configure networking.
6. Configure the system time.
7. Configure language support.
8. Configure user accounts and authentication.
9. Select packages.
10. Install packages.
11. Configure X.
12. Create a boot diskette.
13. Complete the video configuration.
14. Complete the installation.

Although the Linux installation procedure is generally trouble-free, errors or malfunctions that occur during the installation of an operating system can result in loss of data. You should not begin the installation procedure until you have backed up all data on your system and determined that your backup is error-free. You should also create boot floppies or other media that enable you to boot your system even if the boot information on the hard disk is damaged.

Start the Installation

To begin installing Linux, you must boot your system from the installation media. Most recently manufactured PCs can boot the Installation CD 1 Red Hat Linux CD-ROM. However, unless you generally boot from a CD-ROM—which is quite unlikely—you'll need to reconfigure your PC's BIOS so your PC is able to boot from a CD-ROM. To do so, enter your PC's BIOS screen and look for a configuration item titled something like Boot Order or Boot Priority. Change the configuration so that the CD-ROM drive has the highest boot priority. Consult your PC's documentation for details on entering and using its BIOS configuration screens.

Creating a Boot Floppy

If your PC can't boot from a CD-ROM, you must create a boot floppy disk. Creating a boot floppy requires some special measures; you can't simply copy files onto a disk and then boot it. To create a Red Hat Linux installation boot floppy by using a PC that runs Microsoft Windows, perform the following steps:

1. Format a floppy.

2. Insert Disc 1 of Red Hat Linux into your system's CD-ROM drive.

3. Click **My Computer** and then your CD-ROM drive. Navigate to the \dosutils\ rawritewin directory. Double-click the program **rawwritewin**. The RawWrite dialog box appears, as shown in Figure 3-1. Specify the floppy drive and image file (images\boot.img or other), and click **Write**. It takes perhaps a minute or so for the **rawrite** utility to create the floppy diskette.

> If your PC requires one or more PCMCIA or unusual SCSI devices during boot up, you must follow a somewhat more complicated procedure. See Appendix F of *The Red Hat Linux 8.0 Installation Guide*, available at *http://www.redhat.com/docs*, for details.

Boot the Installation Program

To start the installation process, insert Installation CD 1 of Red Hat Linux into your system's CD-ROM drive. If your system cannot boot from a CD-ROM, insert the boot floppy you created and reboot your PC. When the system reboots, you should see a start-up screen featuring a boot: prompt and a series of messages explaining

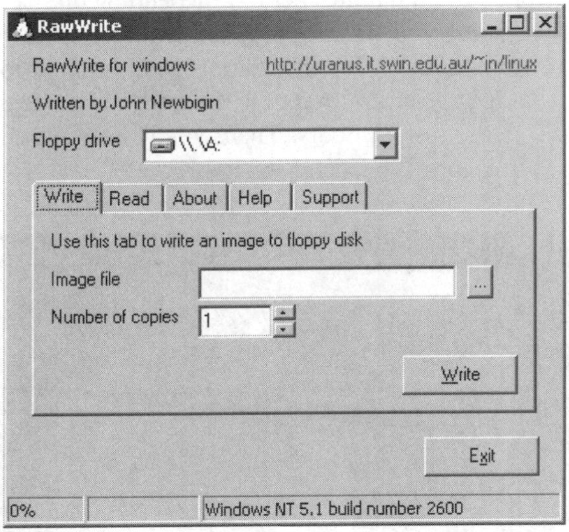

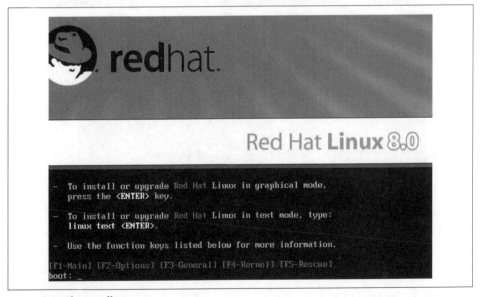

Figure 3-1. Using rawrite to make a boot diskette

how to invoke the graphical and text mode installation and upgrade facilities, as shown in Figure 3-2. This prompt lets you enter special parameters to work around a variety of installation problems. Generally, it's not necessary to do so. Simply press **Enter** or wait about a minute and the installation program will start.

Figure 3-2. The installation start-up screen

If you downloaded your installation media, you'll next see the screen shown in Figure 3-3. This screen lets you verify the contents of the installation CD-ROMs.

Verification takes from 5 to 20 minutes per CD, depending on the speed of your system. However, by verifying your media, you can avoid problems that might otherwise be difficult to troubleshoot. The installation media that accompany this book do not cause the CD Found screen to appear. Instead, for perhaps a minute, you'll see text flashing by as the system boots. Then, you'll see the Red Hat Linux Welcome screen, shown in Figure 3-4. Click Next to proceed.

Figure 3-3. The CD Found screen

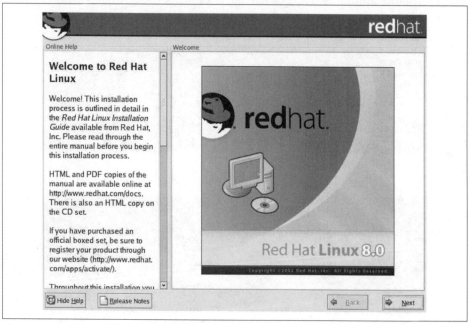

Figure 3-4. The Red Hat Linux Welcome screen

The Installation Program's User Interface

Like other modern Linux distributions, Red Hat Linux includes a graphical installation program that simplifies the installation and initial configuration of Linux. Figure 3-5 shows a typical screen displayed by the installation program. You won't see this particular screen until later in the installation process.

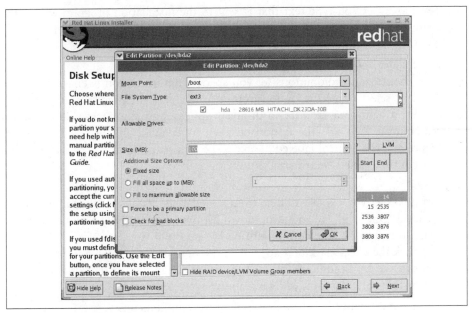

Figure 3-5. A typical installation screen

The installation screen includes the following elements:

A main window

> The installation program runs in a full screen window that contains one or more child windows within it. The upper-left corner of each child window displays the name of the window. You cannot minimize or change the size of the installation program's main window.

The cursor

> The installation program also has an on-screen cursor that resembles a small arrow pointing up and slightly to the left. When you position the cursor above a control and click the mouse, you set the input focus to the selected control. At any time, exactly one control has the input focus, which lets it respond to keyboard input. The control that has the input focus has a dotted rectangle outlining it or has a lighter color than otherwise similar controls. In Figure 3-5, the OK button has the input focus.

Dialog boxes

The installation program uses dialog boxes to obtain user input. In Figure 3-5, a dialog box titled Edit Partition is visible. You can recognize it by the controls it contains, such as Mount Point and Size (MB). You dismiss a dialog box by using its OK or Cancel button. You cannot minimize an installation dialog box.

Text boxes

Text boxes let you type text that is sent to the installation program when you dismiss the dialog box by using the OK button. In Figure 3-5, the field labeled Size (MB) is a text box.

Checkboxes and radiobuttons

Checkboxes and radiobuttons let you specify that an option is enabled or disabled or select a specific option from a list. A dark area indicates an enabled option; a light area indicates a disabled option. You can click a checkbox or radiobutton to toggle the option between its enabled and disabled states. In Figure 3-5, the control labeled "Force to be a primary partition" is a checkbox. The control labeled "Fixed size" is a radiobutton.

List boxes

List boxes let you choose an item from a predefined list. Two kinds of list boxes are used. One kind, called a drop-down list box, displays only a single item at a time. In Figure 3-5, the control labeled Mount Point is a drop-down list box. If you click the checkmark that appears at the right of a drop-down list box, other items in the list become visible. When you select an item by clicking it, the list reverts to its original form, showing only the selected item.

The second kind of list shows multiple items simultaneously. If this kind of list box has more items than can be shown, it will have an associated scrollbar that lets you page through the list. The selected item, if any, is indicated by the item's dark background.

Buttons

When you click a button, the installation program performs a corresponding action. For example, clicking the OK button of a dialog box tells the installation program to accept the dialog box contents and proceed to the next step. Similarly, clicking the Cancel button of a dialog box tells the installation program to ignore the dialog box contents. Many installation screens include a helpful Back button that lets you return to the previous installation step. Most installation screens include a Next button that takes you to the next installation step.

Online Help

The Online Help panel lets you view information that helps you understand what the current installation screen does and how to use it. If you don't understand the installation procedure or if you're curious to learn more, read the information in the Online Help panel.

Graphical Install... What Graphical Install?

If you don't see the Red Hat Linux Welcome screen but instead see a screen with red and blue text areas over a black background, your system is not compatible with the Red Hat Linux graphical install. Perhaps your system lacks sufficient RAM or has an unsupported video adapter.

In that case, you can use a text-based installation procedure. To do so, reboot your system and respond to the *boot:* prompt by typing **linux text** and pressing **Enter**. Because this special installation procedure is text-based, you won't be able to use a mouse. Instead, use **Tab** to move from field to field, use **Space** to select fields, and press **Enter** to click a selected button.

If you need additional help using the text-based installation procedure, see Section 3.2 of *The Red Hat Linux 8.0 Installation Guide*, available at *http://www.redhat.com/docs*.

Use Virtual Consoles to Monitor the Installation

A console is a combination of a keyboard and a display device, such as a video monitor. A console provides a basic user interface adequate to communicate with a computer: you can type characters on the keyboard and view text on the display device.

Although a home computer system seldom has more than one console, Linux systems provide several virtual consoles. By pressing a special combination of keys, you can control which console your system's keyboard and monitor are connected to.

Table 3-1 describes the virtual consoles used by the installation program. The main installation dialog appears in virtual console #7. If you like, you can use the indicated keystrokes to view a different virtual console.

Table 3-1. Virtual consoles used by Red Hat's installation program

Console	Keystroke	Contents
1	Ctrl-Alt-F1	Installation dialog
2	Ctrl-Alt-F2	A shell prompt that lets you enter commands to be processed by Linux
3	Ctrl-Alt-F3	The installation log, containing messages from the install program
4	Ctrl-Alt-F4	The system log, containing messages from the Linux kernel and other system programs
5	Ctrl-Alt-F5	May contain other messages, including those concerning the creation of filesystems
7	Ctrl-Alt-F7	The graphical window, which is the main window used by the installation program

The contents of virtual consoles #1 through #5 can be useful in monitoring and troubleshooting; you will not generally need to switch from one virtual console to another. Nevertheless, you may find it interesting to view the contents of the virtual consoles during the installation procedure.

Choose the Installation Language

Click Next to move from the Installation screen to the Language Selection screen. Figure 3-6 shows that screen, which asks you to specify what language should be used during the installation process. Click the desired language and then click Next. The Keyboard Configuration screen appears.

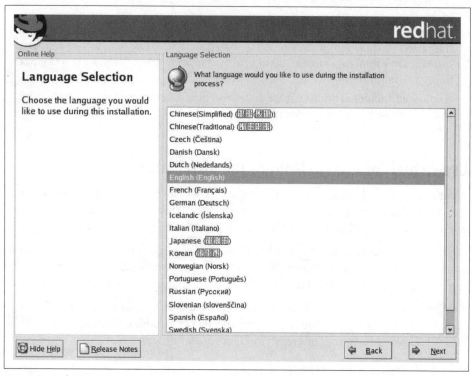

Figure 3-6. The Language Selection screen

Select the Keyboard Type

The Keyboard Configuration screen, shown in Figure 3-7, lets you specify the type of keyboard attached to your system. The preselected choice is appropriate for most U.S. users. If you prefer another keyboard configuration, click the desired model or layout. Then, click Next to proceed. The Mouse Configuration screen appears.

Select the Mouse Type

The Mouse Configuration screen, shown in Figure 3-8, lets you specify the type of mouse attached to your system. The installation program generally determines the type of mouse automatically. If you prefer a different mouse configuration, click the desired mouse type.

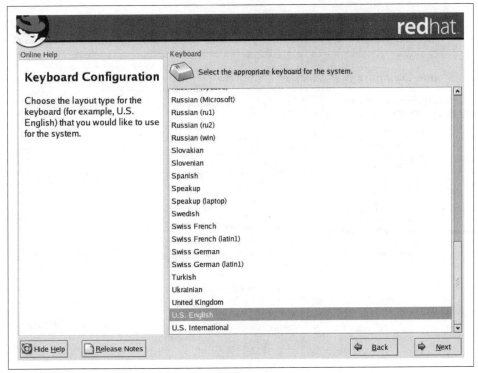

Figure 3-7. The Keyboard Configuration dialog box

Many graphical Linux programs are designed to use a three-button mouse. If your mouse has only two buttons, you should generally enable the Emulate 3 Buttons checkbox. Click Next to proceed to the Installation Type screen.

Select the Installation Type

The Installation Type screen, shown in Figure 3-9, lets you choose whether to perform any of four types of fresh installations or an upgrade of your existing Red Hat system. The Install options—Personal Desktop, Workstation, Server, and Custom—are described in Chapter 2. As explained, the appropriate choice for most users is Custom. Therefore, click the radiobutton next to Custom and click Next to proceed.

> The step-by-step procedure given in this chapter describes only the Custom installation type. The procedures required for other installation types are similar and you can probably complete a non-Custom installation with the help of this chapter. However, if you want a more detailed procedure for performing a non-Custom installation, see *The Red Hat Linux 8.0 Installation Guide*.

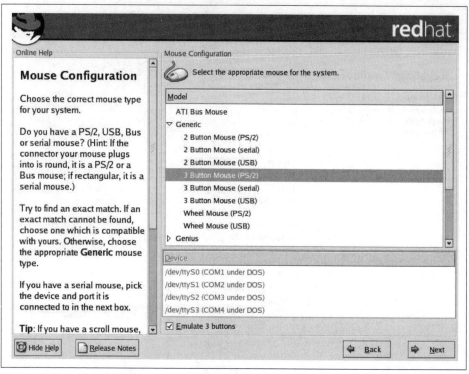

Figure 3-8. The Mouse Configuration screen

Create Partitions

Druids in Red Hat Linux are analogous to wizards in Microsoft Windows. In the next phase of the installation procedure, you use Red Hat's Disk Druid to establish Linux partitions on your hard disk drive. Figure 3-10, the Disk Partitioning Setup screen, appears. Disk Druid is generally capable of automatically creating the necessary partitions.

If you prefer, the installation program lets you manually partition your hard disk using Disk Druid. However, it's generally easier to allow Disk Druid to automatically partition the hard disk and then review and edit the results. No changes are made to the partition table until you accept the final results.

The installation program also provides a third partitioning method, manual partitioning via **fdisk**. However, as the Disk Partitioning Setup screen suggests, this program is suitable only for experts. Unlike Disk Druid, **fdisk** does not check that your partitions have been properly defined. Unless you're familiar with **fdisk**, it's best to avoid using it until you gain more experience with Linux.

So, you can generally click Automatically partition and click Next to proceed. The Automatic Partitioning screen appears, as shown in Figure 3-11.

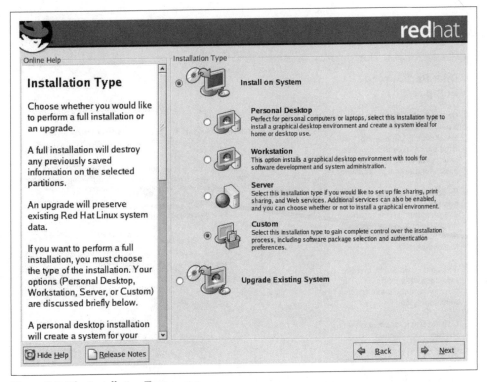

Figure 3-9. The Installation Type screen

Before the Disk Partitioning Setup screen appears, a dialog box may appear, announcing that Disk Druid has found a problem with the partition table of one of your system's hard drives. The dialog box tells you how to resolve the problem. If the hard disk has never been used, its partition table won't be invalid. In that case, you can continue the installation; Disk Druid will write an appropriate partition table to the disk.

Otherwise, you may need to restart the installation and specify the geometry of your hard drive in response to the boot: prompt. Appendix C describes the most common options. If you plan on erasing all the data on your hard drive, you can click Skip Drive and continue with the installation.

The Automatic Partitioning screen lets you choose how any existing partitions are treated. Three choices are available:

- Remove all Linux partitions on this system
- Remove all partitions on this system
- Keep all partitions and use existing free space

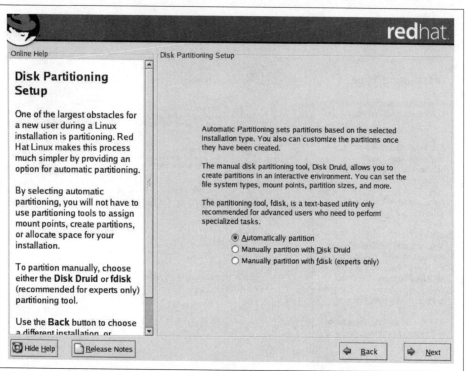

Figure 3-10. The Disk Partitioning Setup screen

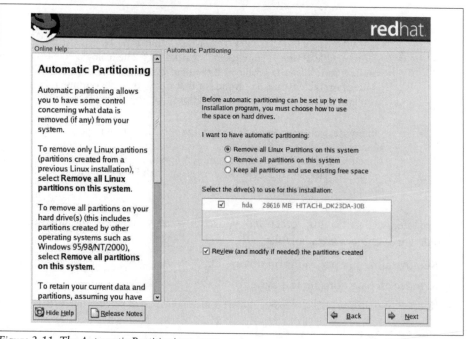

Figure 3-11. The Automatic Partitioning screen

If you want to preserve an existing operating system, you should *not* choose Remove all partitions on this system. If you want to overwrite an existing Linux installation, choose Remove all Linux partitions on this system. Otherwise, choose Keep all partitions and use existing free space.

The Automatic Partitioning screen also lets you specify the hard disks on which the installation program will load Red Hat Linux. You can prevent the installation program from using a hard disk by clearing the checkbox associated with the hard disk.

Finally, the Automatic Partitioning screen lets you specify whether to review the results of automatic partitioning. You should generally leave the associated checkbox set so that you can modify the results, if needed.

Click Next to perform automatic partitioning. If Disk Druid cannot find sufficient free space, you may see a dialog box announcing an error. In that case, you can use the Back button to return to the Disk Partitioning Setup screen and choose manual partitioning with Disk Druid. The following section explains how to review and modify the results of automatic partitioning, and also equips you to perform manual partitioning.

Manual disk partitioning

The Disk Setup screen, shown in Figure 3-12, lets you add, edit, and delete Linux partitions. The bottom part of the screen contains a list box that describes each drive and partition. The middle part of the screen contains buttons that control the operation of Disk Druid, the tool that carries out partitioning. The top part of the screen graphically depicts the partition structure.

What to add

Whereas Windows associates drive letters, such as **D**:, with partitions, Linux associates directories—known as mount points—with partitions. Two such directories, / (the root directory) and /boot, are essential. In addition, a third partition is necessary to manage your system's RAM. This partition has no associated mount point.

During this step of the installation process, you should establish three Linux partitions on your system's hard drive:

- A Linux swap partition to provide a work area used by Red Hat Linux to efficiently manage your system's RAM memory. This partition, which has no mount point, should have a size two times the amount of your PC's installed RAM. However, the swap partition should not be smaller than 190 MB or larger than 2000 MB. This partition is not mounted by Linux and therefore has no associated mount point.

- A Linux native partition to hold the Linux kernel. This partition, which has the mount point /boot, should be at least 75 MB in size. However, there's no advantage to making it larger than 100 MB.

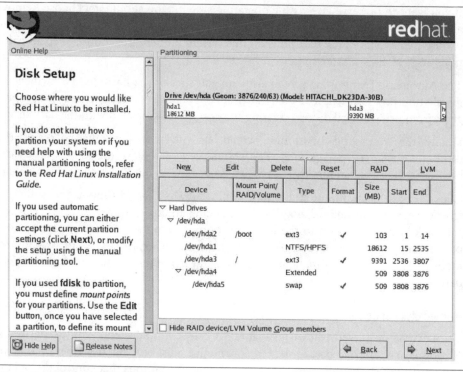

Figure 3-12. The Disk Druid screen

- A Linux native partition to hold the Red Hat Linux operating system. This partition, known as the root partition, has the mount point /. It should be as large as you can afford.

Create the swap partition. From the Disk Setup screen, click New to launch the Add Partition dialog box, shown in Figure 3-13.

Enter the following values in the Add Partition dialog box:

Mount Point
Leave this field blank.

Type
Select Swap.

Allowable Drives
Choose one or more hard disk drives on which to place the partition. If you select more than one hard disk drive, Disk Druid will choose a drive from among those you specify; Disk Druid will never create a partition that spans multiple disk drives.

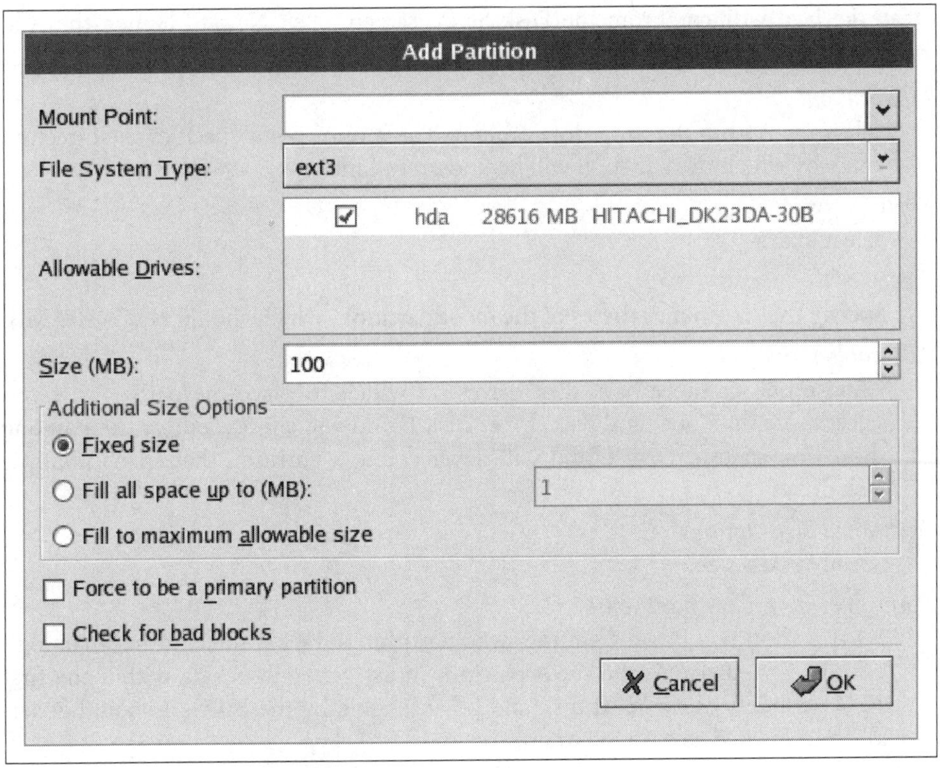

Figure 3-13. The Add Partition dialog box

Size

Specify twice the amount of RAM in your system. However, do not specify less than 190 MB or more than 2000 MB.

Additional Size Options

Specify Fixed size.

Force to be a primary partition

Set this checkbox if you want the swap partition to be a primary rather than logical partition. A primary partition is one that can be accessed by the BIOS and some old versions of operating systems. Because a hard disk can have only four primary partitions and the BIOS need not access the Linux swap partition, it's generally unwise to use a primary partition as a swap partition.

Check for bad blocks

If you want to verify the reliability of the partition, set this checkbox. However, checking for bad blocks can be time-consuming. Depending on the size of the partition and the speed of the hard disk, checking bad blocks may require as much as several hours.

Click OK to accept the input values. The Add Partition dialog box disappears.

Create the /boot partition. From the Disk Setup screen, click New to launch the Add Partition dialog box. Enter the following values:

Mount Point
> Select */boot* from the drop-down menu. The mount point specifies the directory name by which the partition will be known to Linux.

Partition type
> Select ext3.

Size
> Specify the size in megabytes of the */boot* partition, which should be 75–100 MB.

Allowable Drives
> Choose one or more hard disk drives on which to place the partition. If you select more than one hard disk drive, Disk Druid will choose a drive from among those you specify; Disk Druid will never create a partition that spans multiple disk drives.

Additional Size Options
> Specify Fixed size.

Force to be a primary partition
> Set this checkbox if you want the swap partition to be a primary rather than logical partition. Because the */boot* partition must generally reside within the first 1024 cylinders of the hard disk and be accessible by the BIOS, it should generally be allocated as a primary partition.

Check for bad blocks
> If you want to verify the reliability of the partition, set this checkbox. However, checking for bad blocks can be time-consuming. Depending on the size of the partition and the speed of the hard disk, checking bad blocks may require as much as several hours.

Click OK to accept the input values; or, if you don't want to create the partition, click Cancel. The Add Partition Dialog box disappears.

If you enter an inappropriate value, Disk Druid may be unable to create the requested partition. In such a case, it displays a dialog box that explains the reason the partition could not be created. Study the dialog box to determine what you did wrong and try again.

Create the / partition. From the Disk Setup screen, click New to launch the Add Partition dialog box. Enter the following values:

Mount Point
> Type a forward slash (/) to denote the root directory.

Partition Type
> Select ext3.

Allowable Drives
> Choose one or more hard disk drives on which to place the partition.

Size
> Specify the size in megabytes of the / partition, which should be at least 300 MB. More realistically, the size of the partition should be at least 1.2 GB (1200 MB).

Additional Size Options
> Specify Fill to maximum allowable size, so the Linux native partition will be as large as possible. If you prefer to restrict the size of the partition, select Fill all space up to (MB) and specify the maximum desired size in the immediately following text box.

Force to be a primary partition
> Set this checkbox if you want the swap partition to be a primary rather than logical partition.

Check for bad blocks
> If you want to verify the reliability of the partition, set this checkbox. However, checking for bad blocks can be time-consuming. Depending on the size of the partition and the speed of the hard disk, checking bad blocks may require as much as several hours.

Click OK to accept the input values. The Add Partition dialog box disappears.

Editing a partition

If you wish to change one or more values associated with a partition, highlight the partition you wish to change in the Disk Setup screen and click Edit. Disk Druid launches a dialog box that you can use to change the mount point of a previously existing partition or other options of a partition you've just created.

You cannot use the Add Partition dialog box to change the size, grow option, or type of a previously existing partition; instead, you must delete such a partition and re-create it.

Deleting a partition

If you wish to delete a partition, highlight it and click Delete. Disk Druid presents a dialog box that asks you to confirm the operation.

> Deleting a partition destroys all the data it contains. Exercise great care to delete only unneeded partitions.

Starting over

If you determine that you've made mistakes and want to abandon the changes you've specified, simply click Reset. Disk Druid resets all partitions to their original state.

Saving your changes

When you're done, save your changes and proceed with the installation, by clicking Next.

Configure the Boot Loader

Next, the installation program presents the Boot Loader Configuration screen, shown in Figure 3-14. GRUB, the Grand Unified Boot loader, is a special program used to start Linux—or another operating system—when you boot your system. This screen lets you choose an alternative boot loader (LILO) or omit installation of a boot loader altogether. You can also specify the location where GRUB will be installed.

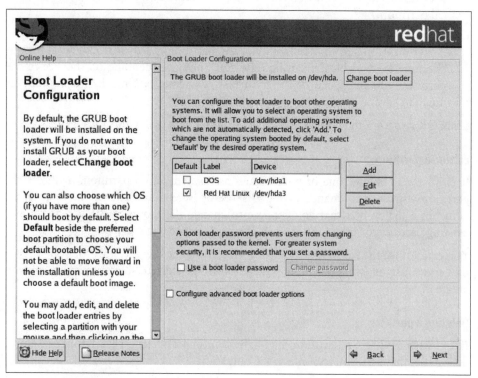

Figure 3-14. The Boot Loader Configuration screen

Most Linux users install GRUB on their PC's primary hard drive. However, doing so poses some risk. For example, some antivirus applications detect changes to the MBR and roll them back. The bottom line is that, for a few Red Hat Linux users, GRUB can present some headaches.

If you're among those bothered by GRUB, you can easily avoid GRUB. To do so you can boot Linux by using the boot floppy prepared near the end of the installation procedure. Linux won't boot as quickly as it might, but you won't face the prospect of disabling your other operating system if you're running a dual-boot system. Switching from GRUB to LILO is unlikely to help, as LILO is vulnerable to the same problems affecting GRUB. The Boot Loader Configuration screen lets you select the operating systems that GRUB will be able to boot. When GRUB boots your PC, GRUB displays a screen that lets you select from among the configured operating systems.

The installation program preselects Linux as the default operating system. To specify a different default operating system, highlight the corresponding partition and click Default.

If you like, you can change the label associated with an operating system by highlighting the corresponding partition and typing the desired label in the text box labeled Boot Label. When you've completely specified the desired boot loader configuration, click Next to proceed.

> The Boot Loader Configuration screen also lets you specify a boot loader password. If you want to prevent unauthorized persons from using your PC, you can use a password to prevent someone from overriding security checks by passing special information to the Linux kernel. However, this level of protection is rarely necessary.

Configure Networking

After you've configured the boot loader, the installation program probes for a network card. If it finds one, the installation program presents the Network Configuration screen, shown in Figure 3-15. If your computer is attached to a Local Area Network (LAN), you can use the Network Configuration screen to configure networking. If your computer is not attached to a LAN, click Next.

If your LAN provides a DHCP server, Red Hat Linux can automatically determine your PC's network configuration when your PC boots. By default, the installer configures your PC to activate its network adapter and obtain its network configuration from a DHCP server whenever your PC is booted.

If you want to assign your PC a static IP address or if you don't want your network adapter to be activate when your system boots, click the Edit button. An Edit Interface dialog box, shown in Figure 3-16, appears. To specify a static IP address, clear the checkbox labeled Configure using DHCP. Then, enter the IP address and netmask in the proper text fields, using the information you recorded in Table 2-1. If you don't want your network adapter to be activated when your system boots, clear the checkbox labeled Active on boot. Click OK to save your changes.

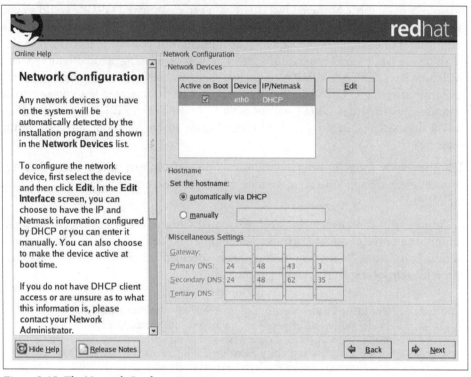

Figure 3-15. The Network Configuration screen

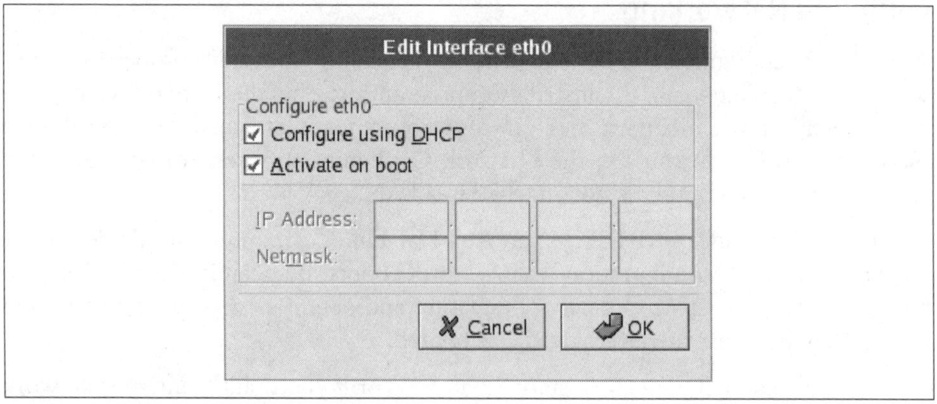

Figure 3-16. The Edit Interface dialog box

If you want to assign your system a static IP address, you should select the radiobutton labeled Set the hostname manually in the Network Configuration Screen. You should also provide the following from Table 2-1:

Hostname

    The hostname of your system, including the domain name (for example, **newbie. redhat.com**)

Gateway

    The host address of the router your system uses to send packets beyond its local network (for example, 192.168.1.1)

Primary DNS

    The IP address of the system that provides hostname lookup services to your system (for example, 192.168.1.1)

Secondary DNS

    The IP address of the system used to look up hostnames if the primary name server is unavailable (optional)

Ternary DNS

    The host address of the system used to look up hostnames if the primary and secondary name servers are unavailable (optional)

When you've entered the desired network configuration, click Next to proceed. The Firewall Configuration screen, shown in Figure 3-17, appears. This screen lets you specify protection against threats originating across the network.

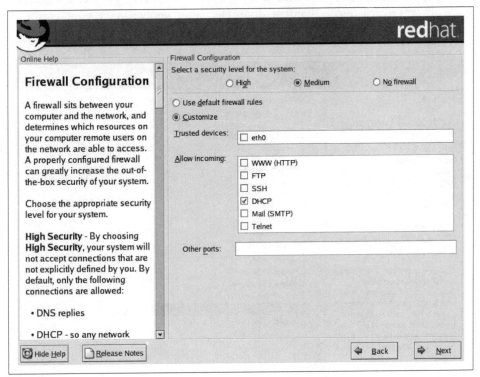

Figure 3-17. The Firewall Configuration screen

Chapter 12 explains the firewall capabilities of Red Hat Linux in more detail. If you're especially concerned about network security, you should select the High security option; otherwise, you should select Medium security. If your system obtains its network configuration from a DHCP server, you should leave the checkbox labeled Allow incoming DHCP enabled. Make your choices and click Next to proceed.

> After installation, you can use the Security Level tool to change your firewall settings, as explained in Chapter 12.

Configure the Language

Next, the installation program presents the Additional Language Support screen, shown in Figure 3-18. You earlier selected the language used during the installation procedure; this screen has a different function. It lets you select the default language in which the desktop is presented. It also lets you install support—including X fonts and spelling dictionaries—for one or more additional languages. As the screen explains, multiple languages consume significant disk space. So, select a single language if you're reasonably content doing so. After you've made your choice or choices, click Next to proceed.

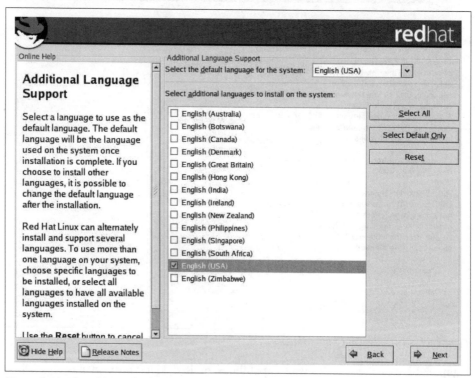

Figure 3-18. The Additional Language Support screen

Configure the System Clock

After you bypass or complete the Network Configuration screen, the installation program presents the Time Zone Selection screen, shown in Figure 3-19. Select a time zone by clicking on the map or by clicking an entry in the list box that appears below the map.

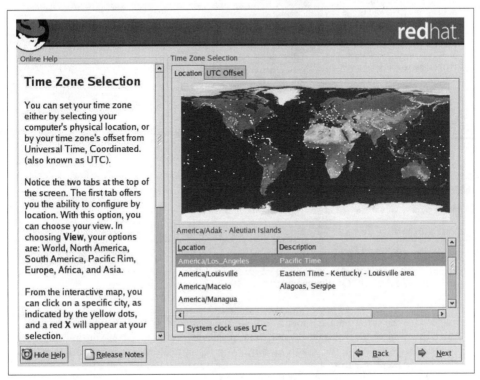

Figure 3-19. The Time Zone Selection screen

If you want to set your system's clock to UTC (Universal Coordinated Time), enable the System Clock Uses UTC checkbox. However, you should not enable this checkbox if your PC is set up to boot an operating system, such as Microsoft Windows 9x, that does not support setting the system clock to UTC. After making your selections, click Next to proceed.

Configure User Accounts and Authentication

The user who administers a Linux system is known as the root user, or simply *root*. To protect your system against mischief and misadventure, you must protect the root user's login with a password. To enable you to do so, the installation program presents the Account Configuration screen, shown in Figure 3-20.

Simply choose a password for the root user and type it twice: in the text field labeled Root Password and the nearby text field labeled Confirm.

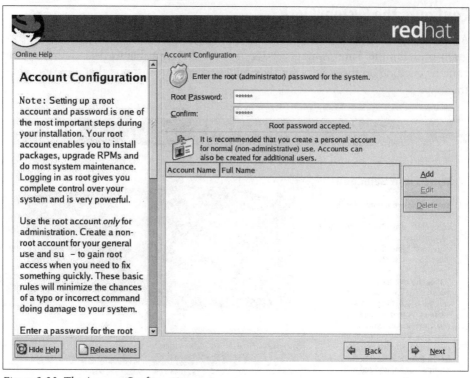

Figure 3-20. The Account Configuration screen

> Be sure to make a mental note of the password, because you'll need it
> in order to log in once system installation is complete. If you must,
> write down the password, but, if you do so, make sure the password is
> kept safe from anyone who might use it to compromise your system.

You should establish at least one additional user account during system installation. You can use this account when not performing system administration, thereby avoiding unnecessary use of the root account, which might lead to a breach of system security or integrity. To create the account, click Add. Then, type the account name, user's full name, and the password (twice). You can establish additional user accounts during system installation if you like, but it's generally easier to establish them after system installation is complete.

Once you've specified the password for the root account and have set up an additional user account, click Next to proceed. The installation program shows the Authentication Configuration screen, shown in Figure 3-21.

Generally, the default options are appropriate: both Enable MD5 Passwords and Enable Shadow Passwords should be enabled. MD5 lets you use passwords longer than eight characters; shadow passwords hides encrypted passwords from ordinary

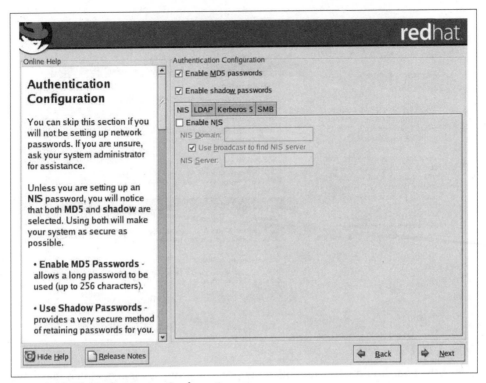

Figure 3-21. The Authentication Configuration screen

users. Only in special circumstances would it be necessary or appropriate to disable either option.

Unless your PC is part of a network that uses NIS, LDAP, Kerberos, or SMB, you don't need to specify options associated with these tabs. Otherwise, consult your network administrator to determine the appropriate settings. Click Next to proceed. The Package Group Selection screen appears.

Select Packages

To install an application under Red Hat Linux, you generally install a package that contains all the files needed by the application. If you like, you can specify the individual packages you want to install; however, the large number of available packages makes it tedious to specify them one at a time. Instead, the installation program lets you specify package groups you want to install. A package group is simply a group of related packages.

The Package Group Selection screen, shown in Figure 3-22, lets you specify which packages should be installed. Simply enable the checkbox associated with each desired package group. The installation program has preselected several package groups for you.

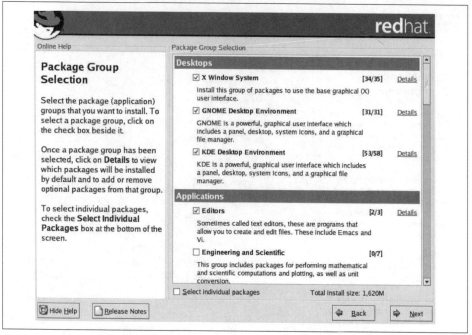

Figure 3-22. The Package Group Selection screen

Generally, you should select the following package groups, some of which may have been preselected for you:

X Window System
The graphical user interface (GUI) used with Red Hat Linux (default option)

GNOME Desktop Environment
The GNOME desktop, the default Red Hat Linux desktop (default option)

KDE Desktop Environment
The KDE desktop, an alternative to GNOME, which can co-exist with GNOME

Graphical Internet and Text-based Internet
Applications for sending and receiving mail, browsing the Web, and reading and posting Internet newsgroup messages (default option)

Office/Productivity
Applications for creating documents, spreadsheets, presentations, and so on (default option)

Sound and Video
Support for audio cards, CD burning, and other multimedia functions (default option)

Graphics
The GIMP (GNU Image Manipulation Program), which lets you perform graphic operations similar to those supported by Adobe Photoshop, and several other graphics programs (default option)

Administration Tools
   Tools for administering user accounts and setting configuration options

System Tools
   Tools for backing up large data sets, monitoring the network, and using network shares

Printing Support
   Lets you print to a local or remote printer (default option)

In addition, you can choose from among the available optional package groups, according to your interests and the characteristics of your system. Peruse the install program's list to see what's available. The Package Group Selection screen shows the approximate size of the selected package groups in its lower-right corner.

If you don't know what package groups to select, don't worry; you can install additional package groups after setting up your Red Hat Linux system. If, on the other hand, you want to be able to select individual packages as well as package groups, enable the Select Individual Packages checkbox. When you're satisfied with your choices, click Next to proceed. If you checked the Select Individual Packages checkbox, the Individual Package Selection screen appears. Select any desired packages. Then, click Next to proceed.

When X Is Obstinate

Sometimes, the installation program can't configure X to work properly. Generally, this is due to video hardware that's not compatible with X. If you find yourself in this situation, you can click the Skip X Installation button. The installation will then proceed, but X will not be installed. After system installation is complete, you can try to achieve a working X configuration. To do so, follow this procedure.

First, read the following:

- Chapter 4
- Chapter 7
- Appendix D

Then, perform the following steps:

1. Boot your system and access virtual console #1.
2. Log in as the *root* user.
3. Reconfigure your system to boot into run level 3 rather than run level 5.
4. Use **redhat-config-xfree86** to attempt to reconfigure X to work with your hardware.

If you requested installation of individual packages, the Unresolved Dependencies screen may appear. You should generally accept the preselected option, Install packages to satisfy dependencies. Click Next to proceed.

Install Packages

When the installation program is ready to begin installing packages, it presents the About to Install screen, shown in Figure 3-23. Up to this point, the installation program has made no changes to your system's hard drive. This is your last chance to terminate the installation procedure before any data is written. To abort the installation procedure, press **Ctrl-Alt-Delete** or press your system's hardware reset button.

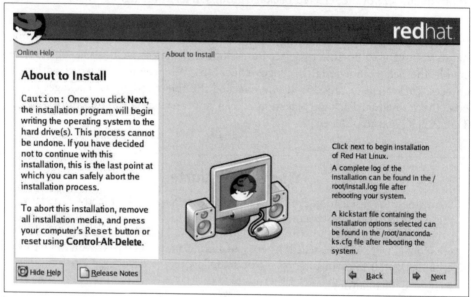

Figure 3-23. The About to Install screen

The installation program now formats any partitions you earlier specified for formatting. Depending on the size of your system's hard drive, it may require several minutes to complete this step. When formatting is done, the Installing Packages screen, shown in Figure 3-24, appears and the installation program begins installing packages.

The Installing Packages screen displays the name of each package as it is installed and presents a progress bar that shows the relative progress of the installation process. You'll likely be asked to insert other installation CDs during the installation process. When all the packages have been installed, you're ready to create a boot diskette. Click Next to proceed.

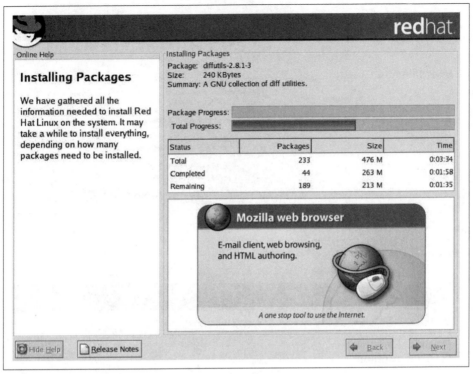

Figure 3-24. The Installing Packages screen

Create a Boot Floppy

The installation program next gives you the opportunity to create a boot floppy, by presenting the Boot Disk Creation screen, shown in Figure 3-25. This floppy is not the same as the one you may have created and used to start the installation procedure. You should take the opportunity to create the boot floppy, because it may enable you to boot your Linux system even if the boot loader fails to install properly or the system boot information is damaged.

To create a boot floppy, click Next. The installation program will prompt you to insert a blank floppy in your system's floppy drive. Insert the diskette and click OK. The installation program may take several minutes to create the boot floppy.

Configure Video

Next, the installation program displays the Graphical Interface (X) Configuration screen, shown in Figure 3-26, which helps you configure X, the Linux graphical user interface. If the installation program was able to determine the type of video card associated with your PC, it will highlight the appropriate item in the X Configuration list box. If you prefer to specify a different video card, click the desired item.

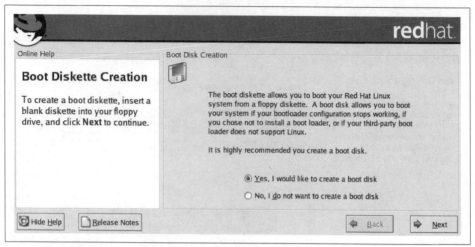

Figure 3-25. The Boot Disk Creation screen

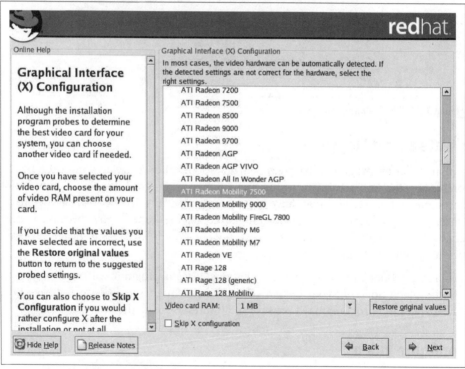

Figure 3-26. The Graphical Interface (X) Configuration screen

If your video card is not listed, you may be able to use the Generic SVGA Compatible entry. This will yield a basic, working X configuration. Later, you can follow the instructions given in Appendix D to achieve a better configuration.

You should specify the amount of video memory installed on your video card. Specifying a value that is too large will probably prevent X from starting. If you followed the procedure given in Chapter 2, you should have learned the amount of video memory installed on your card; otherwise, consult your video card's documentation to determine the proper value. If you can't locate the information, select a conservatively low value; choosing a value that's too low will prevent you from using high-resolution video modes but won't damage your monitor.

Earlier in the installation, you specified the make and model of your system's video card. The next two screens guide you in completing the video configuration.

Identifying your system's monitor

The installation program next presents the Monitor Configuration screen, shown in Figure 3-27. The Monitor Configuration screen includes a list of supported video monitors. If the installation program was able to determine the type of monitor associated with your PC, it will highlight the appropriate item in the Monitor Configuration list box. If you prefer to specify a different monitor, click the desired item.

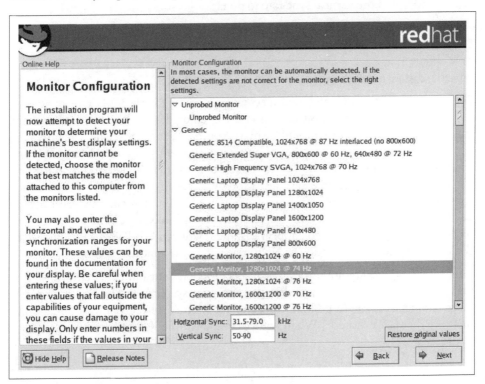

Figure 3-27. The Monitor Configuration screen

Don't select a monitor that has an identifier merely similar to that of your monitor. Similarly identified models often have quite different characteristics.

Failing to select the appropriate monitor may result in permanent damage to your monitor, particularly if your monitor is an older, fixed-frequency model.

If your monitor displays a scrambled image, turn it off promptly and recheck your configuration.

If you can't find your monitor listed, don't despair: you can select the Unprobed Monitor entry. If you do so, the installation program will suggest horizontal and vertical sync (also known as *vertical refresh*) rates or ranges. You should compare these with the characteristics of your monitor, which you can generally obtain from the owner's manual or from the manufacturer's web site; adjust the rates of ranges if necessary. If you fail to find information describing your monitor, you can try some conservative values that are unlikely to damage all but the oldest of monitors. Low values are safer than high values. For example, try setting the horizontal sync range to 50–70 kHz and the vertical sync rate to 60 Hz.

Once you've selected your monitor or specified its sync rates, click Next to proceed. The Custom Graphics Configuration screen appears.

Selecting custom graphics options

The Custom Graphics Configuration screen, shown in Figure 3-28, lets you specify several X-related options. You can choose the color depth, which determines the number of colors your system will display. You can also choose the screen resolution, which determines the number of pixels your system will display. Larger resolutions result in greater detail; however, your system's video adapter and monitor may not operate with all possible settings. Moreover, specifying a high resolution will consume additional system resources, such as RAM. You can click the Test Setting button to see that a given setting works and what it looks like. When testing a setting a small, untitled dialog box appears asking if you can Read This Text; if so, click Yes to accept the current setting or No to reject it and try another setting.

Check the Graphical radiobutton, which specifies that your Linux system will start in graphical mode. Graphical mode lets you use your system's mouse and is therefore more familiar and comfortable for those unaccustomed to the Linux command-line interface than is Text mode. When you've completed the X configuration, click Next to proceed.

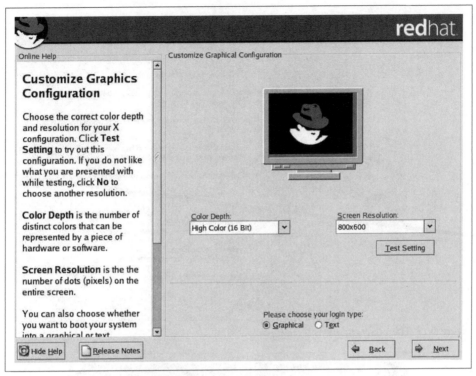

Figure 3-28. The Custom Graphics Configuration screen

Complete the Installation

The installation program then presents its final screen, shown in Figure 3-29, which explains that Red Hat Linux has been successfully installed.

Try booting your system from its hard drive or a Linux boot floppy, as appropriate. If your system successfully boots Linux, you're ready to log in to your Red Hat Linux system.

The Setup Agent

When you boot your system for the first time, the Red Hat Setup Agent is launched to help you configure your system. Figure 3-30 shows the Setup Agent's Welcome screen. Click Forward to continue.

The Date and Time Configuration screen, shown in Figure 3-31, lets you specify the current date and time. You can also specify a time server to which your system can synchronize. However, don't specify a time server at this time. Chapter 10 explains how to do so. After specifying the date and time, click Forward to continue.

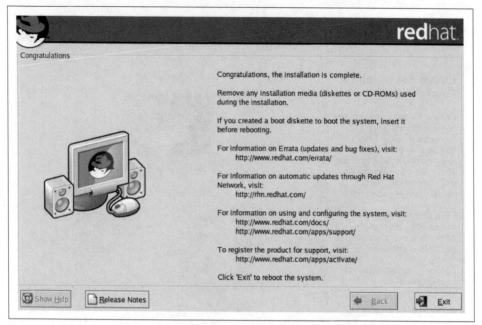

Figure 3-29. The Congratulations screen

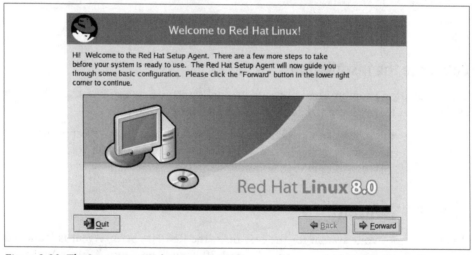

Figure 3-30. The Setup Agent Welcome screen

If the installation program detected a sound card on your system, the Setup Agent displays a Sound Card Configuration screen that reports the vendor and model of the sound card. The screen includes a Play test sound button that lets you test the operation of your sound card. Click Forward to continue.

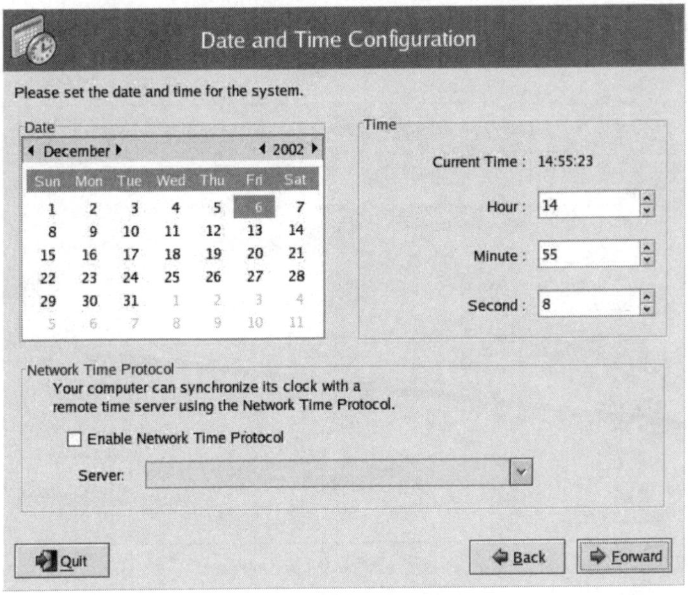

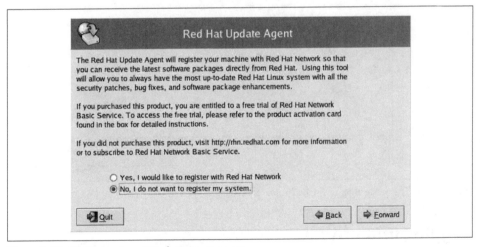

Figure 3-31. The Setup Agent Date and Time Configuration screen

The Update Agent screen, shown in Figure 3-32, lets you register your system to receive updates via Red Hat Network. Chapter 8 explains Red Hat Network and how to use it. Specify "No, I do not want to register my system." Then, click Forward to continue.

Figure 3-32. The Setup Agent Update Agent screen

The Install Additional Software screen, shown in Figure 3-33, lets you install Red Hat Linux documentation from a documentation CD, install package groups you omitted during system installation, or install applications from specially prepared CDs. However, you can easily install documentation, package groups, or applications later. So, merely click Forward to continue.

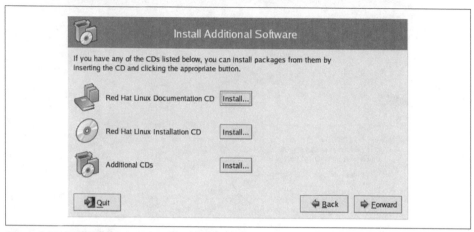

Figure 3-33. The Setup Agent Install Additional Software screen

Finally, the Setup Agent displays the Finished Setup screen, shown in Figure 3-34. Click Forward to log in to your system for the first time.

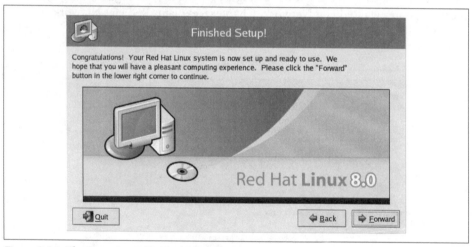

Figure 3-34. The Setup Agent Finished Setup Screen

Logging into GNOME

The login screen should resemble that shown in Figure 3-35. To log in, type **root**, or the name of another user account you created, in the text box labeled Login and press **Enter**. A second login screen appears, requesting your password. Type the password you earlier assigned to the user and press **Enter**.

Figure 3-35. The GNOME login screen

The GNOME desktop, shown in Figure 3-36, appears. If you like, click around the desktop and see what you can discover. Chapter 4 explains how to use the GNOME desktop. However, you should read Chapter 5 before reading that chapter.

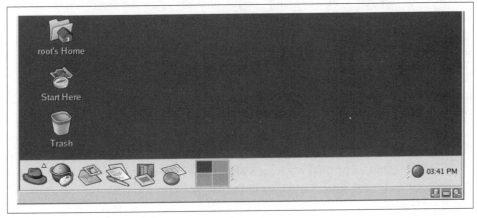

Figure 3-36. The GNOME desktop

To shut down your system, click the red hat at the lower left of the desktop. Then click Shutdown and click OK. Wait for your system to power down; now you're ready to move on to Chapter 4 to begin learning how Linux works.

You may see a flashing red ball at the lower right of the GNOME desktop. The ball is associated with the Red Hat Network Alert Notification facility, which you'll learn about in Chapter 8.

Getting Help

If your system fails to boot or if you're unable to complete the Linux installation process, don't despair: this section will help you troubleshoot your installation.

Failed Graphical Login

Sometimes, the graphical login fails. This is particularly likely if your system wasn't manufactured recently or if it's a laptop rather than a desktop.

If you don't see either display manager's screen, your X configuration isn't appropriate for your system's video hardware. It could be that your X configuration requires revision. In the worst case, your system's video hardware may not be compatible with X; in that event, you'll nevertheless be able to run nongraphical Linux applications.

> *If you see a scrambled image rather than text or images on your monitor, immediately switch off the monitor.* If your monitor is an older model, it can be damaged by the incorrect configuration. To reconfigure your system so that it operates properly, follow the procedures in the sidebar "When X Is Obstinate," earlier in this chapter.

Additional Resources

As much as I'd like to help you solve your problems in installing Red Hat Linux, I get too much email to be able to respond personally. But don't fret: the help you need is probably close by, in one of these sources:

The Red Hat Linux 8.0 Installation Guide
This guide is distributed with retail boxed copies of Red Hat Linux, either on CD-ROM or as a printed book. It's also available online. It provides a step-by-step guide to installing Red Hat Linux that includes more details than given in this chapter.

http://www.redhat.com/docs

Red Hat Linux 8.0 bug fixes
The Red Hat Linux 8.0 bug fixes web page describes bugs discovered in Red Hat Linux 8.0 and provides links to updated packages that resolve known problems. Sometimes, the installation media themselves are found to contain bugs. In that case, you may be able to find and download fixes from this web page.

http://www.redhat.com/apps/support/errata

Linux Installation and Getting Started

Though somewhat out of date, this resource still gives useful information and hints for installing Linux. Though it addresses Linux generally, much of the material is applicable to Red Hat Linux.

http://www.redhat.com/mirrors/LDP/LDP/gs/gs.html

Red Hat Linux Frequently Asked Questions

This FAQ site is maintained by Red Hat. It provides answers to many common questions regarding Red Hat Linux and includes a section on installing it.

http://www.redhat.com/support/docs/faqs/rh3_general_faq/FAQ.html

The Linux Installation HOWTO

This HOWTO resembles *Linux Installation and Getting Started*. It too addresses Linux generally rather than Red Hat Linux, but it contains much useful information and is more current than *Linux Installation and Getting Started*.

http://www.redhat.com/mirrors/LDP/HOWTO/Installation-HOWTO

The Linux on Laptops

Installing Linux on a laptop presents special difficulties, because laptops regularly contain peculiar hardware. Worse, two laptops that have identical model numbers may contain different hardware. The Linux on Laptops web page is an essential resource for those who want to install Red Hat Linux on a laptop.

http://www.cs.utexas.edu/users/kharker/linux-laptop

Bugzilla

This searchable database covers problems reported by users of Red Hat Linux. You can use Bugzilla to determine if someone else has had the same problem you're experiencing. Often, the Bugzilla record will include a workaround or fix for your problem.

http://bugzilla.red.hat.com/bugzilla

Mailing Lists

Red Hat hosts several mailing lists to which you can post questions and expect to receive replies from other list members. In addition, you can view archives of past postings. The Redhat-install-list is dedicated to issues related to the installation of Red Hat Linux.

https://listman.redhat.com/mailman/listinfo

Running Linux

The book *Running Linux*, by Matt Walsh, Matthias Kalle Dalheimer, Terry Dawson, and Lar Kaufman, takes a more advanced look at Linux generally, rather than only at the Red Hat Linux distribution. It's full of insights and techniques that will help you master Linux. You'll find it especially useful for continuing study after completing this book. You may also find it useful in troubleshooting and resolving installation and configuration problems.

CHAPTER 4

How Linux Works

Before you can effectively use a desktop environment, you need to know some Linux fundamentals. This chapter explains basic Linux concepts that underlie graphical and nongraphical system use. It describes Linux user accounts and how Linux organizes data as filesystems, directories, and files. This chapter also explains how to use the X Window System (often known simply as X). Because both GNOME and KDE are built on top of X, an understanding of X is central to using either desktop environment. Even though you're probably eager to get working with your new system, I suggest you at least skim this chapter. I also predict that you'll come back to it when you have some more experience and run into something confusing.

User Accounts

Like other multiuser operating systems, such as Windows NT/2000/XP, Linux uses user accounts to identify users and allocate permissions. Every Linux system has a special user known as the *root user*. The root user is analogous to the Windows user known as Administrator. The root user can perform privileged operations that are forbidden to other users. For instance, only the root user can perform most system administration operations. By default, the username associated with the root user is **root**.

You should be judicious in your use of the root account. For instance, you should safeguard the associated password so that no one uses it to compromise your system. Also, you should log in as the root user only when performing privileged operations. Following this advice will help you avoid disasters such as accidentally deleting important files that are protected against access by ordinary, non-root users.

How Linux Organizes Data

In order to make the most effective use of your Linux system, you must understand how Linux organizes data. If you're familiar with Windows or another operating system, you'll find it easy to learn how Linux organizes data, because most operating systems organize their data in similar ways. This section explains how Linux organizes data and introduces you to several important Linux commands that work with directories and files.

Devices

Linux receives data from, sends data to, and stores data on *devices*. A device generally corresponds to a hardware unit, such as a keyboard or serial port. However, a device may have no hardware counterpart: the kernel creates several *pseudodevices* that you can access as devices but that have no physical existence. Moreover, a single hardware unit may correspond to several devices. For example, Linux defines each partition of a disk drive as a distinct device. Table 4-1 describes some typical Linux devices; not every system provides all these devices and some systems provide devices not shown in the table. The device name often appears in messages and filenames on the system.

Table 4-1. Typical Linux devices

Device	Description
audio	Sound card
cdrom	CD-ROM drive
console	Current virtual console
fd*n*	Floppy drive (*n* designates the drive; for example, fd0 is the first floppy drive)
ftape	Streaming tape drive, not supporting rewind
hd*xn*	Non-SCSI hard drive (*x* designates the drive and *n* designates the partition; for example, hda1 is the first partition of the first non-SCSI hard drive)
lp*n*	Parallel port (*n* designates the device number; for example, lp0 is the first parallel port)
modem	Modem
mouse	Mouse
nrft*n*	Streaming tape drive, supporting rewind (*n* designates the device number; for example, nrft0 is the first streaming tape drive)
nst*n*	Streaming SCSI tape drive, not supporting rewind (*n* designates the device number; for example, nst0 is the first streaming SCSI tape drive)
null	Pseudodevice that accepts unlimited output and throws it away
printer	Printer
psaux	PS/2 mouse
rft*n*	Streaming tape drive, not supporting rewind (*n* designates the device number; for example, rft0 is the first streaming tape drive)
scd*n*	SCSI CD-ROM (*n* designates the device number; for example, scd0 is the first SCSI CD-ROM)
sd*xn*	SCSI hard drive (*x* designates the drive and *n* designates the partition; for example, sda1 is the first partition of the first SCSI hard drive)

Table 4-1. Typical Linux devices (continued)

Device	Description
st*n*	Streaming SCSI tape drive, supporting rewind (*n* designates the device number; for example, st0 is the first streaming SCSI tape drive)
tty*n*	Virtual console (*n* designates the particular virtual console; for example, tty0 is the first virtual console)
ttyS*n*	Modem (*n* designates the port; for example, ttyS0 is an incoming modem connection on the first serial port), serial device (such as Palm Pilot), or some PCMCIA devices
zero	Pseudodevice that supplies an inexhaustible stream of zero-bytes

Filesystems

Whether you're using Windows or Linux, you must format a partition before you can store data on it. The installation procedure automatically formats the partitions you create during system installation. When Linux formats a partition, it writes special data, called a *filesystem*, on the partition. The filesystem organizes the available space and provides a directory that lets you assign a name to each *file*, which is a set of stored data. A filesystem also enables you to group files into *directories*, which function much like the folders you create using the Windows Explorer: directories store information about the files they contain.

Just as every partition must have a filesystem, every CD-ROM and floppy diskette must have a filesystem. The filesystem of a CD-ROM is written when the disk is created; the filesystem of a floppy diskette is rewritten each time you format it.

Windows 98 lets you choose to format a partition as a FAT or FAT32. Windows NT/2000 also support the NTFS filesystem type. Linux supports a wider variety of filesystem types; Table 4-2 summarizes the most common ones. The most important filesystem types are *ext3*, which is used for Linux native partitions; *msdos*, which is used for FAT partitions (and floppy diskettes) of the sort created by MS-DOS and Microsoft Windows; and *iso9660*, which is used for CD-ROMs. Linux also provides the *vfat* filesystem, which is used for FAT32 partitions of the sort created by Windows 9x. Linux also supports reading of Windows NT/2000 NTFS filesystems; however, the support for doing so is not enabled in the standard Red Hat Linux kernel.

Table 4-2. Common filesystem types

Filesystem	Description
ext2	The predecessor of the ext3 filesystem; supported for compatibility.
ext3	The standard Linux filesystem.
iso9660	The standard filesystem used on CD-ROMs.
msdos	A filesystem compatible with Microsoft's FAT filesystem, used by MS-DOS and Windows.
nfs	A filesystem compatible with Sun's Network File System. An nfs filesystem does not reside on a physical partition; it is accessed via the network.
reiserfs	A Linux filesystem designed for high-reliability, large-capacity storage systems.
vfat	A filesystem compatible with Microsoft's FAT32 filesystem, used by Windows 9x.

Directories and Paths

If you've used MS-DOS, you're familiar with the concepts of file and directory and with various MS-DOS commands that work with files and directories. Under Linux, files and directories work much as they do under MS-DOS.

Home and working directories

When you log in to Linux, you're placed in a special directory known as your *home directory*. Generally, each user has a distinct home directory, where the user creates personal files. This makes it simple for the user to find files previously created, because they're kept separate from the files of other users and system files.

The *current directory*—or *current working directory*, as it's sometimes called—is the directory you're currently working in. When you log in to Linux, you're automatically placed in your home directory.

The directory tree

The directories of a Linux system are organized as a hierarchy. Unlike MS-DOS, which provides a separate hierarchy for each partition, Linux provides a single hierarchy that includes every partition. The topmost directory of the directory tree is the *root directory*, which is written using a forward slash (/), not the backward slash (\) used by MS-DOS to designate a root directory.

Figure 4-1 shows a hypothetical Linux directory tree; a real Linux system contains many more directories. The root directory contains six subdirectories: */bin, /dev, /etc, /home, /tmp,* and */usr.* The */home* directory has two subdirectories; each is the home directory of a user and has the same name as the user who owns it. The user named *bill* has created two subdirectories in his home directory: *books* and *school.* The user named *patrick* has created the single *school* subdirectory in his home directory.

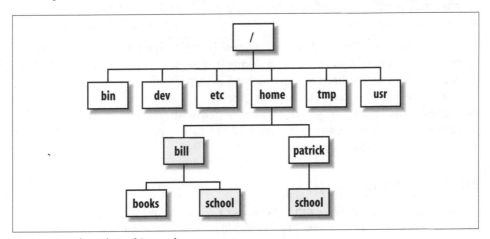

Figure 4-1. A hypothetical Linux directory tree

Each directory (other than the root directory) is contained in a directory known as its parent directory. For example, the parent directory of the *bill* directory is *home*.

 The *root* user has a special home directory, */root*. This directory is commonly called "slash root" to distinguish it from the root directory, */*.

Absolute and relative pathnames

If you look closely at Figure 4-1, you'll see that two directories named *school* exist; one is a subdirectory of *bill* and the other is a subdirectory of *patrick*. To avoid confusion that could result when several directories have the same name, directories are specified using *pathnames*.

There are two kinds of pathnames: *absolute* and *relative*. The absolute pathname of a directory traces the location of the directory beginning at the root directory; you form the pathname as a list of directories, separated by forward slashes (*/*). For example, the absolute pathname of the unique directory named *bill* is */home/bill*. The absolute pathname of the *school* subdirectory of the *bill* directory is */home/bill/school*. The absolute pathname of the identically named *school* subdirectory of the *patrick* directory is */home/patrick/school*.

When a subdirectory is many levels below the root directory, its absolute pathname may be long and cumbersome. In that case, it may be more convenient to use a relative pathname, which uses the current working directory, rather than the root directory, as its starting point. For example, suppose that the *bill* directory is the current working directory; you can refer to its *books* subdirectory by the relative pathname *books*. A relative pathname must never begin with a forward slash, whereas an absolute pathname must begin with a forward slash. As a second example, suppose that the */home* directory is the current working directory. The relative pathname of the *school* subdirectory of the *bill* directory would be *bill/school*; the relative pathname of the identically named subdirectory of the *patrick* directory would be *patrick/school*.

Linux provides two special directory names. Using a single dot (.) as a directory name is equivalent to specifying the working directory. Using two dots (..) within a pathname refers to the directory up one level in the current path; that is, to the parent directory. For example, if the working directory is */home/bill*, then .. refers to the */home* directory. Similarly, if the current working directory is */home/bill* and the directory tree is that shown in Figure 4-1, the path *../patrick/school* refers to the directory */home/patrick/school*.

File Permissions

Unlike Windows 98, but like other varieties of Unix and Windows NT/2000, Linux is a multiuser operating system. Therefore, it includes mechanisms to protect data from unauthorized access. The primary protection mechanism restricts access to directories and files based on the identity of the user who requests access and on access modes assigned to each directory and file.

Each directory and file has an associated user, called the *owner*. The user who initially creates a file is the owner of the file. Each user belongs to one or more sets of users known as *groups*. Each directory and file has an associated group, which is assigned when the directory or file is created. The user and the group can be changed later.

Access permissions, also known as *modes*, determine what operations a user can perform on a directory or file. Table 4-3 lists the most common permissions and explains the meaning of each. Notice that permissions work differently for directories than for files. For example, permission r denotes the ability to list the contents of a directory or *read* the contents of a file. A directory or file can have multiple permissions. Only the listed permissions are granted; any other operations are prohibited. For example, a user who had file permission rw could *read* or *write* the *file* but could not execute it, as indicated by the absence of the execute permission, x.

Table 4-3. Common access permissions

Permission	Operations allowed on a directory	Operations allowed on a file
r	List the directory	Read contents
w	Create or remove files	Write contents
x	Access files and subdirectories	Execute

The access modes of a directory or file consist of three sets of permissions:

User/Owner
    Applies to the owner of the file

Group
    Applies to users who are members of the group assigned to the file

Other
    Applies to other users

The **ls** command, which you'll meet in Chapter 7, lists the file access modes in the second column of its long output format, as shown in Figure 4-2. The GNOME and KDE file managers use this same format. The column contains nine characters: the first three specify the access allowed the owner of the directory or file, the second three specify the access allowed users in the same group as the directory or file, and the final three specify the access allowed to other users (see Figure 4-3).

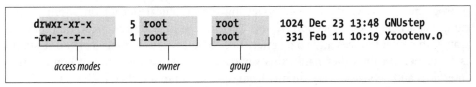

Figure 4-2. Access modes as shown by the ls command

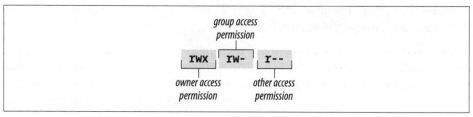

Figure 4-3. Access modes specify three permissions

Mounting and Unmounting Filesystems

You cannot access a hard drive partition, CD-ROM, or floppy disk until the related device or partition is *mounted*. Mounting a device checks the status of the device and readies it for access when it boots or when you launch a desktop environment. By default, the GNOME and KDE desktop environments automatically mount devices that use removable media.

Before you can remove media from a device, you must unmount it. You can unmount a device by using a desktop environment or issuing a command. For your convenience, the system automatically unmounts devices when it shuts down. A device can be unmounted only if it's not in use. For example, if a user's current working directory is a directory of the device, the device cannot be unmounted.

 A common error is attempting to mount a CD-ROM or floppy without first inserting the media. If you're unable to mount a device that uses removable media, check that the media is available.

Using X

X is the standard graphical user interface (GUI) for Linux. Like other GUIs, such as Windows and Mac OS, X lets you interact with programs by using a mouse (or other pointing device) to point and click, providing a simple means of communicating with your computer.

Despite its age, X is a remarkable and very modern software system offering a cross-platform, network-oriented GUI. It runs on a wide variety of platforms including essentially every flavor of Unix, such as Solaris, Linux, and the BSDs (FreeBSD, NetBSD, and OpenBSD). X clients are available for use, for example, under Windows 3.*x*, 9*x*, NT, 2000, and XP. The sophisticated networking capabilities of X let you run a program on one computer while viewing the graphical output on another computer via a network connection. X was designed to provide room for experimentation with new interfaces and so a variety of X-based window managers and desktops is available. On the other hand, this variety can provoke some minor confusion as interfaces and behaviors vary slightly from one system to another.

Most Linux users run XFree86, a freely available software system compatible with X, which is distributed with Red Hat Linux. XFree86 was developed by the XFree86 software team, which began work in 1992. In 1994, the XFree86 Project, Inc. (*http://www.xfree86.org*) assumed responsibility for ongoing research and development of XFree86.

Window Managers

Using X means interacting with Linux on several different levels. X itself merely provides the graphics facility for displaying components of a GUI: X draws the screen, draws objects on the screen, and tracks user input actions such as keyboard input and mouse operations. To organize the desktop into familiar objects like windows, menus, and scrollbars, X relies on a separate program called a window manager. But even more functionality is required. A window manager alone doesn't provide tight integration between applications of the sort required by drag-and-drop operations; that higher degree of integration comes from what's called a desktop environment. While X itself is a single program, X under Linux supports several popular window managers and two popular desktop environments, GNOME and KDE.

Window managers create the borders, icons, and menus that provide a simple-to-use interface. Window managers also control the look and feel of X, letting you configure X to operate almost any way you desire. At one time, it was common for Linux users to separately choose a window manager and desktop environment. However, today most users retain the window manager with which their preferred desktop environment is initially configured. GNOME uses the metacity window manager and KDE uses Kwin, formerly known as the K Window Manager, or simply K. Because of the variety of window managers, scrollbars and other widgets may behave differently from one system to another. But, the differences are minor and determined clicking generally discovers the proper method of interacting with a widget. See the section "Using scrollbars" later in this chapter.

Desktop Environments

A *desktop environment* is a set of desktop tools and applications. The Windows desktop includes applications such as the Windows Explorer, accessories such as Notepad, games such as FreeCell and Minesweeper, and utilities such as the Control Panel and its applets. Although you can run X without a desktop, having a desktop helps you work more efficiently. Both GNOME and KDE are free software and are developed by teams in an open, collaborative manner.

The default Red Hat Linux desktop environment is GNOME. However, you can easily reconfigure KDE as the desktop, if you prefer. The choice between GNOME and KDE is now not so important as in the past. Red Hat has reworked GNOME and KDE to give them a consistent look and feel. Moreover, almost every GNOME application can now be run under KDE and almost every KDE application can now be run under GNOME. So your Linux experience will be similar whether you're using GNOME or KDE.

GNOME

GNOME stands for the GNU Network Object Model Environment (pronounced as *guh-nome* or *gee-nome*). One of GNOME's most interesting features is session awareness. When you re-enter GNOME after logging out, it reconfigures your desktop to match the state at the time you exited by launching each application that was open when you exited. GNOME even restores each application to its former state by, for example, moving to the page that was open when you exited.

Both GNOME and KDE support a myriad of standard and optional desktop tools and applications, such as:

- Games and amusements such as freecell, gnibbles, gnobots, gnomine, mahjongg, and sol
- The GNU Image Manipulation Program (GIMP)
- Ghostview, which lets you view PostScript files and print them on non-PostScript printers
- Internet applications such as Mozilla, gFTP, NcFTP, X-Chat, slrn, and pine
- Multimedia applications such as Audio Player, Sound Mixer, and CD Player
- General applications such as gEdit, a text editor; Mozilla, the popular open source web browser; and OpenOffice, a desktop suite featuring word processing, spreadsheets, presentations, and other facilities
- Utilities for configuring and using your Red Hat Linux system

KDE

KDE (the K Desktop Environment) includes Kwin, the K Window Manager, as an integral component. KDE provides a file manager, a help system, a configuration utility, and a variety of accessories and applications, such as:

- Games such as kasteriods, kmines, and kpoke
- Graphical applications such as Kfract, a fractal generator; and Kview, an image viewer
- Multimedia applications such as Kmix, a sound mixer; and KsCD, a CD player
- Network applications such as Kmail, a mail client; gaim, an instant messenger compatible with AOL's AIM; and KNewsticker, an applet that displays news from web sites of your choice

As with GNOME, new KDE accessories and applications are available almost weekly.

At one time, KDE was distributed under a license that suggested that some users owed a fee to developers of an important library used to develop KDE. This inhibited acceptance of KDE within the free software community. As a result, several releases of Red Hat Linux featured only GNOME, despite the popularity of KDE. Currently, KDE is open source and may be freely distributed.

Keyboard Operations

Using the keyboard with X closely resembles using the keyboard with Windows. X sends your keyboard input to the active window, which is said to have the *input focus*. The active window is usually the window in which you most recently clicked the mouse.

This chapter refers to your pointing device as a *mouse*. However, like Windows, X supports a variety of pointing devices.

While Windows lets you choose to perform most operations by using the keyboard or mouse, X was designed for use with a mouse. If your mouse isn't functioning, you'll find it quite challenging or even impossible to use most X programs. X allows you to perform only a few important functions via the keyboard:

- Switching video modes
- Using virtual consoles
- Abruptly terminating X

Switching video modes

When you configured X, you specified the video modes in which X can operate. Recall that the current video mode determines the resolution and color depth of the image displayed by your monitor—for example, 16 bits per pixel color depth and 1024×768 pixels screen resolution.

By pressing **Ctrl-Alt-+** (using the Plus key on the numeric keypad), you command X to switch to the next video mode in sequence. X treats the video modes as a cycle: if X is operating in the last video mode, this key sequence causes X to return to the first video mode.

The similar key sequence **Ctrl-Alt--** (using the minus key on the numeric keypad) causes X to switch to the previous video model. If you shift to a video mode that your monitor doesn't support—as demonstrated by an unsteady or garbled image—you can use this key sequence to return to a supported video mode, avoiding the inconvenience of terminating X and reconfiguring your system.

Using virtual consoles

Even while X is running, you can access the Linux virtual consoles. For instance, you may find it useful to do so in order to recover from a X-related problem, so long as the problem hasn't frozen the keyboard. To switch from graphical mode to a virtual console running in text mode, type **Ctrl-Alt-F***n*, where **F** is a function key and *n* is the number of the desired virtual console. X uses virtual console #7, so only virtual consoles #1–6 are accessible while running X.

To switch from a virtual console back to X, type **Ctrl-Alt-F7**. Nothing is lost when you switch from X to a virtual console or back, so you can move freely between the graphical and text operating modes.

Terminating X

You can terminate X abruptly by typing **Ctrl-Alt-Backspace**. However, this method of terminating X is appropriate only when X is malfunctioning. Terminating X abruptly closes down running applications, which may result in loss of data.

Terminal Windows and Pop-up Menus

In Windows, you don't need to restart in DOS mode simply to have access to the DOS command line. Similarly, in X you don't need to switch to a virtual console simply to have access to the command line. X enables you to open a terminal window. A terminal window resembles the MS-DOS Prompt window or command-line interface window; like a Linux virtual console, it lets you type commands and view command output. Various window managers support different methods of accessing a terminal window, as described in Chapter 5.

The terminal window is just one example of a frequently used program under X that you'll want to access. Most window managers install with a default set of common programs that can be accessed by right-clicking with the mouse on the desktop. For example, most window managers let you right-click on the desktop and select a terminal window program from the pop-up menu that appears. However, the pop-up menu displayed by a window manager may display program names rather than program functions. In this case, you may have some difficulty determining which entry on the pop-up menu corresponds to a terminal program. Many programs that provide terminal windows have names that include the sequences *xt* or *xterm*. Selecting such an entry will launch a terminal window. You'll learn more about window managers later in this chapter.

Mouse Operations

Mouse operations under X are similar to mouse operations under Windows, although you perform them differently. The most common mouse operations that behave differently are:

- Copying and pasting text
- Using scrollbars

Copying and pasting text

To copy and paste text, you must first mark the text by moving the mouse to the beginning of the text; then click the left mouse button and drag the mouse across the text to be copied. X automatically copies the marked text into a buffer; you don't need to press **Ctrl-C** or perform any other operation. However, for compatibility with Windows, some window managers let you copy text by pressing **Ctrl-C**, or by right clicking and choosing from a pop-up menu. If you find that you need to change the size of the marked text section, you can click the right mouse button and move the mouse to adjust the marked text.

 Some window managers display a pop-up menu when you click the right button, even when the mouse cursor is above text. When using such a window manager, you cannot use the right mouse button to adjust the size of the marked text section.

To paste the text, properly position the insertion point and click the middle mouse button. If your mouse has only two buttons, simultaneously click the left and right buttons to simulate clicking the middle mouse button. You may find that this operation requires a little practice before you get it right, but once you've mastered it, you'll find it works almost as well as having a three-button mouse. Some window managers will let you paste text by pressing **Shift-Ctrl-V**, or by right clicking and choosing from a pop-up menu.

Using scrollbars

Many X programs provide scrollbars that resemble those provided by Windows. However, the operation of scrollbars under X originally differed from that under Windows. Most X programs have been revised to display scrollbars that work like Windows scrollbars, although a few have not.

If you're having trouble using a scrollbar, it may have been programmed to use the original X method of interaction. This problem is more likely to affect old X programs than recent ones. To page forward using the original X method, click the left mouse button on the scrollbar. Clicking near the top of the scrollbar scrolls forward a short distance, as little as a single line. Clicking near the bottom of the scrollbar scrolls the window by a page. To page backward, click the right mouse button on the scrollbar. Again, clicking near the top of the scrollbar scrolls a short distance, as little as a single line. Clicking near the bottom of the scrollbar scrolls the window by a page.

Virtual Desktop

Under X, your desktop can be scrollable; that is, larger than the size of your monitor. For example, even if your monitor has a maximum resolution of 800×600, you might have a desktop of 1600×1200 or even 3200×2400. Such a desktop is known as a *virtual desktop*.

 Don't confuse the term *virtual desktop* with the term *virtual console*. A virtual console is used to log in and enter commands in text mode; a virtual desktop is used to obtain an oversized desktop in graphics mode.

Most desktop environments provide a tool called a *pager*, which lets you move around the virtual desktop. The pager provides a thumbnail view of your virtual desktop; by clicking within the thumbnail, you center your actual desktop on the clicked location. You'll learn more about pagers in the next two chapters.

## CHAPTER 5

Using the GNOME and KDE Desktops

Red Hat Linux supports two desktops, GNOME and KDE. This choice is consistent with the Linux philosophy of having it your own way. But the reasons behind having multiple desktops have more to do with history and law than technology.

At one time, parts of KDE were distributed under a license that some believed required commercial users to pay a license fee. Because Red Hat wanted Red Hat Linux to be freely redistributable and usable, Red Hat included only GNOME in the Red Hat Linux distribution. Red Hat also assisted in the development of the GNOME desktop. However, the KDE license was eventually clarified. At that point, Red Hat warmed toward KDE and included it in the Red Hat Linux distribution. Many users prefer KDE to GNOME, finding it in many ways more mature than GNOME. But GNOME retains a somewhat favored status in Red Hat's eyes, as indicated by Red Hat's use of GNOME's GTK toolset to implement many of Red Hat Linux's system administration tools.

In Red Hat Linux 8, Red Hat has attempted to give GNOME and KDE a more consistent look and feel. This has upset many KDE fans, who prefer KDE's native look and feel to that imposed by Red Hat. An advantage of Red Hat's decision is that most applications work properly under both GNOME and KDE. However, a disadvantage of Red Hat's decision is that KDE now includes applications that lack the distinctive look and feel that unites the KDE desktop.

However, I'm not much interested in justifying or attacking Red Hat's decision. The decision has been made, and the goal of this book is to describe Red Hat Linux as it is, rather than as it might be. Therefore, this chapter describes both desktops, devoting roughly equal space to each. My personal recommendation is that you try each desktop for a while and use the one you prefer.

Some readers of earlier editions of this book claim that I favor one desktop over the other. Yes, I do have a personal favorite. However, almost all such readers have incorrectly identified my preference. So, I believe that my presentation of the desktops is reasonably fair and unbiased.

Using the GNOME Desktop

If you selected GNOME as the default desktop, you will see the GNOME desktop as shown in Figure 5-1 after logging in. The contents of your desktop may be different, of course.

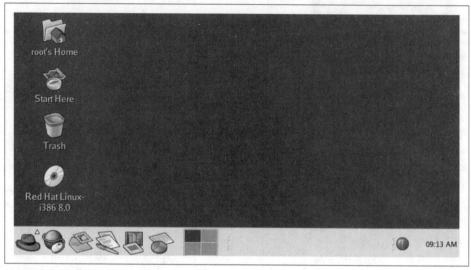

Figure 5-1. The GNOME desktop

If you want to launch a GNOME session, but KDE is configured as the default desktop environment, select Gnome from the Session menu of the system login screen. Of course, GNOME must be installed in order for this to work.

To log out of GNOME, left-click on the main menu, which resembles a red hat. From the pop-up menu that appears, select the Log Out menu item, as shown in Figure 5-2. A Log Out dialog box, shown in Figure 5-3, appears and asks you to confirm your decision to log out. Clicking OK terminates your GNOME session. If you enable the checkbox titled Save Current Setup, the GNOME session manager will save the state of your desktop and restore it when you log in again to GNOME.

There are two other options in the Log Out dialog box. Select the Shut Down button to shut down your system, or the Restart the computer button to restart it.

The GNOME Desktop

The term *desktop* can be used in either of two senses. It can refer either to the entire GNOME display, or to the empty area of the display where no windows or icons appear, as indicated in Figure 5-4. To keep straight these meanings, *GNOME desktop* will be used when referring to the entire display and *desktop* will be used when referring to the empty area of the display.

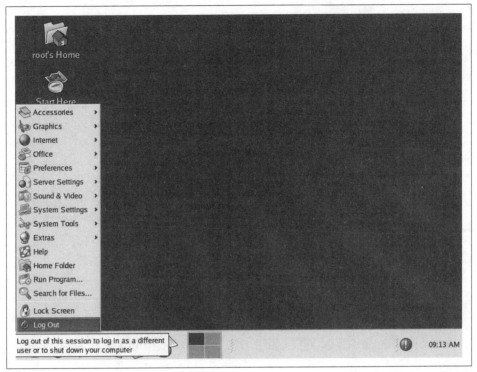

Figure 5-2. Logging out of GNOME

Figure 5-3. The Log Out dialog box

Right-clicking the desktop causes a pop-up menu to appear; this menu lets you perform a variety of operations, such as:

- Creating a new folder
- Creating a new launcher
- Opening a terminal window

Figure 5-4 shows the elements of the GNOME desktop, which are described in the
following sections.

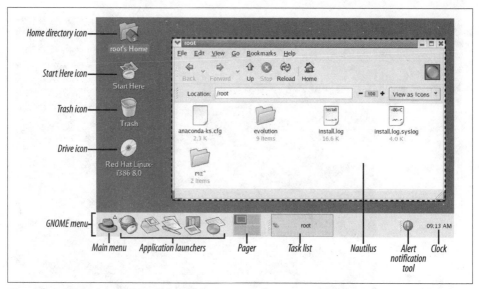

Figure 5-4. Parts of the GNOME desktop

Pager

There's one particular GNOME and KDE feature that I miss when working with Windows: the pager. The pager is the rectangle at the bottom of the screen, just left of center. You can recognize it by the four smaller rectangles nested within it.

The pager provides what's called a *virtual desktop*; that is, a desktop that's larger than the size of your monitor screen. Of course, you can't see the entire virtual desktop at once, since it's larger than your monitor screen. So, you use the pager to select which quadrant of the virtual desktop you're viewing.

To see how the pager works, click on a pager quadrant other than the default, which is the upper-left quadrant. Any open windows vanish. Click on the upper-left pager quadrant to restore them. As a further experiment, click on a quadrant other than the default. Then, launch a program from the menu. When the program's window appears, restore the default desktop view by clicking the upper-left pager quadrant. The new window disappears. Click again on the pager quadrant that was active when you launched the program. The new window reappears.

If you look carefully at the quadrants, you'll see that they provide a bird's eye view of the associated desktop configurations. You may not be able to identify a window from its pager image. But, you can easily distinguish an empty virtual desktop quadrant from one containing one or more windows.

Home Directory icon

The Home Directory icon, which resembles a house superimposed on a file folder, is normally located in the upper-left corner of the display. The icon provides a convenient way to access the file manager: double-clicking the icon with the left mouse button launches Nautilus, GNOME's browser and file manager, which displays the contents of the user's home directory.

Drive icons

If you have permission to mount a CD-ROM or floppy drive, and media is present, your desktop includes an icon representing the drive. Depending on the type of drive, the icon may resemble a CD-ROM or a floppy. If you right-click on the icon, a pop-up menu appears. The menu lets you unmount and eject the media, or open Nautilus to view the files residing on the device. You can also simply double click to launch Nautilus and view the contents of the media.

Start Here icon

By double-clicking the Start Here icon, you can launch Nautilus to view a folder that contains several useful icons. Double-clicking any icon in the folder launches a window containing icons that provide access to GNOME facilities. You can access the same facilities by using the GNOME menu. The icons and a summary of the operators each offers appear in the following list:

Applications
> The Applications icon lets you launch various applications.

Preferences
> The Preferences icon provides access to a folder containing icons that enable you to view and modify a variety of preferences, including those for the desktop, document handlers, user interface look and feel, multimedia, and peripherals.

Server Settings
> The Server Settings icon provides access to tools for configuring servers, such as Apacheconf, a tool for configuring the Apache web server.

System Settings
> The System Settings icon provides access to tools for viewing and modifying the system configuration.

Trash icon

The Trash icon lets you view files that have been deleted by using Nautilus. Files deleted by using the **rm** command are not stored in the trash; they are immediately deleted. Simply double-click the icon, and GNOME launches Nautilus to view the folder where deleted files are stored. To restore a deleted file, you can drag it to a new location. You can permanently delete files stored in the Trash by right-clicking the Trash icon and selecting Empty Trash Bin from the pop-up menu.

The GNOME Panel

By default, the GNOME panel appears along the bottom edge of the display. However, if you prefer a different location, you can move the panel; to do so, click and drag the panel to the desired location. The panel functionally resembles the Windows taskbar; you can use it to launch programs, switch from one program to another, and perform other tasks.

 Moving the mouse cursor over an icon in the panel reveals a message informing you of the function of the icon.

The panel can also contain *applets*, programs represented as panel icons. Applets are typically small programs that display information or take action when clicked. For example, a *launcher applet* launches an application when its button in the panel is clicked.

If you right click the panel and then choose Help from the pop-up menu, GNOME launches Nautilus to view the GNOME Panel Manual. The GNOME Panel Manual explains the function and operation of the GNOME panel in detail.

By default, the GNOME panel contains the following items:

Main menu
> The main menu icon resembles a red hat. Left-clicking the main menu icon presents a menu from which you can choose a variety of programs. Several of the menu entries are submenus; selecting such an entry pops up a new menu to the side of the original entry.

Web browser
> Launches the Mozilla web browser.

Email
> Launches the Evolution email client, described in Chapter 6.

OpenOffice Writer
> Launches the OpenOffice word processor, described in Chapter 6.

OpenOffice Impress
> Launches the OpenOffice presentation creator, described in Chapter 6.

OpenOffice Calc
> Launches the OpenOffice spreadsheet, described in Chapter 6.

Pager
> Described earlier in the "Pager" section.

Task list
> The task list contains a button for each active task. Clicking a task's button raises the task's window to the front of the screen, so that you can view it.

Alert Notification Tool

Alerts you when errata or updates are available via Red Hat Network

Clock

The clock displays your system's current time.

Using Nautilus

To launch the GNOME file manager, double-click the Start Here icon, or a folder or drive icon if one is visible. You can use the GNOME file manager, named Nautilus, to browse any drive, folder, or administrative interface. Nautilus has two main panes, as shown in Figure 5-5. If the left pane is not visible, click View → Side Pane. The left pane may display information about the current folder or a hierarchical folder tree. To switch between these views, click the Tree tab at the bottom of the left pane. If the Tree tab is not visible, right click the left pane and select Tree from the pop-up menu. To select a folder in the left pane, simply left-click it. The right pane then shows the contents of the selected folder.

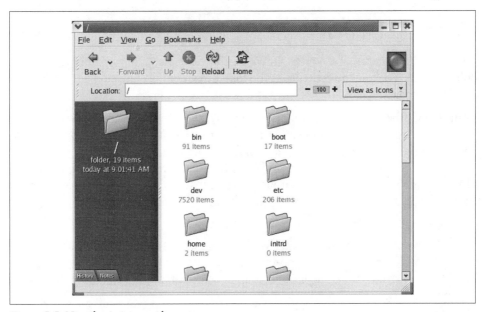

Figure 5-5. Nautilus in icon mode

The right pane can show an icon for each file or detailed information about each file, as shown in Figure 5-6. To switch from icon to detailed mode, left-click the control labeled View as Icons or View as List. You can also select custom mode, which lets you tailor the display appearance according to your own taste.

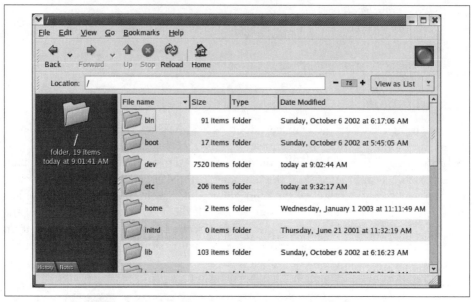

Figure 5-6. Nautilus in list mode

To view the contents of a folder shown in the right pane, simply double-click the folder's icon. To view the contents of the folder that contains the current folder, click the Up toolbar icon.

Nautilus can be used as a file manager to copy, move, rename, and delete files. To perform one of these operations, you must first select the file (or files) by left-clicking in the right pane. To select additional files, hold down the **Ctrl** key as you select individual files. The Edit menu includes a menu item that lets you click on all files that appear in the right pane. Nautilus provides many ways to perform common file manager operations. Here are a few of the most important ones:

- To move a file, simply drag it to its new location.
- To copy a file, hold down **Ctrl** while dragging it. Alternatively, you can right-click on a file and use the pop-up menu to specify the action you want to perform. Nautilus then displays a dialog box that lets you specify additional options.
- To rename a file, right-click on the file's icon and select Rename from the pop-up menu. Simply type the new name and press Enter.
- To delete a file, right-click on the file and select Move to Trash from the pop-up menu.

If you keep Nautilus's left pane open, operations such as the preceding can be performed conveniently. For instance, if you want to move a file from one folder to another, list folders in the left pane and navigate to the folder containing the file in the right pane.

Nautilus lets you double-click on a file to launch the application associated with the file. Alternatively, you can right-click on the file and select Open With from the pop-up menu. Nautilus launches a dialog box that lets you specify the application that should be launched.

Many applications are GNOME-compliant, supporting drag-and-drop operations like those supported by Windows. For example, you can open two file manager windows and drag-and-drop files or folders between them.

The Nautilus menus provide additional functions, including the ability to configure the operation of Nautilus. If you're familiar with the Windows Explorer, you'll find most of these functions and capabilities familiar. To learn more about Nautilus, use the Nautilus Help menu to view the Nautilus Quick Reference.

Using GNOME Terminal

Similar to the MS-DOS Prompt window, the GNOME terminal, shown in Figure 5-7, provides a window in which you can type shell commands and view their output. To launch GNOME terminal, right click the desktop and select New Terminal from the pop-up menu. You can open multiple GNOME terminal windows if you like.

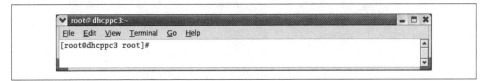

Figure 5-7. The GNOME terminal application

The Edit → Current Profile menu item lets you configure the operation of GNOME terminal, as shown in Figure 5-8. For example, you may find that the default font is too large or too small for your liking. From the Editing profile dialog box, select the General tab and disable the checkbox labelled Use same font as other applications. Click the name of the current font and a second dialog box pops up, from which you can select the font, font style, and font size you prefer.

To exit GNOME terminal, simply type **exit** on the command line and press **Enter**. Alternatively, select Close Window from the File menu or simply type **Ctrl-D**.

Configuring GNOME

Like most GNOME applications, GNOME itself is highly configurable. You can configure GNOME's panel, its main menu, and its overall appearance and function. The following sections briefly show you how.

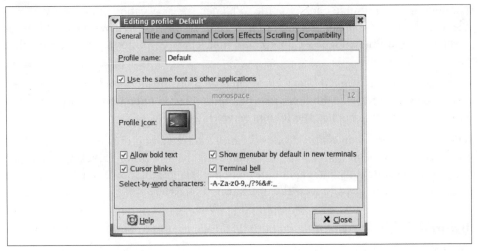

Figure 5-8. Editing terminal settings

The GNOME panel

Clicking on a launcher launches a predetermined application. You can easily add a launcher to the GNOME panel. To do so, right-click on the panel and select Add to Panel → Launcher from the pop-up menu. The Create Launcher dialog box, as shown in Figure 5-9, appears.

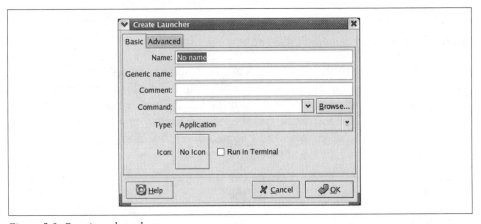

Figure 5-9. Creating a launcher

You can specify a name for the launcher, a comment, and the command that GNOME executes to launch the application. GNOME automatically provides a default icon. If the program to be run is a text-based program, check the Run in Terminal checkbox.

If an application is already on the main menu, you can quickly create a launcher for it. Simply right-click on the application's menu item and select "Add this launcher to panel" or "Add this applet as a launcher to panel" from the pop-up menu.

If your panel contains many launchers, it may become crowded and confusing. To remedy this, you can create one or more drawers, like that shown in Figure 5-10. Drawers act like menus; you click on a drawer to open it and view the launchers it contains. Clicking an open drawer closes it and hides its contents.

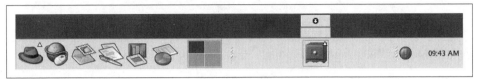

Figure 5-10. A drawer

To add a drawer, right-click on the panel and select Add to Panel → Drawer from the pop-up menu. To move a launcher into the drawer, click on the drawer to open it, right-click on the launcher, and select Move from the pop-up menu. Next, move the cursor over the open drawer and click the left mouse button to drop the launcher on the rectangular box above the drawer icon, not the drawer icon itself.

If you add a launcher or drawer and later decide you don't want it, you can remove it from the panel. Simply right-click on the unwanted launcher and select Remove From Panel from the pop-up menu, as shown in Figure 5-11.

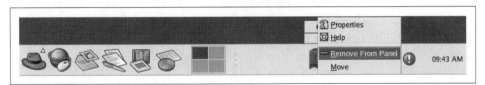

Figure 5-11. Removing a panel item

The GNOME Start Here facility

You can configure the appearance and operation of GNOME and GNOME-compliant applications by using the GNOME Start Here facility, shown in Figure 5-12. The Start Here facility resembles the Windows Control Panel, although it looks and works somewhat differently. To launch the Start Here facility, click the Start Here icon on the desktop or panel.

You can use the Start Here facility to:

- Select background properties
- Configure a screensaver
- Select a desktop theme

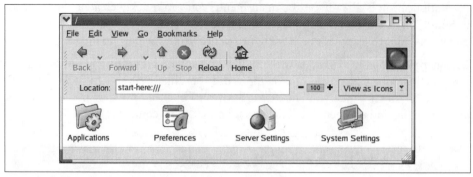

Figure 5-12. The GNOME Start Here facility

- Configure the default web browser, text editor, and terminal application
- Specify MIME types that control the handling of multimedia files
- Configure the keyboard bell and sounds
- Configure keyboard and mouse properties
- Specify applications that GNOME automatically launches when it starts
- Specify a variety of options governing the appearance of GNOME-compliant applications

Simply select the configuration category by double-clicking the appropriate folder in the Start Here window. Like the Windows Control Panel, the Start Here facility uses small programs called *applets* to perform its functions. A Start Here window generally contains a mixture of applets and folders.

When you double-click on an applet, a configuration dialog box appears. You can then revise the configuration parameters by specifying the desired values.

GNOME Resources

Several books have been written on GNOME. This chapter has described only a small fraction of what GNOME can do. The following additional resources are available:

GNOME Desktop 2.0 User's Guide
The official guide to using GNOME, available via the GNOME help system.

http://www.gnome.org/learn

The GNOME FAQ
Written by Telsa Gwynne, the GNOME FAQ provides answers to some of the most commonly asked questions concerning GNOME. However, it's somewhat out of date.

http://www.gnome.org/faqs/users-faq/

Using the KDE Desktop

As explained at the beginning of this chapter, Red Hat Linux initially included only GNOME; however, it now supports both GNOME and KDE. Figure 5-13 shows KDE's desktop. If your system is configured to use GNOME and you want to launch a KDE session, select KDE from the Session menu of the system login screen. Of course, KDE must be installed in order for this to work.

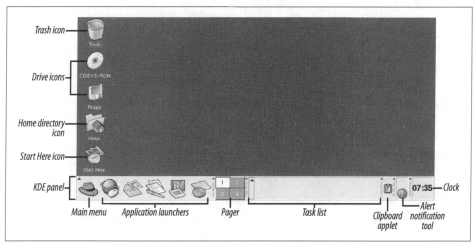

Figure 5-13. The KDE desktop

The KDE Desktop

KDE has a main menu icon in its panel, at the lower left of the screen. The icon is identical to that associated with GNOME's main menu, a red hat. Clicking the icon reveals a menu that includes a Logout menu item. You can use the Logout menu item to terminate KDE.

Right-clicking the KDE desktop causes a pop-up menu to appear. From this menu, you can create desktop shortcuts and perform a variety of other functions. The desktop includes a variety of icons and folders. The specific icons and folders that appear may vary depending on the software installed on your system and your KDE configuration. The most common icons are described in the following subsections.

Start Here icon

By double-clicking the Start Here icon, you can launch Konqueror, KDE's file manager, to view a folder that contains several useful icons. Double-clicking any icon in the folder launches a window containing icons that provide access to KDE facilities.

You can access the same facilities by using the KDE menu. The icons within the Start Here folder include:

Applications
> The Applications icon lets you launch various applications.

Preferences
> The Preferences icon provides access to a folder containing icons that enable you to view and modify a variety of preferences, including those for the desktop, document handlers, user interface look and feel, multimedia, and peripherals.

Server Settings
> The Server Settings icon provides access to tools for configuring servers, such as Apacheconf, a tool for configuring the Apache web server.

System Settings
> The System Settings icon provides access to tools for viewing and modifying the system configuration.

Home Directory icon

The Home Directory icon enables you to view your home directory by using KDE's file manager, Konqueror.

Drive icons

If you have permission to mount a CD-ROM or floppy drive, your desktop includes an icon representing the drive. If you click the icon, a pop-up menu appears. If your system is configured to do so, it will automatically mount media. However, you can use the menu to manually mount or unmount media. Right-clicking the drive icon lets you eject or unmount the media.

Trash icon

Clicking the Trash icon lets you view the contents of the folder in which KDE stores files moved to the Trash bin by Konqueror. Files deleted by the **rm** command are not stored in the trash; they are immediately deleted.

The KDE Panel

KDE's panel normally appears along the bottom edge of the display. However, you can relocate it by dragging it to a side or the top edge of the display. The panel normally contains the main menu icon, launchers, the pager, the task list, the clipboard tool, the alert notification tool, and the clock.

> Moving your mouse over an icon in the Panel displays a message informing you of the icon's function.

Main menu icon

As mentioned, the main menu icon features a red hat. Left-clicking the main menu presents a menu from which you can choose a variety of programs. Several of the menu items are submenus; selecting such a menu item pops up a new menu to the side of the original menu item.

Web browser

Launches the Mozilla web browser.

Email

Launches the Evolution email client, described in Chapter 6.

OpenOffice Writer

Launches the OpenOffice word processor, described in Chapter 6.

OpenOffice Impress

Launches the OpenOffice presentation creator, described in Chapter 6.

OpenOffice Calc

Launches the OpenOffice spreadsheet, described in Chapter 6.

Pager

Like GNOME, KDE features a virtual desktop that's larger than your system's monitor. The pager lets you navigate the virtual desktop. By default, one of four virtual desktop pages is visible. The four pager buttons let you select a different desktop page. The button that shows window contents rather than a numeral indicates the page you're currently viewing as your desktop. To view a different page, simply left-click the button that represents the desktop page you want to view.

Task list

The task list contains a button for each active task. Clicking a task's button raises the task's window to the front of the screen so you can view it.

Clipboard Tool

The clipboard lets you view and manipulate the contents of KDE's clipboard, which holds text during copy-and-paste or cut-and-paste operations.

Alert Notification Tool

Alerts you when errata or updates are available via Red Hat Network.

Clock

The KDE clock gives the current date and time.

Using Konqueror

Konqueror is KDE's file manager and web browser. When you click the icon that resembles a small house superimposed on a larger file folder, Konqueror displays the contents of your */home* folder, as shown in Figure 5-14.

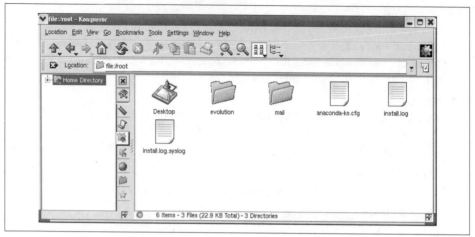

Figure 5-14. Konqueror displaying the contents of a folder

By clicking the Tree View icon, which is the rightmost icon, which is on Konqueror's toolbar, you can cause Konqueror to display information in a format that resembles the familiar two-pane layout used by the Microsoft Windows Explorer and GNOME's Nautilus. Figure 5-15 shows Konqueror in Tree View.

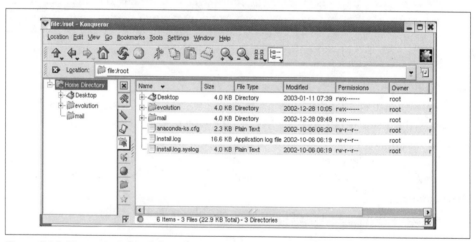

Figure 5-15. Konqueror's detailed mode in Tree View

Konqueror can be used to move, copy, rename, and delete files and folders. You can perform these and other file operations in a variety of ways. To rename a file, right-click on the file's icon and select Rename from the pop-up menu. Simply type the new name and press **Enter**. To delete a file, right-click on the file and select Delete from the pop-up menu. A dialog box asks you to confirm your decision.

You can move, copy, or delete multiple files in a single operation. Select the files by holding down the **Ctrl** key as you select them one at a time. Alternatively, you can click and drag the cursor around a group of files. To move or copy the selected files, simply drag them to the new location. When you release the mouse, a pop-up menu lets you specify whether you want to move or copy the files.

Rather than move or copy a file, you can use the pop-up menu to create a link. Konqueror lets you click on a link to launch an application on the file associated with the link. Alternatively, you can right-click on the file or link and select Open With from the pop-up menu. KDE launches a dialog box that lets you specify the application that should be launched.

Using KDE Terminal

Similar to the MS-DOS Prompt window, the KDE terminal, also known as Konsole, provides a window in which you can type shell commands and view their output. To launch KDE terminal, you can select System Tools → Terminal from the KDE menu. You can open multiple KDE terminal windows if you like.

The Settings menu lets you configure the operation of KDE terminal. For example, you may find that the default font is too large or too small for your liking. If so, select Settings → Font from the KDE terminal window. Then simply select the font size you prefer.

To exit KDE Terminal, simply type **exit** on the command line and press **Enter**. Alternatively, select Quit from the File menu or type **Ctrl-D**.

Configuring KDE

KDE is highly configurable. This section explains how to use the KDE Panel, the KDE Control Panel, the KDE Control Center, and the KDE menu editor.

The KDE Panel

It's simple to add a launcher icon to the KDE Panel. Right-click on the Panel, select Add from the pop-up menu, and choose a program from the menu that appears. To remove a launcher from the Panel, right-click the launcher and select Remove from the pop-up menu.

If your panel contains many launchers, it may become crowded and confusing. To remedy this, you can create a child panel, like that shown at the bottom in Figure 5-16 under the main panel. Right-click the Panel and select Add → Extension → Child Panel. You can move the child panel to a different edge of the screen by dragging its hide panel—the arrowhead that appears at one end of the child panel— to the desired location. Launchers can be added to a child panel, just as you add them to the Panel. To remove a child panel and its contents, right-click the hide button at the end of the child panel and select Remove from the pop-up menu.

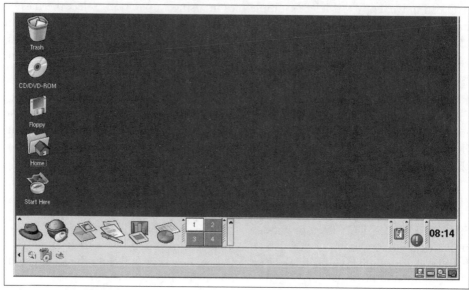

Figure 5-16. A child panel

The KDE Control Center

You can launch the KDE Control Center by choosing Control Center from the KDE main menu. Figure 5-17 shows the KDE Control Center.

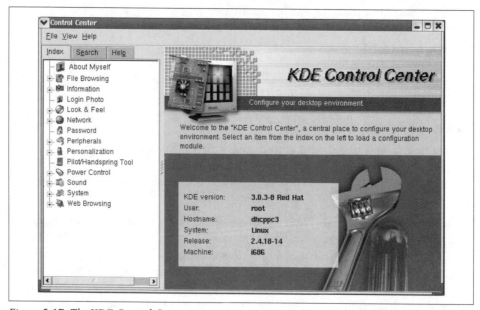

Figure 5-17. The KDE Control Center

The Control Center user interface features two panes. The left pane presents a hierarchically structured set of configuration categories, and the right pane displays information pertaining to the current choice. Control Center categories include:

About Myself
Lets you specify your name and other information that resides in the */etc/passwd* file

File Browsing
Lets you configure file associations, Konqueror (file manager) options, and the copy and move operations

Information
Lets you browse hardware devices and running services

Login Photo
Lets you specify a photo that appears on the login screen (this feature is not enabled by default)

Look & Feel
Lets you configure the desktop background, colors, behavior, and related properties

Network
Lets you configure your email identity, KDE LAN browser options, network options, and SOCKS proxy client options

Password
Lets you change your password

Peripherals
Lets you configure a digital camera, keyboard, and mouse

Personalization
Lets you configure accessibility options, localization options (keyboard and display character sets), encryption options, KDE terminal options, password recall, the KDE session manager, and the spelling checker

Pilot/Handspring Tool
Lets you synchronize local files with a personal digital assistant (PDA)

Power Control
Lets you configure power management options

Sound
Lets you configure audio sources, levels, and other options

System
Lets you configure KDE's alarm, login, and printing features

Web Browsing
Lets you configure Konqueror and Mozilla web browser options

Simply select the configuration category by clicking in the left pane. You can then revise the configuration parameters by specifying the desired values in the right pane. The contents of the right pane vary depending on the current selection in the left pane.

Adding an application link

You can easily add to your desktop an icon called an *application link* that lets you launch an application with a double click. To do so, right-click the desktop and select Create New → Link to Application from the pop-up menu. The Properties for Program dialog box appears, as shown in Figure 5-18.

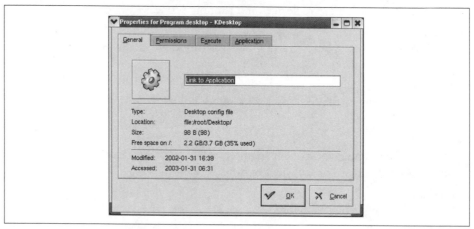

Figure 5-18. The Properties for Program dialog box

In the General tab, type a name for your link, replacing the text "Link to Application." Then, click the Execute tab and the Browse button. An Open dialog box appears. Use it to navigate to the program file you want to launch, click to select the file's icon, and click OK. The Properties for Program dialog box reappears. If the program you chose isn't an X program, enable the checkbox titled Run in terminal. Finally, click OK to close the Properties for Program dialog box.

Move the application link icon to a suitable location. Now, you can launch the configured program simply by double-clicking the icon. Who ever said that Linux is hard to use?

KDE Resources

Entire books have been written on using KDE, so this chapter has provided a mere overview of KDE's many features and facilities. The following additional resources are available via KDE's help information function:

The Konqueror Handbook

An overview of Konqueror.

http://docs.kde.org/en/3.1/kdebase/konqueror

KDE Quickstart Guide: An Introduction to KDE

A fast-paced introduction to KDE's most important features.

http://www.kde.org/documentation/quickstart/index.html

KDE User's Guide

KDE's most complete reference, "a detailed overview of the basic workings of KDE."

http://www.kde.org/documentation/userguide/index.html

The KDE FAQ

Answers to some of the most commonly asked questions concerning KDE can be found online.

http://www.kde.org/documentation/faq/index.html

Use these resources to learn more about KDE. Also, visit the KDE web site, *http://www.kde.org*. There you'll find more information—and more current information—about KDE and the KDE project.

CHAPTER 6
Using Linux Applications

Red Hat Linux includes a plethora of applications. This chapter introduces you to several of the most popular and useful applications. These include: OpenOffice.org, a desktop suite; Evolution, an email client and personal scheduler; Pilot/Handspring Tool, an application for syncing a personal digital assistant (PDA) with your system; and CD Writer, an application for burning CDs.

OpenOffice.org

OpenOffice.org is a desktop suite that functionally resembles Microsoft Office. That is, OpenOffice.org can perform many of the functions performed by Microsoft Office and includes many of the familiar features of Microsoft Office. The distinctive advantage of a desktop suite is that its component applications are designed to work together. The applications of a desktop suite have a similar look and feel, which makes them easy to learn and use.

Linux users have long had access to applications that help them prepare documents. However, development of Linux desktop suites has lagged behind that of Microsoft Office. The applications and suites have tended to be somewhat clumsy to use, unreliable, and poor in features. OpenOffice.org sets a new standard for Linux desktop suites, providing features and capabilities that are adequate to satisfy most computer users, not merely Linux fans.

OpenOffice.org began as a commercial desktop suite known as StarOffice, created by StarDivision. When Sun Microsystems acquired StarDivision in 1999, Sun soon thereafter released a freely available version of StarOffice. More recently, Sun has made certain StarOffice technologies available to the open source community, which created the freely redistributable OpenOffice.org desktop suite. Sun plans to continue development of StarOffice as a commercial product. At the same time, the open source community plans to continue development of OpenOffice.org.

OpenOffice.org is a multi-platform product, and is currently available for Linux, PPC Linux, Solaris, and Windows. Work is underway to support other platforms, including Mac OS X, FreeBSD, and IRIX. OpenOffice.org is also a global product, currently supporting 27 languages. Support for new languages is added regularly.

OpenOffice.org includes translating filters that let you share documents with users of Microsoft Office and other popular applications. It also includes convenient features such as Print to PDF (Adobe Portable Document Format); AutoPilot, which assists you in creating complex documents; and Stylist, which helps you take control of the look of your document.

OpenOffice.org includes word processor, spreadsheet, graphics, presentation manager, and drawing applications. The next several sections describe these applications. You can learn more about OpenOffice.org at *http://www.openoffice.org*.

Writer: The OpenOffice.org Word Processor

Writer is available via the Office menu item of the GNOME and KDE menus and, still more conveniently, has its own panel icon, which resembles a pen superimposed on two sheets of paper. When you launch Writer, you see a window resembling that shown as Figure 6-1. If you're launching Writer for the first time, a dialog box invites you to register as an OpenOffice.org user. Your registration is invited, but not required.

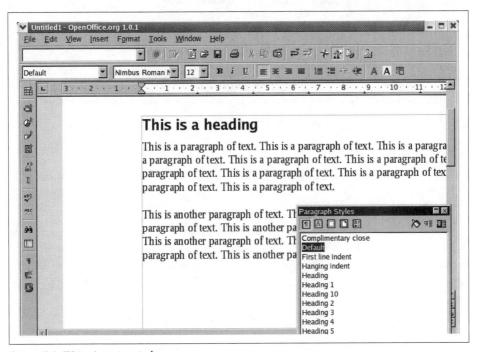

Figure 6-1. Writer's main window

If—as is likely the case—you've used Microsoft Word or another word processor, you'll find Writer's user interface intuitive and easy to use. You can type text in the middle area of the window. To style text, highlight the text and double-click a style in the Stylist, the window titled Paragraph Styles that appears in Figure 6-1. If the Stylist is not visible, you can summon it by pressing F11 or choosing Format → Stylist.

As mentioned, Writer includes many impressive features, some of which are available to users of Microsoft Office only at significant cost. For instance, Writer makes it simple to create PDF documents. To create a PDF document, prepare and save your document as usual. Then choose File → Printer Settings. The Printer Setup dialog box appears, as shown in Figure 6-2.

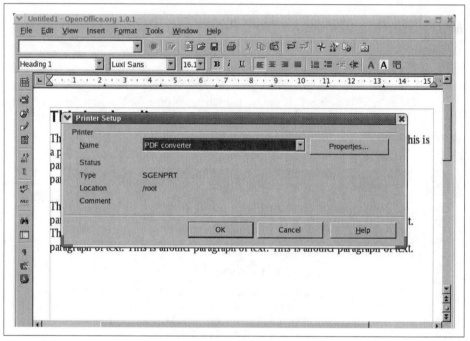

Figure 6-2. The Printer Setup dialog box

Choose PDF converter from the Name list box and click OK. Then, choose File → Print. When the Print dialog box appears, review the Options and Properties as necessary and then click OK. The PDF document is created and stored as a file in your home directory. Launch Nautilus or another file browser and click on the file to view the PDF document.

Here are some other Writer features you may enjoy exploring and using:

AutoPilot

Choose File → AutoPilot. From the submenu, choose the type of document you want to compose, such as a fax, agenda, web page, or form. AutoPilot will assist you in composing the document.

Address Book
> Choose File → Template → Address Book Source. Writer can access your Netscape or Mozilla address book, an LDAP or SQL database, or other data sources and obtain names, addresses, and other information.

Navigator
> Choose Edit → Navigator. The Navigator helps you find bookmarks, sections, hyperlinks, references, indexes, and notes. It's especially helpful when working on a large document.

To sample Writer's ability to work with documents prepared using Microsoft Word, I opened a draft version of this chapter—which was converted from DocBook to Microsoft Word—in Writer. In previous editions of this book, Linux word processors were not fully up to this challenge. They generally mangled the manuscript and sometimes crashed.

Writer, however, did not balk. The only problem I found was that curly quotes had been replaced by question marks throughout the document, because the default font used by Writer (Times) does not include the necessary characters. This problem was easily remedied by choosing another font.

Calc: The OpenOffice.org Spreadsheet

Like Writer, Calc is available via the Office menu item of the GNOME and KDE menus. It too has a convenient panel icon, which resembles a pie chart superimposed on a tabular spreadsheet. Calc's main window appears in Figure 6-3.

Just as Writer resembles Microsoft Word, Calc resembles Microsoft Excel. In particular, the language used in writing cell formulas is similar to that used by Excel. Moreover, the resemblance between the products is not merely syntactic. If your fingers are so accustomed to Excel that they race to perform operations in the familiar way, disaster will not likely ensue: many of Calc's keyboard shortcuts are identical to those used by Excel. You may need to look up from the keyboard to realize you're using Calc rather than Excel.

Like Excel, Calc can produce tables, graphs, and charts. Like other OpenOffice.org applications, Calc can send your work product to a printer or write it as a PDF document. Again, like Writer, Calc can obtain data from databases and other external sources. Choose View → Data Sources to view available data sources. To configure a new data source, right-click in the left pane of the window that appears. To return to the standard view, choose View → Data Sources a second time.

Here are some interesting Calc features for you to explore:

Detective
> Select a cell. Choose Tools → Detective. Then, choose from the submenu. Calc will show you cells that determine the value of the selected cell (Precedents), cells with values determined by the selected cell (Dependents), or other relationships.

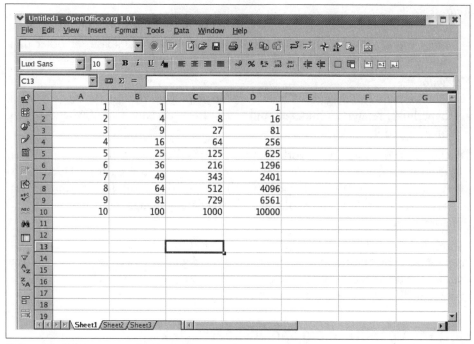

Figure 6-3. Calc's main window

Goal Seek

Select a cell. Choose Tools → Goal Seek. Specify a target value. Specify a precedent cell as the Variable cell. You can do so by typing the cell's name or by clicking the cell. Click OK. Calc determines the value of the variable cell that causes the selected cell to have the specified target value and offers to enter the value in the variable cell.

Subtotals

Select a block of cells in which the left column designates an entity (such as a department) and the right column or columns designate characteristics of the entity (such as sales, sales returns, and net sales). Ideally, the top row of the block should contain a name for each column. Choose Data → Subtotals. On the 1st Group tab, enable the checkboxes associated with the right column or columns. Click the left column name and choose the function count. Click each right column name and choose the function Sum. Click OK. The block now includes subtotals and a grand total.

Input Validation

Select a cell. Choose Data → Validity. On the Criteria tab, specify rules that govern valid cell values. On the Error Alert tab, enable Show error message when invalid values are entered. Optionally, specify an action, title, and error message. Click OK. Enter an invalid value for the cell and press Enter. Calc presents a dialog box warning you that the value is invalid.

Draw: The OpenOffice.org Drawing Program

Draw is the OpenOffice.org drawing program, available via the Office submenu of the GNOME and KDE menus. Unlike its sister programs Writer and Calc, Draw has no panel icon. Figure 6-4 shows Draw's main window.

Figure 6-4. Draw's main window

Draw enables you to draw two- and three-dimensional objects, and specify their color and other characteristics. Using Draw, you can move, align, and manipulate your objects to arrive at a complete composition. You can use Draw to create graphics that you incorporate into documents prepared using other OpenOffice.org applications, such as Impress, the presentation manager. You can save your work product using GIF, JPEG, PNG, or other popular graphics formats.

The GIMP (Gnu Image Manipulation Program), also included in Red Hat Linux, is a more sophisticated drawing program. However, Draw integrates smoothly with other OpenOffice.org applications. So, you may find it the more convenient tool for graphics of everyday complexity.

Here are some fun operations to try out:

3D object manipulation
>   3D manipulations are impressive but can be challenging to create. Here's a sample 3D manipulation you can perform. On the drawing toolbar on the left edge,

select the 3D tool, which resembles a cube. Drag twice within the document window to create two solid cubes. Convert one solid cube to a wire frame cube by choosing Format → Area and specifying None as the Fill and by choosing Format → Line and specifying Continuous as the Style. To see other 3D effects, select the other cube and choose Format → 3D Effects. Experiment with the effects to see what's possible. The Favorites tab is particularly fun when working with solid objects.

FontWork

On the drawing toolbar, select the text tool, which resembles the letter T. Click in the document window and type some text. Choose Format → FontWork. Click one of the arcs visible in the list at the top of the FontWork dialog box. The text is bent in the direction indicated by the arc. Click other buttons and specify other values as desired. As you'll quickly see, you can easily create dynamic and attention-grabbing visuals using FontWork.

Impress: The OpenOffice.org Presentation Manager

Impress is OpenOffice.org's presentation manager, which functionally resembles Microsoft PowerPoint. Impress is available via the Office submenu of the GNOME and KDE menus. Impress has a convenient panel icon, which resembles a slide superimposed on a bar chart. Figure 6-5 shows Impress's main window.

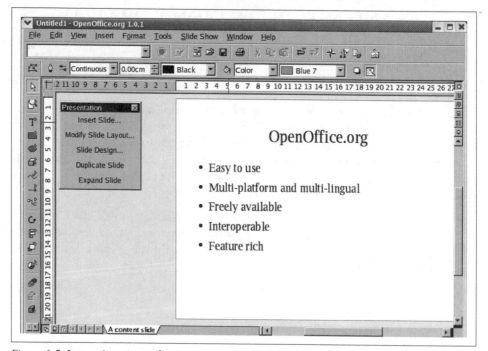

Figure 6-5. Impress's main window

When you launch Impress for the first time, it fires up AutoPilot to lead you through creating a presentation. AutoPilot lets you specify the presentation medium (paper, slides, and so on), and select a presentation template, slide design, and slide transition appropriate for your presentation. Currently, Impress is distributed without templates. A few templates are available on the OpenOffice.org web site, *http://www. openoffice.org*. However, Impress also lets you model a presentation on an existing presentation. Until a variety of templates is available, you'll likely find this capability useful and convenient.

When the AutoPilot is finished, Impress presents the Modify Slide dialog box, shown in Figure 6-6. This dialog box is the main means of creating the slides that comprise a presentation. Select the desired layout and click OK. An empty slide appears in the window, ready for your customization.

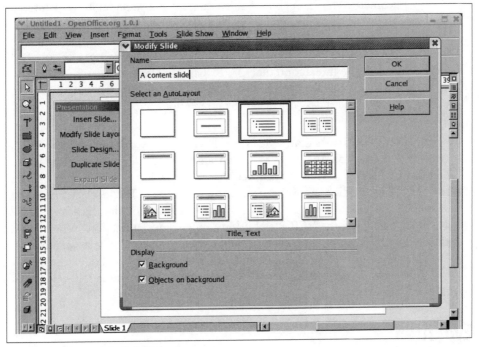

Figure 6-6. The Modify Slide dialog box

Impress is not as featureful as Microsoft PowerPoint. In particular, it lacks support for video clips. However, many experts believe that overly sophisticated presentations can work to the disadvantage of the presenter. Impress is more than adequate to create simple and clear presentations that help you communicate persuasively.

Impress includes the FontWork and 3D Effects tools explained in the section on Draw, as well as other facilities common to many OpenOffice.org applications.

Here's some fun you can have with Impress:

Effects

Create a geometric shape, such as a filled circle, within a slide. Select the shape and choose Slide Show → Effects. Choose the Favorites menu and click one of the effects that appear in the large selection box. Click the Assign button, which resembles a green checkmark. Then, click the Preview button, which appears to the right of the Assign button. A preview window appears. Click the preview window to see how your effect looks. Choose Slide Show → Slide Show to view the slide show. During the slide show, click the slide to trigger the effect. A single slide can contain multiple effects, which play sequentially when triggered, in the order they were created.

Interaction

Create a geometric shape, such as a filled circle. Choose Slide Show → Interaction. Use the Action at mouse click list to associate an action, such as playing a sound, with the shape. Depending on the action you selected, Impress may present additional options from which you can select. When you're satisfied, click OK to exit the Interaction dialog box. Choose Slide Show → Slide Show to view the slide show. During the slide show, click the object—not merely an unrelated part of the slide—to trigger the interaction.

Animation

Create a series of shapes that, when quickly viewed in sequence, will resemble a cartoon. To assemble the shapes into an animation, select the first shape and choose Slide Show → Animation. Click the Apply Object button that appears at the left of the middle row of the Animation dialog box. Then, select the second shape and click Apply Object. Repeat this procedure for the third and subsequent shapes. Click the VCR Play button to view your animation. When you're satisfied with the animation, click Create to place it in your slide as an animated GIF. Delete the component shapes and choose Slide Show → Slide Show to view the slide show. When you click the slide containing your animation, the animation will play.

Evolution

Ximian's Evolution is an email client and personal scheduler. Previously, Evolution was available from Ximian as an add-on to Red Hat Linux. However, conflicts between Ximian's RPM packages and those distributed by Red Hat sometimes made life complicated for Ximian users. Red Hat is now distributing Evolution as part of Red Hat Linux, so Ximian users can expect more trouble-free operation and fewer problems when upgrading to new versions of Red Hat Linux. You can learn more about Evolution at *http://www.ximian.com*.

Evolution has four main functions:

Email client
Evolution receives email from POP and IMAP servers and sends email via SMTP servers.

Calendar
Evolution provides daily and monthly calendars to help you plan your time.

Task list
Evolution provides a to-do list that helps you keep track of projects and deadlines.

Contact database
Evolution provides a contact list that you can conveniently use when composing email.

Evolution is available via the Internet → Email submenu of the GNOME and KDE menus. It also has a convenient panel icon, which resembles a postage stamp superimposed on an envelope. When launched for the first time, Evolution provides a wizard to help you configure its operation, as shown in Figure 6-7.

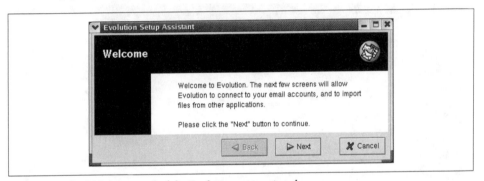

Figure 6-7. The Welcome panel of the Evolution setup wizard

Click Next to move on to the Identity panel. There, you specify your full name and email address. Optionally, you can specify the name of your organization, a plain text email signature file, and an HTML email signature file.

Click Next to move on to the Receiving Email panel. There, you specify the type of server you use to receive email, the hostname of the server, your username, and information on the security and authentication characteristics of the server. You can obtain this information from your email provider or determine the correct values by experimentation.

Click Next to move on to a second Receiving Email panel. This panel lets you specify options about checking for new email and using folders and filters. You can specify the values according to your preferences.

Click Next to move on to the Sending Email panel. There, you specify the type of server you use to send mail, its hostname, and security and authentication options.

You can obtain this information from your email provider or determine the correct values by experimentation.

Clicking Next takes you to the Account Management panel. This panel lets you associate a name with the account, so that you can distinguish from accounts you may add later. You can also specify whether the account is the default account. If you have only one account, you should specify that it is the default account.

Clicking Next takes you to the Timezone panel. Click the map or use the drop-down list to specify your time zone.

Finally, Next takes you to the Importing Files panel. The appearance of this panel depends on what other email clients and applications you have previously configured. Its purpose is to let you specify whether and how information from other email clients and applications should be imported into Evolution.

Clicking Next takes you to the Done panel. From there, click Finish to save your configuration. At last, Evolution appears as shown in Figure 6-8.

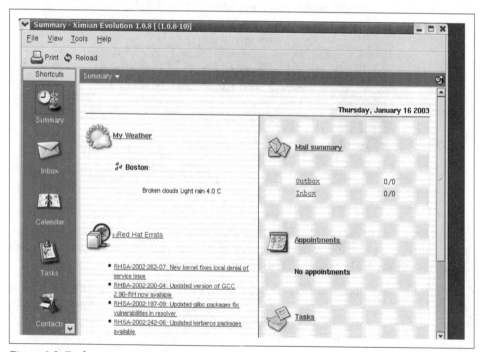

Figure 6-8. Evolution's main window

The left pane of Evolution's window is a menu that lets you choose the contents of the right pane. The Summary pane, which appears initially, presents weather, news, and a status summary of Evolution. Clicking Inbox, Calendar, Tasks, or Contacts selects the corresponding Evolution function.

Pilot/Handspring Tool

Red Hat Linux includes gnome-pilot, a tool that lets you synchronize your Palm or Handspring PDA (personal digital assistant) with your Linux system using your system's serial port and your PDA's serial hot sync cradle. By default, Red Hat Linux is configured to enable you to back up your PDA to your Linux system or restore a backup from your Linux system to your PDA. You can also synchronize Evolution's calendar, task list, and contact list with your PDA. These functions are broken under Red Hat Linux 7.3 and 8.0; however, it's simple to work around the problem.

To set up your system to communicate with your PDA, choose Accessories → Pilot/Handspring Tool from the GNOME or KDE menu. The Welcome panel appears, as shown in Figure 6-9.

Figure 6-9. The gnome-pilot Welcome panel

Plug your PDA into its cradle and plug the cradle into your system's serial port. Click Next to continue. The Cradle Settings panel, shown in Figure 6-10, appears. Specify the serial port to which the cradle is attached. If you've synched your PDA by using a Microsoft Windows host, you can use the information in Table 6-1 to determine the serial port.

Table 6-1. Linux and Windows serial port designations

Windows designation	Linux designation
COM1	/dev/ttyS0
COM2	/dev/ttyS1
COM3	/dev/ttyS2
COM4	/dev/ttyS3

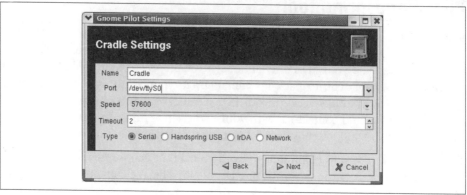

Figure 6-10. The Cradle Settings panel

Click Next to continue. The Pilot Identification panel appears, as shown in Figure 6-11. If you've already stored a username and ID in PDA, enable the No radiobutton and specify them. Otherwise, enable the Yes radiobutton.

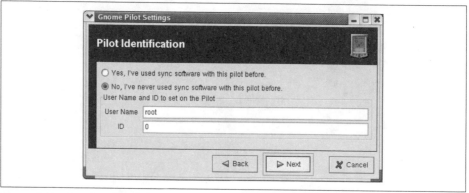

Figure 6-11. The Pilot Identification panel

Click Next to continue. The Initial Sync panel appears. As directed, press the PDA's HotSync button. Check the PDA's screen to determine if the hot sync succeeded. If it failed, use the Back button to return to a previous screen and correct the problem. Also, check the cable connecting the HotSync cradle to the PC.

If the hot sync succeeded, the Pilot Attributes panel appears. If you like, you can change the Pilot Name and Local basedir values.

Click Next to continue and a Success panel should appear.

When the GNOME Pilot Settings wizard completes, the Pilot Conduits dialog box remains on the desktop. Its purpose is to show the available conduits, small programs that let you move information between your system and PDA. Although several conduits are installed along with gnome-pilot, a bug prevents them from appearing and therefore prevents you from using them.

To view all the conduits, close the Pilot Conduits dialog box. Then, open a terminal window and issue the following command:

```
gpilotd-control-applet --cap-id=1
```

A Pilot Conduits dialog box appears, as shown in Figure 6-12. Note that five conduits now appear. By default, the conduits are disabled. You can enable a conduit by clicking Enable. When enabled, some conduits present a small configuration dialog box, as shown in Figure 6-13. Generally, the dialog box lets you configure the direction of information transfer: either from the PDA to the system or from the system to the PDA. Configure each conduit as you prefer and then click OK to close the Pilot Conduits dialog box.

 You can create a launcher that makes it convenient to launch gpilot-control-applet. See Chapter 5 to learn how.

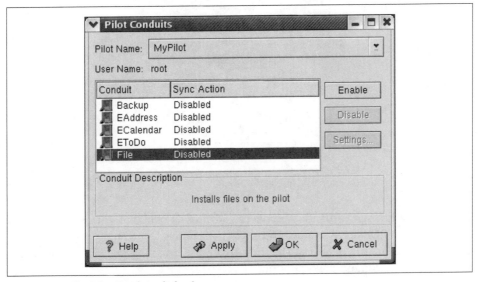

Figure 6-12. The Pilot Conduits dialog box

The conduits have the following functions:

Backup
Backs up your PDA contents to a file on your system or restores the PDA contents from a file on your system.

EAddress
Sends Evolution's contact list to your PDA or your PDA's contact list to Evolution.

ECalendar
Sends Evolution's calendar to your PDA or your PDA's calendar to Evolution.

EToDo

Sends Evolution's task list to your PDA or your PDA's task list to Evolution.

File

Transfers files from your system to your PDA or from your PDA to your system. You shouldn't enable this conduit unless you have a specific purpose in mind, in which case you should be careful to properly configure it.

Be sure to properly configure the direction of transfer—the Action—for each conduit. Otherwise, you may destroy important information by performing a transfer in an inappropriate direction. For instance, you could inadvertently transfer old data from your PC onto your PDA, destroying more recent data in the PDA.

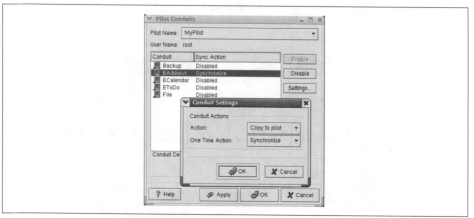

Figure 6-13. A conduit configuration dialog box

To perform a hot sync operation, connect your PDA's cradle to your system's serial port, place the PDA in its cradle, and press the HotSync button on the cradle. The enabled conduits run and transfer information between your PDA and system according to the conduit configurations.

CD Writer

At one time, writing a CD by using Linux was a common rite of passage for new Linux users. The command used to write a CD, **cdrecord**, is a sophisticated command having many options. Getting all the options just right was a challenge for many. However, GnomeToaster makes it easy to write CDs. GnomeToaster can create data and audio CDs. It can duplicate CDs on the fly, create CDs from ISO images, and create bootable El Torito CDs, such as those used to distribute Red Hat Linux. GnomeToaster can create multisession CDs and can erase CD-RW media. For more information on GnomeToaster, see its web site, *http://gnometoaster.rulez.org*.

To launch GnomeToaster, choose Extras → System Tools → CD Writer from the GNOME or KDE menu. GnomeToaster presents the Choose Recorder dialog box, shown in Figure 6-14. Highlight your CD-R or CD-RW drive and click OK.

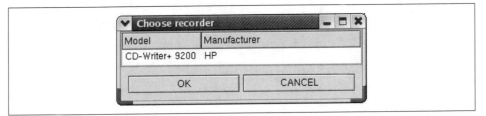

Figure 6-14. The Choose Recorder dialog box

GnomeToaster's main screen, which may have been partially obscured by the Choose Recorder dialog box, is now plainly visible. Figure 6-15 shows the main screen.

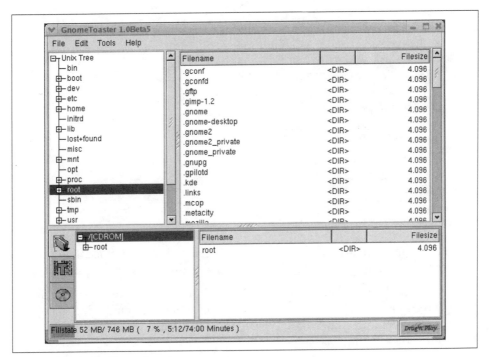

Figure 6-15. GnomeToaster's main screen

To specify the files to be written to the CD, simply navigate the filesystem using the left and right panes at the top of the GnomeToaster window. Then drag the desired files or directories into the panes at the bottom of the window.

When you've specified all the files to be written, click the CD icon at the bottom left of the window. The appearance of the bottom panes changes to resemble that shown in Figure 6-16.

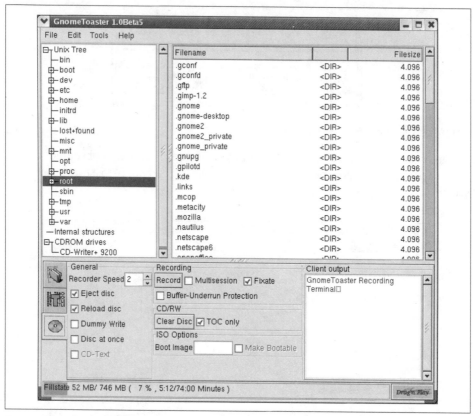

Figure 6-16. The CD drive specifications

Use the bottom panel to specify the recorder speed and other options. If your drive supports buffer underrun protection, you can enable the corresponding check box.

To create the CD, put blank media in the drive and click Record. The Writing CD dialog box appears, as shown in Figure 6-17. Your CD is a standard ISO9660 CD and should be readable under Windows, Linux and other Unix and Unix-like systems, Mac OS, and other platforms.

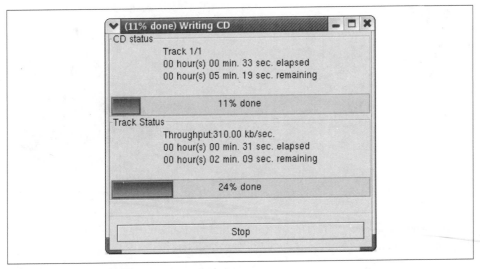

Figure 6-17. Burning a CD

## CHAPTER 7

Conquering the bash Shell

Linux provides two user interfaces: the graphical user interface (GUI) hosted by X and an older, command-line interface (CLI) called the shell.

Those who're familiar with the MS-DOS command-line interface will recognize the shell, which you use by typing text commands to which the system responds by displaying text replies. But the comparison with the MS-DOS command line doesn't do justice to the Linux shell, which is vastly more powerful. And, *older* doesn't necessarily imply *inferior*.

GUIs are stylish primarily because they're easy to learn and use. But they're not always the most efficient way of operating a computer. A skilled user of the shell can often outrace a competitor using a GUI. Moreover, a GUI enables its user to perform only the functions the GUI's programmers provided. In contrast, the shell is expandable. The shell enables users to define entirely new operations based on sequences of existing operations.

The real power of Linux lies in the shell. So, if you aspire to master Linux, you must conquer the shell. Even if your ambition falls short of gurudom, you'll find knowledge of the shell helpful. Many procedures from sources other than this book assume that you know how to use the shell. And, if X fails, you can't easily repair it without knowing how to use the shell.

Linux supports a variety of shells, but the most popular is the *bash* shell, described in this chapter. The chapter explains how to issue shell commands, and how to use shell commands to manipulate files and directories, work with removable media, and launch programs. The chapter also explains pico, a simple text editor that operates in text mode.

Issuing Shell Commands

The most common way to access the shell is via a terminal window, as explained in Chapters 5 and 6. However, a terminal window isn't the only way to access the shell.

The section ""Using virtual consoles" in Chapter 4 explains how to access the shell by using a virtual console.

As your first Linux command, launch a terminal window, type **w**, and press **Enter**. Your contents of the terminal window should look something like this:

```
[bill@home bill]$ w
11:12am  up 6 min,  1 user,  load average: 0.00, 0.08, 0.05
USER     TTY     FROM      LOGIN@   IDLE   JCPU   PCPU  WHAT
bill     tty1              11:11am  0.00s  0.20s  0.11s -bash
```

The **w** command tells Linux to display the system status and a list of all system users. In the example, the output of the command tells you that it's now 11:12 a.m., that the system has been up for six minutes, and that only one user—*bill*—is currently logged in. Notice that the command output is very terse, packing much information into a few lines. Such output is typical of Linux commands. At first, you may find Linux output cryptic and difficult to read, but over time you'll grow to appreciate the efficiency with which Linux communicates information.

 Linux command output is not terse owing to an oversight or laziness on the part of the creators of Linux. Instead, Linux command output is designed so that it can be processed by programs as well as by humans. The structure of the output simplifies the task of programmers who write programs to process command output.

Linux provides many commands besides the **w** command—so many that you may despair of learning and recalling them. Actually, the number of commands you'll use regularly is fairly small. Soon, they will become second nature to you.

Try a second command, the **date** command:

```
[bill@home bill]$ date
Fri Oct 5 11:15:20 PST 2002
```

The **date** command displays the current date and time.

If you find working with MS-DOS distasteful or intimidating, you may not immediately enjoy working with the Linux command line. However, give yourself some time to adjust. The Linux command line has several features that make it easier to use, and more powerful, than MS-DOS.

Correcting Commands

Sometimes you may type a command incorrectly, causing Linux to display an error message. For example, suppose you typed **dat** instead of **date**:

```
[bill@home bill]$ dat
bash: dat: command not found
```

In such a case, carefully check the spelling of the command and try again. If you notice an error before pressing **Enter**, you can use the **Backspace** or **Left** arrow key to return to the point of the error and then type the correct characters. The **Backspace** key erases characters whereas the **Left** arrow key does not. You can also use the **Del** key to delete unwanted characters.

Just as a web browser keeps track of recently visited sites, the *bash* shell keeps track of recently issued commands in what's known as the *history list*. You can scroll back through *bash*'s history by using the Up arrow key, or back down using the Down arrow key, just as you would with the Back and Forward buttons on a web browser. To reissue a command, scroll to it and press **Enter**. If you like, you can modify the command before reissuing it. When typing shell commands, you have access to a minieditor that resembles the DOSKEY editor of MS-DOS. This minieditor lets you revise command lines by typing key commands. Table 7-1 summarizes some useful key commands interpreted by the shell. The key commands let you access a list of the 500 most recently executed commands. *bash*'s history is saved in the *~/.bash_ history* file.

Table 7-1. Useful editing keystrokes

Keystroke(s)	Function
Up arrow	Move back one command in the history list.
Down arrow	Move forward one command in the history list.
Left arrow	Move back one character.
Right arrow	Move forward one character.
Backspace	Delete previous character.
Tab	Attempt to complete the current word, interpreting it as a filename or command, as determined by the context.
Alt-B	Move back one word.
Alt-D	Delete current word.
Alt-F	Move forward one word.
Ctrl-A	Move to beginning of line.
Ctrl-D	Delete current character.
Ctrl-E	Move to end of line.
Ctrl-K	Delete to end of line.
Ctrl-L	Clear the screen, placing the current line at the top of the screen.
Ctrl-U	Delete from beginning of line.
Ctrl-Y	Retrieve last item deleted.
Esc .	Insert last word of previous command (note that Esc is pressed before the dot, rather than at the same time).
Esc ? or Tab	List the possible completions (note that Esc is pressed before the question mark, not at the same time).

One of the most useful editing keystrokes, **Tab**, can also be used when typing a command. If you type the first part of a filename and press **Tab**, the shell will attempt to locate files with names matching the characters you've typed. If something exists, the shell fills out the partially typed name with the proper characters. You can then press **Enter** to execute the command or continue typing other options and arguments. This feature, called either *filename* or *command completion*, makes the shell much easier to use.

In addition to keystrokes for editing the command line, the shell interprets several keystrokes that control the operation of the currently executing program. Table 7-2 summarizes these keystrokes. For example, typing **Ctrl-C** generally cancels execution of a program. This keystroke command is handy, for example, when a program is taking too long to execute and you'd prefer to try something else.

Table 7-2. Useful Control keystrokes

Keystroke	Function
Ctrl-C	Sends an interrupt signal to the currently executing command, which generally responds by terminating itself.
Ctrl-D	Sends an end-of-file to the currently executing command; use this keystroke to terminate console input.
Ctrl-Z	Suspends the currently executing program.

Several other special characters control the operation of the shell, as shown in Table 7-3. The # and ; characters are most often used in shell scripts, which you'll learn about in more detail later in this chapter. The & character causes the shell prompt to return immediately instead of waiting for a command to finish; the command runs in the background and you can continue to enter more commands.

Table 7-3. Other special shell characters

Character	Function
#	Marks the line as a comment, which the shell ignores.
;	Separates commands, letting you enter several commands on a single line.
&	Placed at the end of a command, causes the command to execute as a background process, so that a new shell prompt appears immediately after the command is entered.
>	Stores output from the command in the file whose name follows.
<	Takes input from the file whose name follows.
\	At end of line, continues command on the following line.

Working with the Linux Command Prompt

Linux commands share a simple, common structure. This section describes their common structure and explains how you can obtain helpful information about the commands available to you.

Commands and Arguments

The general form of a shell command line is this:

```
command [options] [arguments]
```

The **command** determines what operation the shell will perform and the *options* and *arguments* customize, or fine-tune, the operation. The *options* and *arguments* may or may not appear, as indicated by the square brackets. Sometimes the **command** specifies a program file that will be launched and run; such a command is called an *external command*. Linux generally stores these files in */bin*, */usr/bin*, or */usr/local/bin*. System administration commands are generally stored in */sbin* or */usr/sbin*, which are included by default in the path of the root user. When a command specifies a program file, the shell passes any specified arguments to the program, which scans and interprets them, adjusting its operation accordingly.

Some commands are not external program files; instead they are built-in commands interpreted by the shell itself. One important way in which shells differ is in the built-in commands that they support. Later in this section, you'll learn about some of *bash*'s built-in commands.

The name of a Linux command almost always consists of lowercase letters and digits. Most commands let you specify options or arguments. However, in any given case, you may not need to do so. For example, typing the **w** command without options and arguments causes Linux to display a list of current users.

 Remember, Linux commands are case sensitive; be sure to type each character of a command in the proper case.

Options modify the way that a command works. Many options consist of a single letter, prefixed by a dash. Often, you can specify more than one option; when you do so, you separate each option with one or more spaces. For example, the **-h** option of the **w** command causes the output of the command to omit the header lines that give the time and the names of the fields:

```
[bill@home bill]$ w -h
```

Arguments specify filenames or other targets that direct the action of the command. For example, the **w** command lets you specify a username as an argument, which causes the command to list logins that pertain only to the specified user:

```
[bill@home bill]$ w bill
```

Some commands let you specify a series of arguments; you must separate each argument with a space between them. For example, the following command prints a list of logins by the root user, without header lines:

```
[bill@home bill]$ w -h bill
```

When a command includes several arguments, a command may not fit on a single line. However, you can continue typing when you reach the end of a line, because the shell will automatically wrap your input to the next line. If you find line wrapping disconcerting, you can type a backslash (\) at the end of a line, press **Enter**, and continue typing on the next line. The backslash is the shell's line continuation character; the shell sees lines joined by a backslash as though they were a single line. Don't type anything after the backslash or the continuation feature won't work correctly.

Getting Help

Because Linux provides so many commands and because Linux commands provide so many possible options, you can't expect to recall all of them. To help you, Linux provides the **man** and **apropos** commands, which let you access a help database that describes commands and their options.

Using man

Each Linux command is described by a special file called a *manual page*. The manual pages (or *manpages*) are stored in a group of subdirectories comprising a help database. To access this database, you use the **man** command, which resembles the MS-DOS **help** command. For example, to get help on using the **w** command, type:

```
[bill@home bill]$ man w
```

Figure 7-1 shows the resulting output, which the command displays one page at a time. Notice the colon prompt that appears at the bottom left of the screen. To page forward, press the **Space** key; to page backward, press the **b** key. To exit the **man** program, press the **q** key.

Manpages are organized according to a common format. At the beginning of a manpage, you'll find the name of the page and the section of the database from which the page comes, shown in parentheses. For example, Figure 7-1 shows "W(1)" in the upper-left and -right corners. This means that you're looking in section 1 of the manpage (the section pertaining to commands) for the **w** command. Table 7-4 describes the sections of the manual page database; most sections are primarily of interest to programmers. As a user and system administrator, you'll be interested primarily in sections 1 and 8.

Table 7-4. Manual page sections

Section	Description
1	Executable programs and shell commands
2	System calls (provided by the kernel)
3	Library calls (provided by system libraries)
4	Special files (for example, device files)
5	File formats and conventions

Table 7-4. Manual page sections (continued)

Section	Description
6	Games
7	Macro packages and conventions
8	System administration commands
9	Nonstandard kernel routines

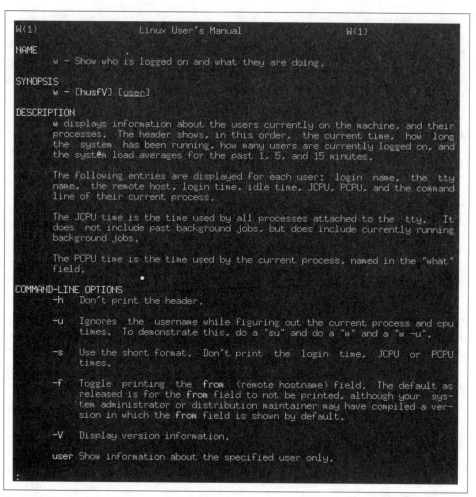

Figure 7-1. A typical manpage

Next in the output comes the name and a brief description of the command. Then comes a synopsis of the command, which shows the options and arguments that you can specify. Brackets enclose parts of a command that you can choose to include or omit. Next comes a detailed description of the operation of the command, followed by a description of its options.

As you're learning your way around Linux, you may find it convenient to reserve a terminal window or virtual console for running the **man** command. Alternatively, you can browse manpages using Konqueror. Browsing the URI *man://index* will present the Unix manual index, from which you can jump to other manpages. That way, you can enter commands in a separate virtual console, switching between windows or consoles to refresh your recollection of the options and arguments of commands as you type them.

Using apropos

The **man** command searches the manual pages and displays detailed information about a specified command. The **apropos** command also searches the manual pages, but it displays just a one-line summary of each. You have to supply **apropos** with a keyword that indicates the information you're looking for; it simply displays each summary line that contains the keyword. For example, typing the command:

```
[bill@home bill]$ apropos samba
```

will display a list of manpages containing the word *samba*, as shown in Figure 7-2.

The **apropos** command uses a special database to store information about commands. Before using the command for the first time, you must create the database by issuing the command:

> **makewhatis**

The command may require several minutes to complete. After installing a package that includes commands, you can update the database to include information about the new commands by issuing the same command.

The **apropos** command is useful when you don't recall the name of a Linux command. By typing a related keyword, you can obtain a list of commands and search the list for the command you need.

Using Commands That Work with Directories

Now that you understand the fundamentals of issuing Linux commands, you're ready to learn some commands that work with directories. Rather than simply reading this section, you should log in to your Linux system and try the commands for yourself. By doing so, you will begin to develop skill in working with shell commands.

Displaying the working directory

To display the current working directory, issue the **pwd** (print working directory) command. The **pwd** command requires no options or arguments:

```
[bill@home bill]$ pwd
/root
```

```
utime               (2)  - change access and/or modification times of an inode
utimes [utime]      (2)  - change access and/or modification times of an inode
wtimeout [curs_inopts] (3x)  - curses input options
zdump               (8)  - time zone dumper
zic                 (8)  - time zone compiler
XDeviceTimeCoord [XGetDeviceMotionEvents] (3x)  - get device motion history
XTimeCoord [XSendEvent] (3x)  - send events and pointer motion history structure
XtAddInput          (3x)  - register input, timeout, and workprocs
XtAddTimeout [XtAddInput]  (3x)  - register input, timeout, and workprocs
XtAppAddTimeOut     (3x)  - register and remove timeouts
XtAppGetSelectionTimeout (3x)  - set and obtain selection timeout values
XtAppSetSelectionTimeout [XtAppGetSelectionTimeout] (3x)  - set and obtain selection timeou
t values
XtGetMultiClickTime [XtSetMultiClickTime] (3x)  - set and get multi-click times
XtGetSelectionTimeout (3x)  - set and obtain selection timeout values
XtLastEventProcessed (3x)  - last event, last timestamp processed
XtLastTimestampProcessed [XtLastEventProcessed] (3x)  - last event, last timestamp processe
d
XtRemoveTimeOut [XtAppAddTimeOut]  - register and remove timeouts
XtSetMultiClickTime (3x)  - set and get multi-click times
XtSetSelectionTimeout [XtGetSelectionTimeout] (3x)  - set and obtain selection timeout valu
es
t3d                 (1)  - clock using flying balls to display the time
Benchmark           (3)  - benchmark running times of code
CPAN::FirstTime     (3)  - Utility for CPAN::Config file Initialization
Time::Local         (3)  - efficiently compute time from local and GMT time
Time::gmtime        (3)  - by-name interface to Perl's built-in gmtime() function
Time::localtime     (3)  - by-name interface to Perl's built-in localtime() function
Time::tm            (3)  - internal object used by Time::gmtime and Time::localtime
base                (3)  - Establish IS-A relationship with base class at compile time
fields              (3)  - compile-time class fields
lib                 (3)  - manipulate @INC at compile time
timeit [Benchmark]  (3)  - run a chunk of code and see how long it goes
timethese [Benchmark] (3)  - run several chunks of code several times
timethis [Benchmark] (3)  - run a chunk of code several times
[root@linux RPMS]# apropos samba
Samba [samba]       (7)  - A Windows SMB/CIFS fileserver for UNIX
lmhosts             (5)  - The Samba NetBIOS hosts file
make_smbcodepage    (1)  - Construct a codepage file for Samba
make_unicodemap     (1)  - Construct a unicode map file for Samba
smb.conf [smb]      (5)  - The configuration file for the Samba suite
smbpasswd           (5)  - The Samba encrypted password file
smbstatus           (1)  - report on current Samba connections
swat                (8)  - Samba Web Administration Tool
[root@linux RPMS]#
```

Figure 7-2. Output of the apropos command

The **pwd** command displays the absolute pathname of the current working directory.

Changing the working directory

To change the working directory, issue the **cd** (change directory) command, specifying the pathname of the new working directory as an argument. You can use an absolute or relative pathname. For example, to change the working directory to the /bin directory, type:

```
[bill@home bill]$ cd /bin
[bill@home /bin]$
```

Notice how the prompt changes to indicate that /bin is now the working directory.

You can quickly return to your home directory by issuing the **cd** command without an argument:

```
[bill@home /bin]$ cd
[bill@home bill]$
```

Again, notice how the prompt changes to indicate the new working directory.

If you attempt to change the working directory to a directory that doesn't exist, Linux displays an error message:

```
[bill@home bill]$ cd nowhere
bash: nowhere: No such file or directory
```

Displaying directory contents

To display the contents of a directory, you use the **ls** (list) command. The **ls** command provides many useful options that let you tailor its operation and output to your liking.

The simplest form of the **ls** command takes no options or arguments. It simply lists the contents of the working directory, including files and subdirectories (your own output will differ, reflecting the files present in your working directory):

```
[bill@home bill]$ ls
GNUstep              firewall               sniff
Xrootenv.0           linux                  ssh-1.2.26
audio.cddb           mail                   ssh-1.2.26.tar.gz
audio.wav            mirror                 support
axhome               mirror-2.8.tar.gz      temp
conf                 nlxb3181.tar           test
corel                openn                  test.doc
drivec.img           scan                   tulip.c
dynip_2.00.tar.gz    screen-3.7.6-0.i386.rpm  win98
```

Here, the output is presented in lexical (dictionary) order, as three columns of data. Notice that filenames beginning with uppercase letters appear before those beginning with lowercase letters.

A more sophisticated form of the **ls** command that includes the **-l** option displays descriptive information along with the filenames, as shown in Figure 7-3.

The first line of the output shows the amount of disk space used by the working directory and its subdirectories, measured in 1 KB blocks. Each remaining line describes a single file or directory. The columns are:

Type
> The type of file: a directory (d), or an ordinary file (-). If your system supports color, Linux displays output lines that pertain to directories in blue and lines that pertain to files in white.

Access modes
> The access mode, which determines which users can access the file or directory. You'll learn more about access modes, links, and groups in subsequent sections of this chapter.

Links
> The number of files or directories linked to this one.

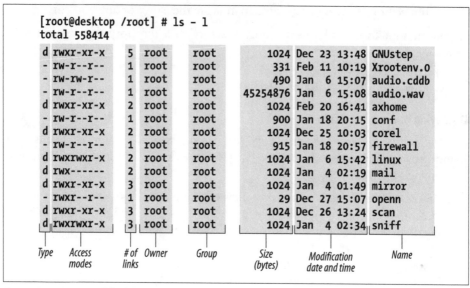

```
[root@desktop /root] # ls - l
total 558414
d rwxr-xr-x   5  root    root      1024 Dec 23 13:48 GNUstep
- rw-r--r--   1  root    root       331 Feb 11 10:19 Xrootenv.0
- rw-rw-r--   1  root    root       490 Jan  6 15:07 audio.cddb
- rw-r--r--   1  root    root  45254876 Jan  6 15:08 audio.wav
d rwxr-xr-x   2  root    root      1024 Feb 20 16:41 axhome
- rw-r--r--   1  root    root       900 Jan 18 20:15 conf
d rwxr-xr-x   2  root    root      1024 Dec 25 10:03 corel
- rw-r--r--   1  root    root       915 Jan 18 20:57 firewall
d rwxrwxr-x   2  root    root      1024 Jan  6 15:42 linux
d rwx------   2  root    root      1024 Jan  4 02:19 mail
d rwxr-xr-x   3  root    root      1024 Jan  4 01:49 mirror
- rwxr--r--   1  root    root        29 Dec 27 15:07 openn
d rwxr-xr-x   3  root    root      1024 Dec 26 13:24 scan
d rwxrwxr-x   3  root    root      1024 Jan  4 02:34 sniff
```

| Type | Access modes | # of links | Owner | Group | Size (bytes) | Modification date and time | Name |

Figure 7-3. Output of the ls command

Owner
> The user who owns the file or directory.

Group
> The group that owns the file or directory.

Size
> The size of the file or directory, in bytes.

Modification date
> The date and time when the file or directory was last modified.

Name
> The name of the file or directory.

If a directory contains many files, the listing will fill more than one screen. To view the output one screen at a time, use the following command:

```
[bill@home bill]$ ls | less
```

This command employs the pipe redirector, sending output of the **ls** subcommand to the **less** subcommand, which presents the output one screen at a time. You can control the operation of the **less** command by using the following keys:

- **Space** moves you one page forward.
- **b** moves you one page back.
- **q** or **Q** exits the program and returns you to the command prompt.

If you want to list a directory other than the working directory, you can type the name of the directory as an argument of the **ls** command, like so:

```
ls /bin
```

Linux displays the contents of the directory but does not change the working directory. Similarly, you can display information about a file by typing its name as an argument of the **ls** command. Moreover, the **ls** command accepts an indefinite number of arguments, so you can type a series of directories and filenames as arguments, separating each with one or more spaces.

When the name of a directory or file begins with a dot (.), the output of the **ls** command does not normally include the directory or file, because the file is *hidden*. To cause the output of the **ls** command to include hidden directories and files, use the **-a** option. For example, to list all the files and subdirectories in the current directory—including hidden ones—type:

```
[bill@home bill]$ ls -a -l
```

If you prefer, you can combine the **-a** and **-l** options, typing the command like this:

```
[bill@home bill]$ ls -al
```

A user's home directory generally includes several hidden files containing configuration information for various programs. For example, the *.profile* file contains configuration information for the Linux *bash* shell.

The **ls** command provides a host of additional useful options; see its manual page for details.

Creating a directory

You can create directories by using the **mkdir** (make directory) command. Just type the name of the new directory as an argument of the command. Linux creates the directory as a subdirectory of the working directory. For example, this command creates a subdirectory named *office*:

```
[bill@home bill]$ mkdir office
```

If you don't want to create the new directory as a subdirectory of the working directory, type an absolute or relative pathname as the argument. For example, to create a directory named */tmp/documents*, type:

```
[bill@home bill]# mkdir /tmp/documents
```

The name of a directory or file must follow certain rules. For example, it must not contain a slash (/) character. Directory names and filenames usually include letters (either upper- or lowercase), digits, dots, and underscores (_). You can use other characters, such as spaces and hyphens, but such names present problems, because the shell gives them special meaning. If you simply must use a name containing special characters, enclose the name within single quotes ('). The quotes don't become part of the name that is stored on the disk. This technique is useful when accessing files on a Windows filesystem; otherwise, you'll have trouble working with files in directories such as *My Documents*, which have pathnames containing spaces.

Most MS-DOS filenames contain a dot, but most Linux filenames do not. In MS-DOS, the dot separates the main part of the filename from a part known as the extension, which denotes the type of the file. For example, the MS-DOS file *memo.txt* would contain text. Most Linux programs ignore file extensions, so Linux filenames don't require an extension. However, if you plan to send a file to someone using an operating system other than Linux, you should include an appropriate file extension, such as *.txt* for a text file.

Removing a directory

To remove a directory, use the **rmdir** command. For example, to remove *unwanted*, a subdirectory of the working directory, type:

```
[bill@home bill]$ rmdir unwanted
```

If the directory you want to delete is not a subdirectory of the working directory, remove it by typing an absolute or relative pathname.

You cannot use **rmdir** to remove a directory that contains files or subdirectories; you must first delete the files in the directory and then remove the directory itself. Hidden files can present a puzzle, because a directory containing hidden files may look empty even though it's not. You must delete hidden files before you can delete the directory containing them.

Working with Files

Directories contain files and other directories. You use files to store data. This section introduces you to several useful commands for working with files.

Displaying the contents of a file

Linux files, like most Windows files, can contain text or binary information. The contents of a binary file are meaningful only to skilled programmers, but you can easily view the contents of a text file. Simply type the **cat** command, specifying the name of the text file as an argument. For example:

```
[root@desktop /root]# cat /etc/passwd
```

displays the contents of the */etc/passwd* file, which lists the accounts on the system.

If a file is too large to be displayed on a single screen, the first part of the file will whiz past you and you'll see only the last few screenfulls of lines of the file. To avoid this, you can use the **less** command:

```
[root@desktop /root]# less /etc/passwd
```

This command displays the contents of a file in the same way the **man** command displays a manual page. You can use **Space** and the **b** key to page forward and backward through the file, and the **q** or **Q** key to exit the command.

Removing a file

To delete a file, type the **rm** (remove) command, specifying the name of the file as an argument. For example:

```
[bill@home bill]$ rm badfile
```

removes the file named *badfile* contained in the working directory. If a file is located elsewhere, you can remove it by specifying an absolute or relative pathname.

 Once you remove a Linux file, its contents are likely lost forever. Be careful to avoid removing a file that contains needed information. Better yet, be sure to have a backup copy of any important data.

The **-i** option causes the **rm** command to prompt you to verify your decision to remove a file. If you don't trust your typing skills, you may find this option helpful. If you log in as the root user, Linux automatically supplies the **-i** option even if you don't type it.

Copying a file

To copy a file, use the **cp** command, specifying the name (or path) of the file you want to copy and the name (or path) to which you want to copy it. For example:

```
[root@desktop /root]# cp /etc/passwd sample
```

copies the */etc/passwd* file to a file named *sample* in the working directory.

If the destination file already exists, Linux overwrites it. You must therefore be careful to avoid overwriting a file that contains needed data. Before copying a file, use the **ls** command to ensure that no file will be overwritten; alternatively, use the **-i** option of the **cp** command, which prompts you to verify that you want to overwrite an existing file. If you log in as the root user, Linux automatically supplies the **-i** option even if you don't type it.

Renaming or moving a file

To rename a file, use the **mv** command, specifying the name (or path) of the file and the new name (or path). For example:

```
[bill@home bill]$ mv old new
```

renames the file named *old* as *new*. If the destination file already exists, Linux overwrites it, so you must be careful. Before moving a file, use the **ls** command to ensure that no file will be overwritten or use the **-i** option of the **mv** command, which prompts you to verify that you want to overwrite an existing file. If you log in as the root user, Linux automatically supplies the -i option even if you don't type it.

The **mv** command can rename a directory but cannot move a directory from one device to another. To move a directory to a new device, first copy the directory and its contents and then remove the original.

Finding a file

If you know the name of a file but do not know which directory contains it, you can use the **find** command to locate the file. For example:

```
[bill@home bill]$ find . -name 'missing' -print
```

attempts to find a file named *missing*, located in (or beneath) the current working directory (.). If the command finds the file, it displays its absolute pathname.

If you know only part of the filename, you can surround the part you know with asterisks (*):

```
[bill@home bill]$ find / -name '*iss*' -print
```

This command will find any file whose name includes the characters *iss*, searching every subdirectory of the root directory (that is, the entire system).

Another command useful for finding files is **locate**. The **locate** command uses a database that is updated only daily. So it can't find recently created files and it shows files that may have been recently deleted. But it operates much more quickly than the **find** command. To use the **locate** command, specify as the command's argument a string of characters, which need not be enclosed in quotes. The command will list all filenames in its database that contain the specified characters. For example, the command:

```
locate pass
```

lists all files containing the characters *pass*.

 The **locate** command depends on a database built by the **updatedb** command. You must run **updatedb** before running **locate** for the first time and as often thereafter as you feel that your system's file structure has changed significantly. The *cron* and *anacron* services will generally take care of this for you. However, you can run the **updatedb** command manually if you feel the results of the **locate** command seem out of date.

Printing a file

If your system includes a configured printer, you can print a file by using the **lpr** command. For example:

```
[root@desktop /root]# lpr /etc/passwd
```

sends the file */etc/passwd* to the printer. See Chapter 9 for information on configuring a printer.

You can send other files to the printer while a file is printing. The **lpq** command lets you see what files are queued to be printed:

```
[root@desktop /root]# lpq
lp is ready and printing
Rank   Owner     Job  Files              Total Size
active root       155  /etc/passwd        1030 bytes
```

Each waiting or active file has an assigned print job number. You can use **lprm** to cancel printing of a file, by specifying the print job number. For example:

```
[root@desktop /root]# lprm 155
```

cancels printing of job number 155. However, only the user who requested that a file be printed (or the root user) can cancel printing of the file.

Working with compressed files

To save disk space and expedite downloads, you can compress a data file. By convention, compressed files are named ending in *.gz*; however, Linux doesn't require or enforce this convention.

To expand a compressed file, use the **gunzip** command. For example, suppose the file *bigfile.gz* has been compressed. Typing the command:

```
[bill@home bill]$ gunzip bigfile.gz
```

extracts the file *bigfile* and removes the file *bigfile.gz*.

To compress a file, use the **gzip** command. For example, to compress the file *bigfile*, type the command:

```
[bill@home bill]$ gzip bigfile
```

The command creates the file *bigfile.gz* and removes the file *bigfile*.

A different compression format is provided by the **bzip2** command; files compressed this way usually have *.bz2* extensions and can be uncompressed with **bunzip2**.

Sometimes it's convenient to store several files (or the contents of several subdirectories) in a single file. This is useful, for example, in creating a backup or archive copy of files. The Linux **tar** command creates a single file that contains data from several files. Unlike the **gzip** command, the **tar** command doesn't disturb the original files. To create a tarfile, as a file created by the **tar** command is called, issue a command like this:

```
tar -cvf tarfile files-or-directories
```

Substitute *tarfile* with the name of the tarfile you want to create and *files-or-directories* with a list of files and directories, separating the list elements by one or more spaces. You can use absolute or relative pathnames to specify the files or directories. By convention, the name of a tarfile ends with *.tar*, but Linux does not require or enforce this convention. Some people refer to tarfiles as *tarballs*, because they often contain multiple files.

For example, to create a tarfile named *backup.tar* that contains all the files in all subdirectories of the directory */home/bill*, type:

```
[bill@home bill]$ tar -cvf backup.tar /home/bill
```

The command creates the file *backup.tar* in the current working directory.

You can list the contents of a tarfile by using a command that follows this pattern:

```
tar -tvf tarfile | less
```

The | **less** causes the output to be sent to the **less** command, so that you can page through multiple pages. If the tarfile holds only a few files, you can omit | **less**.

To extract the contents of a tarfile, use a command that follows this pattern:

```
tar -xvf tarfile
```

This command expands the files and directories contained within the tarfile as files and subdirectories of the working directory.

 If a file or subdirectory already exists, the **tar** command silently overwrites it.

The **tar** command provides a host of useful options; see its manpage for details.

It's common to compress a tarfile, which you can do by specifying the options **-czvf** instead of **-cvf**. Compressed tarfiles are conventionally named ending with *.tgz*. To expand a compressed tarfile, specify the options **-xzvf** instead of **-xvf**.

The **tar** command doesn't use the ZIP method of compression common in the Windows world. However, Linux can easily work with, or even create, ZIP files.

To create a ZIP file that holds compressed files or directories, issue a command like this one:

```
zip -r zipfile files_to_zip
```

where *zipfile* names the ZIP file that will be created and *files_to_zip* specifies the files and directories to be included in the ZIP file.

To expand an existing ZIP file, issue a command like this one:

```
unzip zipfile
```

Working with links

Windows supports shortcuts, which let you refer to a file or directory (folder) by several names. Shortcuts also let you include a file in several directories or a subdirectory within multiple parent directories. In Linux, you accomplish these

---

results by using the **ln** command, which links multiple names to a single file or directory. These names are called *symbolic links*, *soft links*, *symlinks*, or simply *links*.

To link a new name to an existing file or directory, type a command that follows this pattern:

```
ln -s old new
```

For example, suppose that the current working directory contains the file *william*. To be able to refer to this same file by the alternative name *bill*, type the command:

```
[bill@home bill]$ ln -s william bill
```

The **ls** command shows the result:

```
[bill@home bill]$ ls -l
lrwxrwxrwx  1 root    root       7 Feb 27 13:58 bill->william
-rw-r--r--  1 root    root    1030 Feb 27 13:26 william
```

The new file (*bill*) has type 1, which indicates it's a link rather than a file or directory. Moreover, the **ls** command helpfully shows the name of the file to which the link refers (*william*). Notice the file size of the link *bill*. Creating a link merely creates a pointer to a file rather than a duplicate of the file, thereby saving disk space.

If you omit the -s option, Linux creates what's called a *hard link*. A hard link must be stored on the same filesystem as the file to which it refers, a restriction that does not apply to symbolic links. The link count displayed by the **ls** command reflects only hard links; symbolic links are ignored. Hard links are seldom used, because soft links are more flexible.

Working with file permissions

As explained in Chapter 4, access permissions determine which operations a user can perform on a directory or file. Table 7-5 lists the possible permissions and explains the meaning of each. Recall from Chapter 4 that permissions work differently for directories than for files. For example, permission r denotes the ability to list the contents of a directory or *read* the contents of a file. A directory or file can have more than one permission. Only the listed permissions are granted; any other operations are prohibited. For example, a user who had file permission rw could *read* or *write* the *file* but could not execute it, as indicated by the absence of the execute permission, x. Look back to Figure 7-3 to see how the **ls** command displays permissions.

Table 7-5. Access permissions

Permission	Meaning for a directory	Meaning for a file
r	List the directory	Read contents
w	Create or remove files	Write contents
x	Access files and subdirectories	Execute

The access modes of a directory of file consist of three permissions:

User/Owner
  Applies to the owner of the file
Group
  Applies to users who are members of the group assigned to the file
Other
  Applies to other users

The **ls** command lists the file access modes in the second column of its long output format, as shown in Figure 7-3. The column contains nine characters: the first three specify the access allowed the owner of the directory or file, the second three specify the access allowed users in the same group as the directory or file, and the final three specify the access allowed to other users (see Figure 7-4).

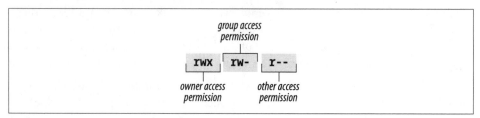

Figure 7-4. Access modes specify three permissions

You set the access modes of a directory or file by using the **chmod** command, which has the following pattern:

    chmod *nnn directory-or-file*

The argument *nnn* is a three-digit number, which gives the access mode for the owner, group, and other users. Table 7-6 shows each possible digit and the equivalent access permission. For example, the argument **751** is equivalent to rwxr-x--x, which gives the owner every possible permission, gives the group read and execute permission, and gives other users execute permission.

Table 7-6. Numerical access mode values

Value	Meaning
0	---
1	--x
2	-w-
3	-wx
4	r--
5	r-x
6	rw-
7	rwx

If you're the owner of a file or directory (or if you're the root user), you can change the ownership of the file or directory by using the **chown** command. For example, the following command assigns *newuser* as the owner of the file *hotpotato*:

```
[bill@home bill]$ chown newuser hotpotato
```

The owner of a file or directory (and the root user) can also change the group of a file. For example, the following command assigns *newgroup* as the new group of the file *hotpotato*:

```
[bill@home bill]$ chgrp newgroup hotpotato
```

The group you assign to a file or directory must have been previously established by the root user. And, unless the command is issued by the root user, the user must be a member of the new group to which the file is assigned. The valid groups appear in the file */etc/group*, which only the root user can alter. The root user can assign each user to one or more groups. When you log on to the system, you are assigned to one of these groups—your *login group*—by default. To change to another of your assigned groups, you can use the *newgrp* command. For example, to change to the group named *secondgroup*, use the following command:

```
[root@desktop /root]# newgrp secondgroup
```

If you attempt to change to a group that does not exist or to which you have not been assigned, your command will fail. When you create a file or directory, it is automatically assigned your current group as its owning group.

Running programs

In Linux, as in MS-DOS and Windows, programs are stored in files. Often, you can launch a program by simply typing its filename. However, this assumes that the file is stored in one of a series of directories known as the *path*. A directory included in this series is said to be *in the path* or *on the path*. If you've worked with MS-DOS, you're familiar with the MS-DOS path, and the Linux path works much like it.

If the file you want to launch is not stored in a directory on the path, you can simply type the absolute pathname of the file. Linux will then launch the program even though it's not on the path. If the file you want to launch is stored in the current working directory, type *./* followed by the name of the program file. Again, Linux will launch the program even though it's not on the path.

For example, suppose the program **bigdeal** is stored in the directory */home/bob*, which is the current directory and which happens to be on the path. You could launch the program with any of these commands:

```
bigdeal
./bigdeal
/home/bob/bigdeal
```

The first command assumes that the program is on the path. The second assumes that the program resides in the current working directory. The third explicitly specifies the location of the file.

Mounting and Unmounting Drives

To mount a device or partition, you use the **mount** command, which has the following pattern:

    mount options device directory

The **mount** command provides many options. However, you can generally use the **mount** command without any options; consult **mount**'s manpage to learn about the available options.

 The reason you can often use the **mount** command without options is that the file /etc/fstab describes your system's devices and the type of filesystem each is likely to contain. When you reboot your system after adding a new device, the kudzu service detects the new device and updates /etc/fstab to include an entry for the device, if necessary. However, you can edit the /etc/fstab by hand to add new entries or revise entries placed there by kudzu.

You must specify the device that you want to mount and a directory, known as the mount point. To make it convenient to access various devices, Linux treats a mounted device as a directory; mounting the device associates it with the named directory. For example, the following command is used to mount a CD-ROM:

    [root@desktop /root]# mount -t iso9660 /dev/cdrom /mnt/cdrom -o ro

The file /dev/cdrom is a link that points to the actual device file associated with your system's CD-ROM drive. The directory /mnt/cdrom is a directory created by the install program; this directory is conventionally used as the mounting point for CD-ROMs. The type of filesystem found on most CD-ROMs is **iso9660**, the value of the -t argument. The -o argument, **ro**, specifies that the filesystem is read-only; that is, it can be read but not written. The file /etc/fstab can supply most of these arguments if they're omitted. Generally, you can mount a CD-ROM by issuing the abbreviated command:

    [root@desktop /root]# mount /dev/cdrom

After the command has completed, you can access files and directories on the CD-ROM just as you would access ordinary files and directories on the path /mnt/cdrom. For example, to list the top-level files and directories of the CD-ROM, simply type:

    [root@desktop /root]# ls /mnt/cdrom

To mount an MS-DOS floppy disk in your a: drive, type:

    [root@desktop /root]# mount -t msdos /dev/fd0 /mnt/floppy

To unmount a device, specify its mount point as an argument of the **umount** command (note the missing *n* in *umount*). For example, to unmount a CD-ROM diskette, type:

```
[root@desktop /root]# umount /mnt/cdrom
```

Generally, only the root user can unmount a device. However, Red Hat Linux allows ordinary users to mount and unmount devices when logged in locally. Nevertheless, a device can be unmounted only if it's not in use. For example, if a user's working directory is a directory of the device, the device cannot be unmounted.

 If you can't unmount a device, check each terminal window and virtual console to see if one of them has a session that's using the device as its working directory. If so, either exit the session or change to a working directory that isn't associated with the device.

Formatting a Floppy Disk

Before you can write data on a floppy disk, you must format it. The Linux command to format a floppy disk is **fdformat**. Simply follow the command with an argument that specifies the floppy drive and the capacity of the floppy disk; the available arguments are listed in Table 7-7.

Table 7-7. Floppy drive designators

Designation	Meaning
/dev/fd0	3.5-inch disk in *a:* (1.44 MB)
/dev/fd0H1440	3.5-inch disk in *a:* (1.44 MB)
/dev/fd1	3.5-inch disk in *b:* (1.44 MB)
/dev/fd1H1440	3.5-inch disk in *b:* (1.44 MB)
/dev/fd1H2880	3.5-inch disk in *b:* (2.88 MB)

For example, to format a 1.44 MB floppy disk, log in as *root* and issue the command:

```
[root@desktop /root]# fdformat /dev/fd0H1440
```

The **fdformat** command performs only a low-level format. Before the floppy disk can be used, you must place a filesystem on it. Floppy disks containing an MS-DOS filesystem are useful for transferring data between Windows and Linux. To place an MS-DOS filesystem on a formatted floppy disk, issue the command:

```
[root@desktop /root]# mkdosfs /dev/fd0
```

Once the floppy disk has been formatted and given a filesystem, you can mount it and then read and write it.

Be sure you unmount the floppy disk before you remove it. Unmounting the floppy disk ensures that all pending data has been written to it; otherwise, the floppy disk may be unusable due to corrupt data.

Useful Linux Programs

This section presents several programs you may find helpful in working with your Linux system. You'll learn several commands that report system status and you'll learn how to use *pico*, a simple text editor.

Viewing System Information

Linux provides a number of commands that report system status. The most commonly used commands are shown in Table 7-8. These commands can help you troubleshoot system problems and identify resource bottlenecks. Although each command can be used without options or arguments, each supports options and arguments that let you customize operation and output; consult the appropriate manpage for details.

Table 7-8. Useful system commands

Command	Function
df	Shows the amount of free disk space (in 1 KB blocks) on each mounted filesystem.
du	Shows the amount of disk space (in 1 KB blocks) used by the working directory and its subdirectories. With the -s option, displays just a summary without listing all the subdirectories and files.
free	Shows memory usage statistics, including total free memory, memory used, physical memory, swap memory, shared memory, and buffers used by the kernel.
ps	Shows the active processes (instances of running programs) associated with this login session. Use the -a option to list all processes.
top	Shows a continually updated display of active processes, and the resources they are using. Type the **q** key to exit.
uptime	Shows the current time, the amount of time logged in, the number of users logged in, and system load averages.
users	Shows each login session.
w	Shows a summary of system usage, currently logged-in users, and active processes.
who	Shows the names of users currently logged in, the terminal each is using, the time each has been logged in, and the name of the host from which each logged in (if any).

Using the pico Editor

If you're working under X, you have access to a variety of GUI text editors. However, GUI text editors cannot be used from a virtual console. The *pico* editor is a simple text editor that you can think of as the Linux equivalent of the Windows program named Edit, because it can be used in graphical or text mode.

Unfortunately, the *pico* text editor is not a part of the standard Red Hat Linux installation. The standard Red Hat Linux installation does include the text editor *vi*; however, *vi* is more difficult to learn than *pico*. To install the *pico* editor, install the *pine* package that contains the editor and the *pine* email client. To do so, mount installation CD 3, open a terminal window, and issue the command:

```
$ redhat-install-packages /mnt/cdrom/RedHat/RPMS/pine-*.rpm
```

 If X is not running, this command to install the *pine* package will fail. Instead, issue the following commands to mount the CD and install the package:

```
$ mount -t iso9660 /dev/cdrom /mnt/cdrom -o ro
$ rpm -Uvh /mnt/cdrom/RedHat/RPMS/pine-*.rpm
```

To start *pico*, simply type **pico** at the shell prompt, or if you want to edit a particular file, type **pico** followed by the name of the file (or the file's path, if the file is not in the working directory). For example, to edit the file *mydata*, type:

```
[bill@home bill]$ pico mydata
```

Figure 7-5 shows *pico*'s standard display. At the top of the display is a status line, which shows the version of the program and the name of the file being edited (or New Buffer, if the file is new). If the file has been modified, the upper-right corner of the display contains the word *Modified*. The bottom two lines of the display list the available editing commands. Most of the commands require you to type a control character, so that commands can be distinguished from characters you want to add to the buffer, as *pico*'s work area is termed. Typing an ordinary character inserts it at the current cursor position. You can use the cursor keys to move around the display; you can use the Delete or Backspace key to erase unwanted characters. Some commands use the third line from the bottom to report status and obtain additional input.

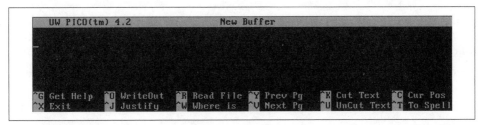

Figure 7-5. The pico editor

Table 7-9 summarizes *pico*'s commands. Notice that the command **Ctrl-G** accesses *pico*'s help system. You can access several of the commands by using function keys; for example, pressing **F1** has the same result as typing **Ctrl-G**.

Table 7-9. Summary of pico commands

Command	Description
Ctrl-^	Mark the cursor position as beginning of selected text.
Ctrl-A	Move to the beginning of the current line.
Ctrl-B	Move backward one character.
Ctrl-C (F11)	Report the current cursor position.
Ctrl-D	Delete the character at the cursor position.
Ctrl-E	Move to the end of the current line.
Ctrl-F	Move forward one character.
Ctrl-G (F1)	Display help.
Ctrl-I	Insert a tab at the current cursor position.
Ctrl-J (F4)	Format the current paragraph.
Ctrl-K (F9)	Cut selected text.
Ctrl-L	Refresh the display.
Ctrl-N	Move to the next line.
Ctrl-O (F3)	Save the current buffer to a file.
Ctrl-P	Move to the previous line.
Ctrl-R (F5)	Insert an external file at the current cursor position.
Ctrl-T (F12)	Invoke the spelling checker.
Ctrl-U (F10)	Paste text at the current cursor position.
Ctrl-V (F8)	Move forward one page of text.
Ctrl-W (F6)	Search for text, neglecting case.
Ctrl-X (F2)	Exit *pico*, saving the edit buffer.
Ctrl-Y (F7)	Move backward one page of text.

Here's a simple exercise that will give you a quick tour of *pico*. Start *pico* by issuing the command:

```
pico
```

Then type the following short paragraph of text, including the typographical errors:

```
Pico is is a greet editor. I use it for my light-duty tasks editing. However, when I
need to really get down to business, I prefer vi.
```

Notice that three errors appear:

- The word *is* appears twice
- *Great* is misspelled as *greet*
- The words *editing* and *tasks* appear in the wrong order.

To correct the first error, use the up and left arrow keys to position the cursor on the letter *i* of the first instance of the word *is*. Then, press **Del** three times to erase the word and the following space.

Next, use the right arrow key to place the cursor on the second (incorrect) letter *e* in the misspelled word *greet*. Type an *a* and press **Del** to correct the error by replacing the *e* with an *a*.

Now, let's revise the phrase "for my" to read "for all my." Simply use the right arrow keys to move to the letter *m* in the word *my*. Type *all* and a space.

Finally, let's cut and paste to move the words *tasks* and *editing* into their proper sequence. Use the arrow keys to position the cursor on the letter *t* in the word *tasks*. Type **Ctrl-^** to mark the beginning of a selection. Use the right arrow key to select the remainder of the word and the following text, positioning the cursor on the letter *e* in the word *editing*. Cut the selected word by typing **Ctrl-K**. Now, use the right arrow key to move the cursor past the word *editing* and type **Ctrl-U** to paste the text that was cut. The paragraph is now error-free.

Save the paragraph to a file by typing **Ctrl-X**, responding *y* to the question "Save modified buffer?", typing the desired filename, and pressing **Enter**. Use the **less** command to verify that the file was created and has the proper contents.

CHAPTER 8

Installing Software Using the RPM Package Manager

This chapter explains the Red Hat Package Manager (RPM), a tool that facilitates installing, uninstalling, and upgrading software for your Red Hat Linux system. The chapter explains how to use RPM to find the package associated with an application and how to quickly and easily install the package. It also explains how to use RPM to upgrade packages and query the status of installed packages.

An RPM package (or more simply, an *RPM* or a *package*) is a file that contains executable programs, scripts, documentation, and other files needed by an application or software unit. RPM packages are generally named using a convention that lets you determine the name of the package, the version of the software, the release number of the software, and the system architecture for which the application is intended. Figure 8-1 shows how the components of a package name are arranged.

Figure 8-1. The structure of a package name

The Package Management Tool

Red Hat Linux 8.0 features a new package management tool that's much easier to use than GnomeRPM, the tool included in previous versions of Red Hat Linux. To launch the package management tool, choose System Settings → Packages from the GNOME or KDE menu. Only the root user can manipulate packages. If you're not logged in as the root user, the tool helpfully prompts you for the root user's password. The tool checks the status of install packages, as shown in Figure 8-2. This process may require a minute or two. Then, the Add or Remove Packages window appears, as shown in Figure 8-3.

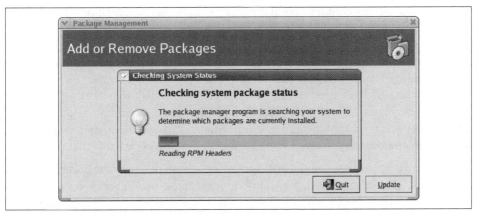

Figure 8-2. The package management tool

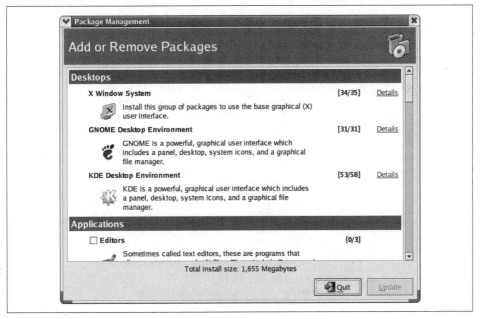

Figure 8-3. The Add or Remove Packages window

Installing Package Groups and Packages

To specify that a package group should be installed, select the checkbox next to the name of an uninstalled package group. In Figure 8-3, the Editors package group is not installed, as indicated by the unchecked checkbox to the left of the package group's name. By enabling the checkbox, you can specify that you want to install the package group. Installation does not begin until you click the Update button.

Most package groups contain optional packages that you can install or omit, according to your preference. The numbers to the right of the package group name indicate how many of the optional packages are installed. If you've just specified that a package group should be installed, the numbers indicate how many of the optional packages will be installed when you click the Update button. For example, in Figure 8-3, the 0/3 associated with the Editors package group indicates that none of the three associated packages is currently installed. If you enable the checkbox associated with the Editors package group, the numbers immediately change to 2/3, meaning that two of the three associated packages will be installed when you click the Update button.

To learn more about the optional packages associated with a package group, click the Details link. The Package Details window appears, as shown in Figure 8-4. This window provides checkboxes that you can use to specify which optional packages you want installed. If you can't see the list of package names, expand the tree by clicking the triangle next to the text Extra Packages. When you're done viewing the package details, close the window by clicking Close. You can then install the selected packages by clicking Update. The package management tool will prompt you to insert the appropriate installation CD, in necessary. To close the Add or Remove Packages window without installing or removing any packages, click the Quit button.

 The package management tool only installs official Red Hat Linux packages that are distributed on the installation media. However, you can use the **rpm** command to install packages from other sources, as described later in this chapter.

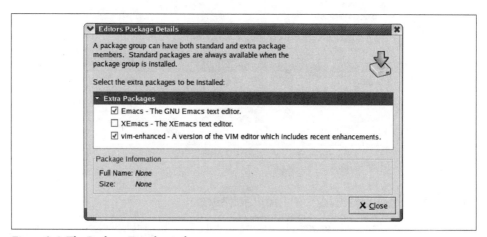

Figure 8-4. The Package Details window

Removing Package Groups and Packages

You can also delete package groups and packages by using the package management tool. To remove a package group, disable the checkbox associated with the package group. To remove a package, open the Package Details window and disable the checkbox associated with the package. No changes are made until you click the Update button of the Add or Remove Packages window.

 You can't use the package management tool to remove the package groups for the X Window System, GNOME desktop environment, or KDE desktop environment. Neither can you use the package management tool to delete standard packages associated with a package group. These restrictions protect you against unintended deletion of packages necessary for system operation. If, however, you do want to delete one or more such packages, you can do so using the **rpm** command. If you do use the **rpm** command to remove packages, be sure you avoid removing packages necessary for system operation.

Installing Packages from the Hard Disk

If you have several free gigabytes of disk storage, you may prefer to copy the Red Hat Linux installation media to your hard disk. Doing so avoids the need to insert CDs when installing packages.

To set up your system for installing packages from the hard disk, open a terminal window, become the root user, and issue the following command to create the directory */redhat-tree/RedHat*:

```
mkdir -p /redhat-tree/RedHat
```

The **-p** flag enables you to create the directory and its parent directory in a single command. Without the flag, the command will fail because the */redhat-tree* directory does not exist.

Next, mount installation CD 1 and copy the contents of the *RedHat* directory (*/mnt/ cdrom/RedHat*) to the new directory:

```
cp -a /mnt/cdrom/RedHat/* /redhat-tree/RedHat
```

Finally, copy the files from installation CD 2 and CD 3 to the same location.

 You can create the directories and copy the files using a file manager, if you prefer.

To install packages, launch the package management tool by issuing the command:

```
redhat-config-packages --tree=/redhat-tree
```

The tool will no longer prompt you to insert a CD; instead, it will obtain package files from the */redhat-tree* directory. To avoid typing this command to install packages, you can create a panel launcher or menu item, as explained in Chapters 5 and 6.

The redhat-install-packages Command

The package management tool uses a special command, **redhat-install-packages**, to install packages. Although the package management tool can install only packages that reside on the installation media, the **redhat-install-packages** command can install RPM packages from any source. For example, you can use this command to install packages that you've downloaded from a web or FTP server.

RPM package names generally end with a *.rpm* extension. To install a package using the **redhat-install-packages** command, issue the command:

```
redhat-install-packages package-file.rpm
```

where *package-file.rpm* is the name of the package you want to install. You can install multiple packages by listing several filenames, separating each from the next with a space, like so:

```
redhat-install-packages package-file1.rpm package-file2.rpm package-file3.rpm
```

If a desired package requires other packages in order to operate correctly, the other packages must already be installed or must be installed at the same time as the desired package. Otherwise, installation of the desired package will fail. See the upcoming section "Failed Dependency" for more information on this potential problem. However, the **redhat-install-packages** command will attempt to automatically install necessary packages that reside on the installation media.

 Several Linux distributions publish their software as RPMs. Although the **redhat-install-packages** command is generally capable of installing foreign packages—that is, packages not created for Red Hat Linux—installing foreign packages may leave your system in an unusable state. You should generally install only packages created for Red Hat Linux. You can safely use the **redhat-install-packages** command to install such packages.

The rpm Command

RPM packages are built, installed, uninstalled, and queried with the **rpm** command. Like other command-line facilities, the **rpm** command gives you almost complete control over its operation. So, you can use the **rpm** command to accomplish feats not possible using the package management tool. For instance, you can use the **rpm** command to install or remove individual packages, install packages from non-Red Hat media, and install packages other than those built by Red Hat. On the other hand, the **rpm** command is sometimes much less convenient to use than the package management tool. So, Red Hat Linux lets you use either the GUI or command line, according to your need and preference.

rpm has several modes, each with its own options. The general format of the **rpm** command is:

```
rpm [options] [packages]
```

The first option generally specifies the **rpm** mode (e.g., install, query, update, build, etc.); any remaining options pertain to the specified mode.

The **rpm** command has built-in FTP and HTTP clients. So, you can specify an *ftp://* or *http://* URL to identify an RPM package stored on a remote host.

Unless the system administrator has specially configured the system, any user can query the RPM database. Most other RPM functions require root privileges. Strictly speaking, it's not necessary for you log in as root to install an RPM package; however, your user account must be authorized to access and modify the files and directories required by the package, including the RPM database itself. Generally, the easiest way to ensure such access is by logging in as root.

General rpm Options

The following **rpm** options can be used with all modes:

--dbpath *path*
> Use *path* as the path to the RPM database.

--ftpport *port*
> Use *port* as the FTP port.

--ftpproxy *host*
> Use *host* as a proxy server for all transfers. Specified if you are FTPing through a firewall system that uses a proxy.

--help
> Print a long usage message (running **rpm** with no options gives a shorter usage message).

--justdb
> Update only the database; don't change any files.

--pipe *command*
> Pipe the **rpm** output to *command*.

--quiet
> Display only error messages.

--rcfile *filename*
> Use *filename*, instead of the system configuration file */etc/rpmrc* or *$HOME/.rpmrc*, as the configuration file.

--root *dir*
> Perform all operations within directory *dir*.

--version

> Print the version number of **rpm**.

-vv

> Print debugging information.

Querying the RPM Database

You can query RPM's database, which lists the packages installed on your system. For example, to display a simple description of an installed package, use a command like this one:

```
rpm -q package
```

In this command, *package* is the name of the package you want RPM to describe. In response, RPM prints the package name, version, and release number.

Rather than use the **-q** option and the package name, you can use any of the following alternative options:

-a

> Causes RPM to display information about all installed packages

-f *file*

> Causes RPM to display information about the package that owns *file*

-p *packagefile*

> Causes RPM to display information about the package contained in *packagefile*

You can also tailor the output of an RPM query, by specifying one or more of the following options:

-c   Causes RPM to display a list of configuration files included in the package

-d   Causes RPM to display a list of documentation files included in the package

-i   Causes RPM to display the package name, description, release number, size, build date, installation date, vendor, and other information

-l   Causes RPM to display the list of files that the package owns

-s   Causes RPM to display the state of all the files in the package—normal, not installed, or replaced

For example, the command:

```
rpm -qid rhide
```

displays information about the *rhide* package, including a list of documentation files included in the package.

Installing a Package

To install a package, log in as root and issue the following command from a shell prompt:

```
rpm -ivh package
```

where *package* specifies the name of the file that contains the package. You can specify multiple packages, as long as you include a space to separate each package name from its neighbor. For example, the following command installs both the *pine* and *mutt* packages from files in the current directory:

```
rpm -ivh pine-4.44-13.i386.rpm mutt-1.4-4.i386.rpm
```

The options used with the **rpm** command include:

-i   This option specifies that RPM should install the package or packages given as arguments.

-h   This option specifies that RPM should print hash marks (#) as it installs the package as a visible indication of progress.

-v   The verbose option specifies that RPM should print messages that summarize its actions and progress.

Generally, RPM will successfully install the specified package. However, errors can occur. RPM may report:

- That the package is already installed
- That a package file conflicts with a file from another package
- A failed dependency

The next three sections explain how to resolve these errors.

Package Is Already Installed

If a package has already been installed, RPM will not overwrite the package without your permission:

```
# rpm -ivh bad-1.0-1.i386.rpm
bad package bad-1.0-1 is already installed
```

If you want to overwrite the package, add the **--replacepkgs** option to your command:

```
rpm -ivh --replacepkgs bad-1.0-1.i386.rpm
```

It may be more appropriate to update the package. Updating the package leaves its configuration files intact, whereas overwriting the package replaces the configuration files with files containing default options. An upcoming section shows you how to update a package.

Of course, it's also possible that you should do nothing. You may have attempted to install the package without first checking whether it's already installed and operational. In that case, you can use RPM to verify that the package is installed correctly and update or overwrite the package only if RPM reports problems.

To verify a package against a package file, issue the following command from a shell prompt:

rpm -Vp *package*

In the command, *package* specifies the name of the file that contains the package; for example, *basesystem-8.0-1.rpm*. In verifying a package, RPM compares the installed files with the original package contents. If RPM detects no discrepancies, no output will appear. Otherwise, RPM displays a line for each file that differs from the original package contents. Figure 8-5 shows the structure of such a line. The first eight characters report discrepancies; each character has the meaning described in Table 8-1. Following the list of discrepancies, you may see the letter *c*, which denotes that this is a configuration file. Finally, the filename appears.

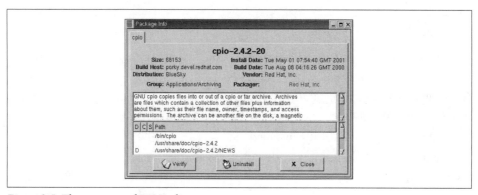

Figure 8-5. The structure of RPM's discrepancy report

Table 8-1. Package file discrepancy codes

Code	Meaning
.	No discrepancy
5	MD5 checksum discrepancy
D	Device discrepancy
G	Group discrepancy
L	Symbolic link discrepancy
M	Access mode or file type discrepancy
S	File size discrepancy
T	File modification time discrepancy
U	User discrepancy

The configuration files associated with a package are generally modified during installation and use, so it's not unusual for the content of configuration files to differ from that of the original files. You should generally ignore MD5 checksum and file size discrepancies that pertain to configuration files.

You can verify a package against the information recorded in the RPM database when the package was installed. To do so, issue a command of the form:

```
rpm -V package
```

Here, *package* specifies the name the package, for example, *basesystem*. Another form of the **rpm** command lets you verify packages that contain a specified file:

```
rpm -Vf path
```

In this form, *path* specifies the absolute pathname of the file. The output of this command is the same as that given earlier.

Conflicting File

Conflict is RPM's term for a situation in which two packages include one or more identically named files that have different contents. For example, suppose that package **a** contains a file named */etc/superconfig* having 12 lines and that package **b** contains a file named */etc/superconfig* having 13 lines. The two packages conflict, because the two instances of */etc/superconfig* are inconsistent.

In the event of a conflict, only one of the two conflicting packages is likely to work properly. If you instruct RPM to install a package and RPM finds that one or more of the package files conflict with existing files, RPM reports the conflict and terminates without installing the package:

```
# rpm -ivh bad-1.0-1.i386.rpm
bad /bin/badfile conflicts with file from good-1.0-1
```

In its report, RPM gives the name of the file and the name of the package that originally installed the file. You can force RPM to install the package, by using the **--replacefiles** option:

```
rpm -ivh --replacefiles package
```

In response, RPM saves and then replaces any conflicting configuration files; it overwrites other types of files. However, using the **--replacefiles** option is a bit like hitting a malfunctioning mechanical device with a hammer. Sometimes, it's what you must do; but, more often, it merely causes damage. The better way to resolve a conflict is to decide which of the two conflicting packages you prefer. Then, delete the unwanted package and install the preferred one.

Failed Dependency

Packages are not always self-contained: some packages require that other packages be installed before they operate correctly. RPM can identify such dependencies. If you attempt to install a package before you install other packages it requires, RPM reports a "failed dependency" and terminates without installing the package:

```
# rpm -ivh bad-1.0-1.i386.rpm
failed dependencies:
    mefirst is needed by bad-1.0-1
```

To resolve a failed dependency, you should install the missing package (or packages) and then install the desired package. If you prefer, you can force RPM to install the package; however, the package may not operate correctly. To force package installation, specify the **--nodeps** option:

```
rpm -ivh --nodeps bad-1.0-1.i386.rpm
```

However, a forcibly installed package is unlikely to work correctly.

Uninstalling a Package

To uninstall a package, type:

```
rpm -e package
```

In this command, *package* is the name of the package, not the name of the package file. The name should omit the architecture; it can also omit the package version or package version and release number. For example, you can erase the **pine** package by issuing either of the following commands:

```
rpm -e pine-4.44-13
rpm -e pine
```

If you attempt to uninstall a package on which another package depends, RPM will report a dependency error and terminate without uninstalling the package. You can force RPM to uninstall the package by using the **--nodeps** option:

```
rpm -e --nodeps package
```

However, doing so will probably cause the dependent package to cease working properly. Therefore, you shouldn't use the **--nodeps** option very often.

Updating a Package

When you update (upgrade) a package, RPM installs the new version of the software but attempts to leave your existing configuration files intact. You can update a package by using the **-U** option of the **rpm** command:

```
rpm -Uvh package
```

When you update a package, RPM automatically uninstalls the old version of the package before installing the new one.

If no old version of the specified package exists, RPM simply installs the new version. Therefore, you can use the -U option to install or update a package; many Linux users avoid the -i (install) option, always using the -U option instead. However, you should not use the -U option when installing a package containing an updated Linux kernel.

If RPM determines that your existing configuration files may be incompatible with those of the new version of the package, RPM will save a copy of the existing files. In that case, you need to examine the old and new files and determine what the proper configuration should be. The documentation that accompanies the package should assist you in this process.

If you attempt to update an existing package using an older version of the package, RPM will report an error and terminate without performing the update. To force RPM to perform the update, use the **--oldpackage** option:

```
rpm -Uvh --oldpackage package
```

Freshening a Package

From time to time, Red Hat issues updated packages that correct functional or security-related problems with released packages. You can use Red Hat Network, described later in this chapter in "Red Hat Network," to obtain and install updated packages. However, if you prefer, you can download updated packages via FTP and install them using the **rpm** command. Red Hat makes updated packages available on the public FTP servers *ftp.redhat.com* and *updates.redhat.com*.

To install an updated package, use the -F flag, which stands for *freshen*. For instance, to install a updated version of the **gv** package, issue the command:

```
rpm -Fvh gv-3.5.8-19.i386.rpm
```

By specifying -F rather than -U, you instruct RPM to install the updated package only if an earlier version of the package is already present. This lets you use wildcards to specify entire sets of updated packages:

```
rpm -Fvh *.rpm
```

This command will not install packages that aren't already installed. But, it will install updated versions of any existing packages.

Advanced RPM Techniques

Because you invoke the **rpm** command by using the shell, just as you do any other program, you can combine options and arguments to perform a variety of useful tasks. Consider the following examples:

rpm -Va
> Verifies every installed package. You might find this command useful if you accidentally deleted some files. The output of the command would help you determine what packages, if any, suffered damage.

rpm -qf /usr/bin/mystery
> Displays the name of the package that owns the specified file.

rpm -Vf /usr/bin/mystery
> Verifies the package that owns the file */usr/bin/mystery*.

rpm -qdf /usr/bin/puzzle
> Lists the documentation files associated with the package that owns the file */usr/ bin/puzzle*. This could be helpful, for example, if */usr/bin/puzzle* is a program you're having difficulty using.

Red Hat Network

Red Hat provides a service known as Red Hat Network (*http://rhn.redhat.com*), designed to help you keep your Red Hat Linux system up-to-date and secure. If you purchased the official boxed-set release of Red Hat Linux, you're entitled to a 30-day subscription to Red Hat Network for one system. You can purchase additional subscriptions for $60 per year, per system. Any Red Hat Linux user is eligible for a Demo account, which provides complimentary access to software updates and update notifications. Unlike paid accounts, a Demo account does not provide priority access during periods of high load. Moreover, only a single computer can be associated with a Demo account.

The Red Hat Network provides access to security alerts, bug fix alerts, and enhancement alerts published by Red Hat. Updated packages can be downloaded or automatically installed via the Red Hat Update Agent. The Red Hat Network is of significant benefit to administrators of multiple systems, who might otherwise have difficulty applying patches to close security loopholes and fix problems quickly.

Using Red Hat Network

To use Red Hat Network, your computer must be able to access the Internet. To set up your computer, you must perform two steps:

1. Sign up for Red Hat Network.
2. Create a system profile for your computer.

Once your computer is set up to use Red Hat Network, updates can be accomplished automatically based on a schedule or manually, by using the Red Hat Update Agent.

The following sections describe these procedures as they existed at the time of writing. However, Red Hat may revise the operation of Red Hat Network at any time.

For more information on using Red Hat Network, see the *Red Hat Network User Reference Guide*, available at *http://www.redhat.com/docs/manuals/RHNetwork*.

Signing up

To sign up for Red Hat Network, point your browser to the main Red Hat Network web page, *http://rhn.redhat.com*. Then click the link marked "Sign Up." The web page shown as Figure 8-6 appears.

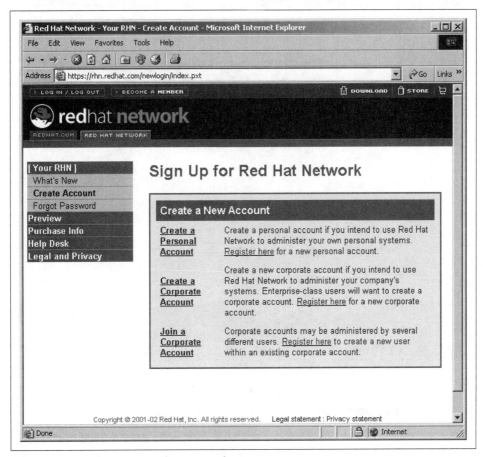

Figure 8-6. The Red Hat Network sign up web page

Click the link marked "Create a Personal Account." The web page shown in Figure 8-7 appears. Fill in the requested information and then click the Create Login button at the bottom of the form.

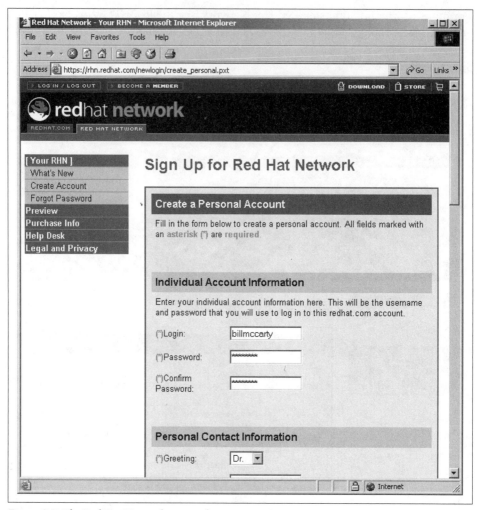

Figure 8-7. The Red Hat Network personal account sign up page

Creating a system profile

Once you've signed up for Red Hat Network, you can create a profile describing your system. To do so, click the Red Hat Network Alert Notification Tool icon that appears near the right of the desktop panel. If you've not yet created a profile, the icon will resemble a red ball with a superimposed exclamation mark. Otherwise, it may take the form of a green, blue, or gray ball.

Clicking the Notification Tool icon starts a configuration dialogue. First, the dialogue asks you to read and accept the Red Hat Network terms of service. Then, it presents the Proxy Configuration dialog box, shown in Figure 8-8. If your computer is behind a firewall that requires you to use a proxy sever to access the Web, you must enable the HTTP proxy and specify its hostname and port. Most users don't require a proxy. If you suspect that you do, you can likely obtain the proper information by inspecting the configuration of your Windows web browser, if any. Otherwise, you can obtain the necessary configuration information from your network administrator.

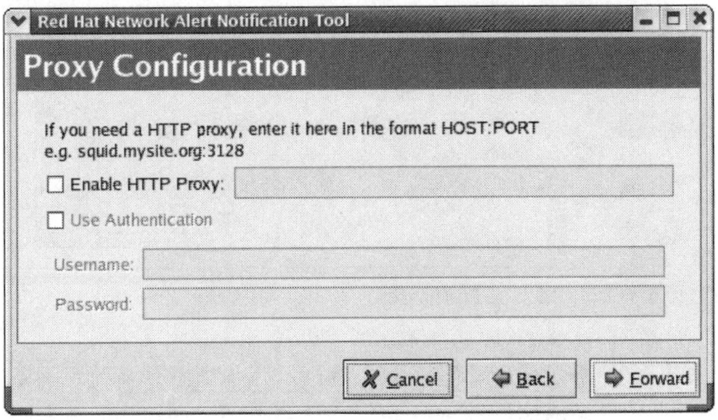

Figure 8-8. The Proxy Configuration dialog box

After you complete the dialogue, the Notification Tool will attempt to access Red Hat Network. Unless you've already configured a profile for your system, the Red Hat Network Registration dialog box shown in Figure 8-9 appears. To register your computer with Red Hat Network by creating a system profile describing it, click Register with RHN. The configuration dialog box shown in Figure 8-10 appears.

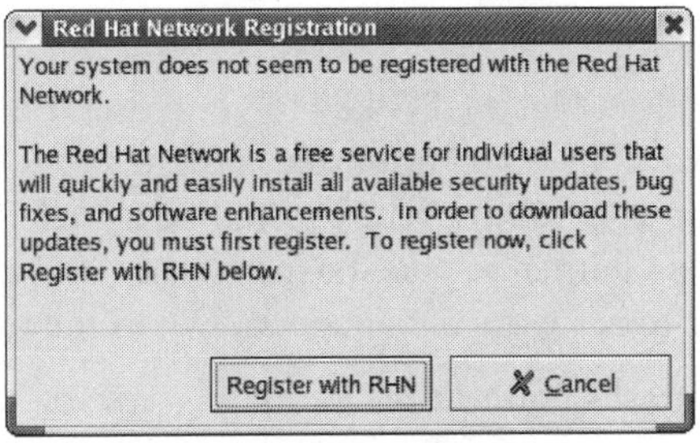

Figure 8-9. The Red Hat Network Registration dialog box

The configuration dialog box includes three tabs: General, Retrieval/Installation, and Package Exceptions. Generally, the default settings are appropriate. However, systems on your network require a proxy server in order to access the Web, so you must enable and specify an HTTP proxy just as you did for the Notification Tool. Click OK to continue. Unless you've installed Red Hat's GPG key on your GPG keyring, the dialog box shown in Figure 8-11 appears.

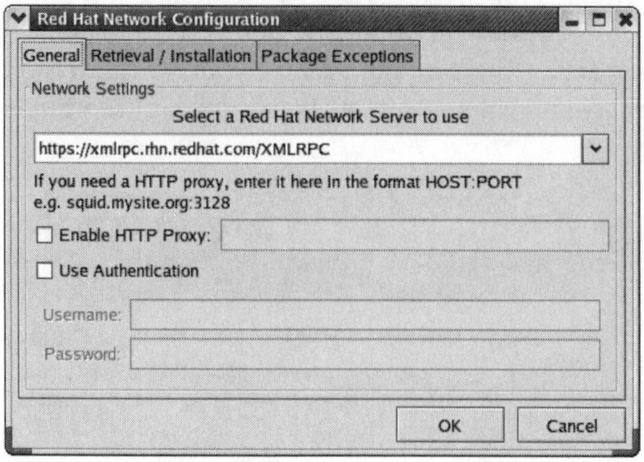

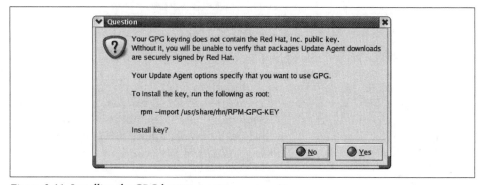

Figure 8-10. Configuring the Red Hat Network

Figure 8-11. Installing the GPG key

The Update Agent uses Red Hat's GPG key to verify that package updates originate from Red Hat and that they have not been altered. This security mechanism is intended to prevent you from inadvertently installing a package that a malicious person has substituted for an authentic one. To install the GPG key, simply click the Yes button. You don't need to issue the command shown in the text of the dialog box.

Next, the Update Agent asks you to read Red Hat's privacy statement. Clicking Forward takes you to the next step, registering or updating a user account, as shown in Figure 8-12.

To register your user account, specify the username, password, and email address you used when you signed up for Red Hat Network. Then, click Forward. The Registering a System Profile—Hardware dialog box appears, as shown in Figure 8-13. This dialog box enables you to specify a name to be associated with the profile you're about to create. Enter a profile name and click Forward to continue.

The Registering a System Profile—Packages dialog box appears, as shown in Figure 8-14. If you're unwilling to transmit the package configuration to Red Hat,

Loan Receipt
Liverpool John Moores University
Learning and Information Services

Borrower: Vijay Mani
Borrower ID: ID65500
Loan Date: 02/06/2008   Loan Time: 14:18

Learning Red Hat Linux
McCarty, B
Barcode: 31111010523601   Loan Type: 7 Day Loan
Due Date: 19/09/2008   Due Time: 23:59

Fines will be charged on late returns.
Please retain receipt in case of dispute.

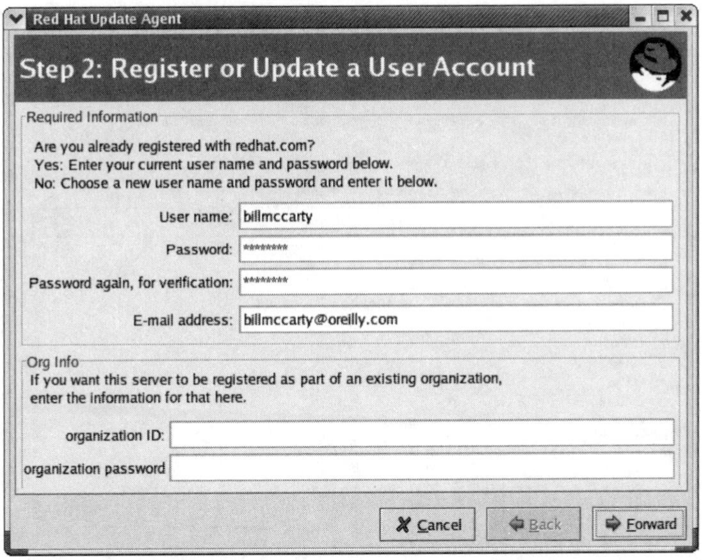

Figure 8-12. Registering or updating a user account

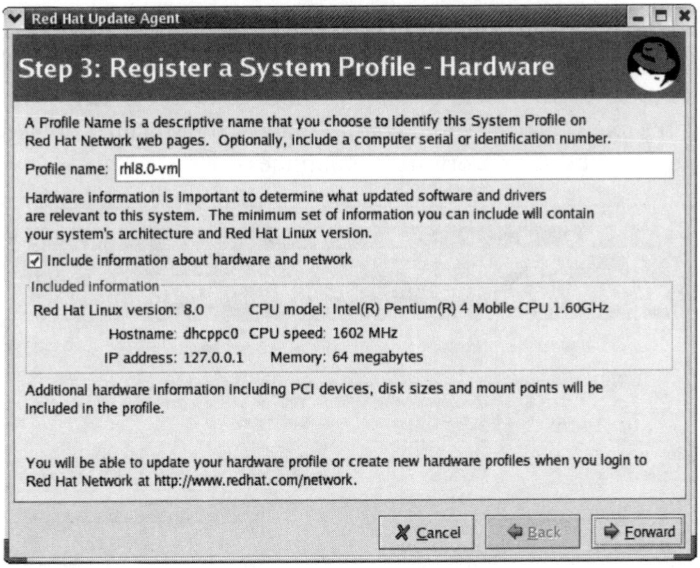

Figure 8-13. Registering a system profile—hardware

you can disable one or more checkboxes. However, Red Hat Network will not be able to properly update your system unless you transmit full and accurate information on the installed packages. So, you should not generally disable any checkboxes on this form. Click Forward to continue.

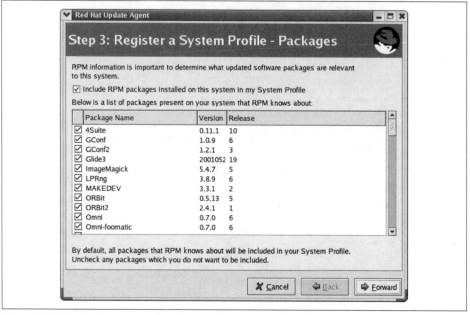

Figure 8-14. Registering a system profile—packages

The Send Profile Information to Red Hat Network dialog box appears, as shown in Figure 8-15. Click Forward to continue. The next dialog box, shown in Figure 8-16, lets you subscribe to the channel that provides updates to Red Hat Linux 8.0. Normally, only one channel should appear and you should not need to make changes to the defaults. Click Forward to continue.

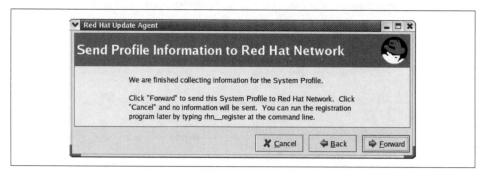

Figure 8-15. Sending the profile information

If you aren't given the opportunity to subscribe to a channel, it's likely that you've already registered all the system profiles to which you're entitled. Red Hat provides you with only a single complimentary account. If you've used all your entitlements, you can log in to Red Hat Network and remove the entitlement of an existing system or purchase an additional entitlement for the new system.

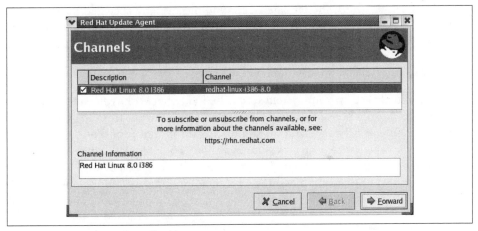

Figure 8-16. Specifying channels

As shown in Figure 8-17, the Update Agent obtains and displays a list of installed packages for which updates are available. To update a package, enable the associated checkbox. You can view information about the updates associated with a package by selecting the package name and clicking View Advisory. Select the packages you want to update and then click Forward. If you do not want to update any packages at this time, click Cancel.

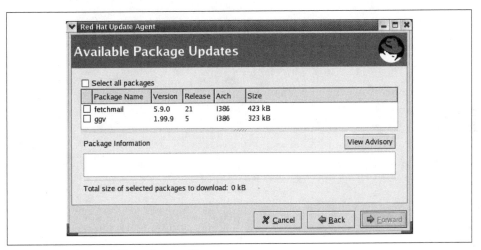

Figure 8-17. The available package updates

The Update Agent may first present a similar dialog box titled Packages Flagged to be Skipped. By default, the Update Agent does not automatically update the Linux kernel, since a failed kernel update can result in an unbootable system. If you want to update a kernel package or other package that is flagged to be skipped, enable the associated checkbox and click Forward.

After you click Forward, the Update Agent will retrieve any specified packages and update your system. Separate dialog boxes present the progress and completion of package retrieval and installation.

Updating your system

After you initially set up your system to use Red Hat Network, you can update it at any time. To do so, choose System Tools → Red Hat Network from the GNOME or KDE menu. Or, click the ball icon that represents the Notification Tool. If the icon is red, this tells you that new updates are available. To avoid a security breach, you should download and install the updates right away. Timely installation of updates is one of the most important measures in defending your system against possible attack.

## CHAPTER 9

Configuring and Administering Linux

GNOME and KDE include three menus that provide access to utilities for configuring and administering your system: System Settings, System Tools, and Server Settings. Most of these utilities are also available via the Start Here folder. This chapter explain the utilities, equipping you to perform common system administration tasks. In particular, the chapter explains how to manage user accounts, how to configure a printer, how to configure your system's sound adapter, how to view system log files, and how to administer services. Many of these operations require root access. If you launch one of the Red Hat Linux tools when not logged in as root, the tool will conveniently ask you for the root password. Once you've logged in as the root user, the desktop will display an icon resembling a set of keys. So long as this icon appears, the system will automatically extend you root privileges when necessary. You can cancel this authorization by clicking on the icon and then clicking Forget Authorization.

Configuring Red Hat Linux by Using the System Settings Menu

The GNOME and KDE System Settings menu provides access to 15 utilities that help you configure your system. Chapter 8 explained one of these, the package management tool. The tools available are:

Authentication
> Provides access to the Authentication Configuration tool, which lets you configure password settings

Date & Time
> Provides access to the Date/Time Properties tool, which lets you configure the time zone, date, and time

Display
> Provides access to the Display Settings tool, which lets you configure monitor resolution, color depth, and other display characteristics

Keyboard

Provides access to the Keyboard tool, which lets you choose the keyboard appropriate to your system

Language

Provides access to the Language Selection tool, which lets you choose the current language from among those for which you've installed support

Login Screen

Provides access to the GDM (GNOME Display Manager) Setup tool, which lets you configure how people log in under X

Mail Transport Agent Switcher

Provides access to the redhat-switchmail tool, which lets you choose between the Sendmail and Postfix mail servers

Mouse

Provides access to the Mouse Configuration took, which lets you choose the mouse appropriate to your system and enable or disable 3-button emulation

Network

Provides access to the Network Configuration tool, which lets you configure network, modem, VPN (virtual private network), and wireless connections and related settings

Packages

Provides access to the Package Management tool, which lets you install and remove RPM packages

Printing

Provides access to the Red Hat Printer Config tool, which lets you configure printers and control print queues

Root Password

Provides access to a tool that enables you to change the root password

Security Level

Provides access to the Security Level Configuration tool, which lets you configure a firewall to protect your system from network attacks

Soundcard Detection

Provides access to the Sound Card Configuration tool, which lets you configure and verify the operation of your sound card

Users and Groups

Provides access to the Red Hat User Manager, which lets you configure user accounts and groups

 Depending on the packages installed on your system, you may see fewer or more items on the System Settings menu.

In addition, the Extras menu contains a System Settings submenu, on which you can find two more tools: Desktop Switching Tool and Printer System Switcher. The Desktop Switching Tool lets you choose between the GNOME and KDE desktop. The Printer System Switcher lets you choose between the LPRng and CUPS printing system. Neither tool will let you choose a facility that's not installed. So, for example, unless you've installed both LPRng and CUPS, the Printer System Switcher tool won't actually function.

Most of the System Settings tools function like similar steps in the Red Hat Linux installation procedure. This section focuses on tools that do not resemble installation procedure steps, namely:

- GDM Setup tool
- redhat-switchmail tool
- Red Hat Printer Config tool
- Sound Card Configuration tool
- Red Hat User Manager
- Desktop Switching Tool

The Network Configuration tool provides many settings and functions. Explanation of the Network Configuration tool is deferred to Chapters 10 and 11. Similarly, explanation of the redhat-switchmail tool is deferred to Chapter 12

Setting Up X Logins

The GDM Setup tool, accessible via System Settings → Login Screen from the GNOME or KDE menu, lets you specify options related to X logins. Figure 9-1 shows the tool. Most of the options are cosmetic. For example, you can choose whether times are displayed in 12-hour or 24-hour format. However, the Security and XDMCP tabs provide options that you should consider changing.

By default, the XDMCP tab disables XDMCP, the facility that provides remote X terminals and sessions the ability to login to your system. If you have X terminals or additional Linux or Unix hosts, you may find it convenient to be able to remotely log in to your Red Hat Linux system. To provide this capability, enable the Enable XDMCP checkbox. The change takes effect when you close the GDM Setup tool. Thereafter, X terminals and X sessions on your local network should be able to remotely log in to your Red Hat Linux system.

 If you've enabled XDMCP but are unable to obtain an X login screen, check your firewall settings by using the Security Level Configuration tool. It's likely that your firewall is configured to block remote X access.

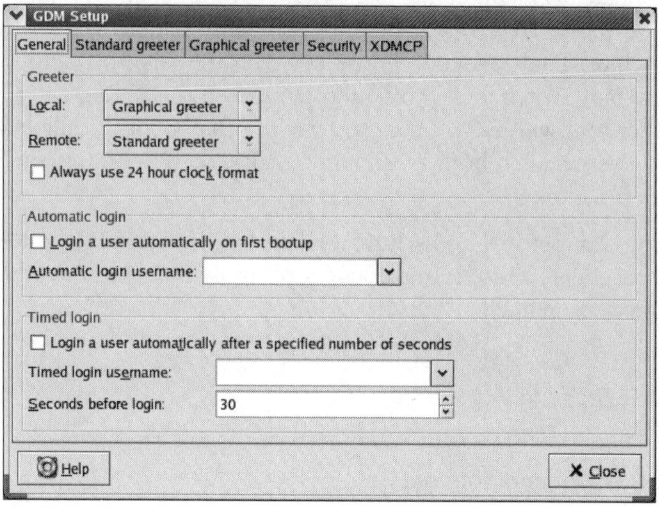

Figure 9-1. The GDM Setup tool

If you enable XDMCP, you should generally make a second configuration change. By default, the Security tab enables the setting Allow root to login remotely with GDM. Most users do not need to remotely login as root and therefore don't require this setting to be enabled. By disabling the setting, you can prevent unauthorized persons from successfully logging in as root from remote X terminals or sessions. Therefore, you should generally disable this setting.

Configuring a Printer

Before you can print from Red Hat Linux, you must configure a printer. Red Hat Linux supports local printers attached to your system's parallel port and remote printers that your system accesses via the network. Before you can configure a remote printer, you must first configure networking, as explained in Chapter 11.

To configure a local printer, launch the printer configuration tool by selecting System Tools → Printing. The Red Hat Printer Config Tool, as shown in Figure 9-2, appears.

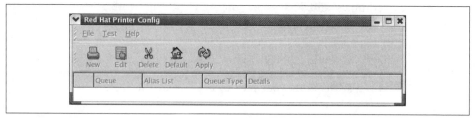

Figure 9-2. The printer configuration tool

First, create a new printer by clicking the New icon. The Add a New Print Queue wizard appears. Click Forward to proceed. The Set the Print Queue Name and Type dialog box, as shown in Figure 9-3, appears.

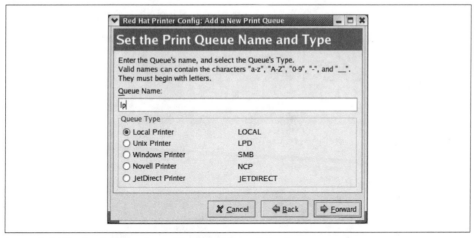

Figure 9-3. The Set the Print Queue Name and Type dialog box

Every print queue has a name. The most commonly used name for the default print queue is *lp*. Type **lp** or another print queue name of your choice in the text box labeled Queue Name. Select the Local Printer radio button and click Forward. The Configure a Local Printer dialog box, as shown in Figure 9-4, appears.

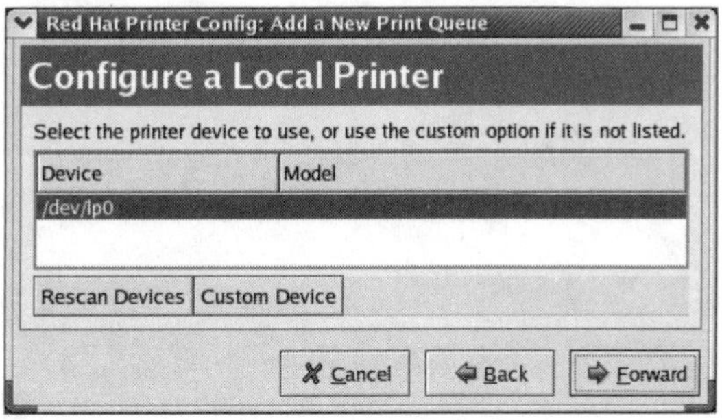

Figure 9-4. The Configure a Local Printer dialog box

The dialog box shows the parallel ports associated with your system. Linux numbers parallel ports starting with zero, so the port designated */dev/lp0* corresponds to the device known by Microsoft Windows as LPT1. Select the parallel port to which your printer is attached and click Forward.

The Select a Print Driver dialog box, as shown in Figure 9-5, appears. Select the make of your printer by clicking the triangle that appears at the left of its name.

From the sublist that appears, select the model of your printer and choose a print driver, as shown in Figure 9-6. More than one driver may be available for your printer. Some drivers work better than others, so you'll eventually want to try each driver in order to locate the one that works best. For now, merely choose a driver arbitrarily from among those listed for your printer. Then click Forward.

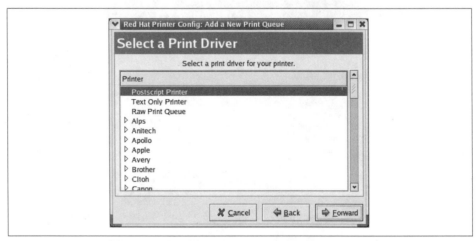

Figure 9-5. The Select a Print Driver dialog box

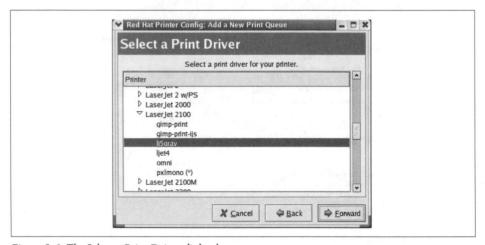

Figure 9-6. The Select a Print Driver dialog box

The Finish and Create the New Print Queue dialog box, as shown in Figure 9-7, appears. Check the information and use the Back button to correct any errors. When you're satisfied with your specifications, click Apply.

The printer configuration tool reappears with the new printer, as shown in Figure 9-8. To verify the configuration, click Test and choose ASCII Text Testpage. Doing so

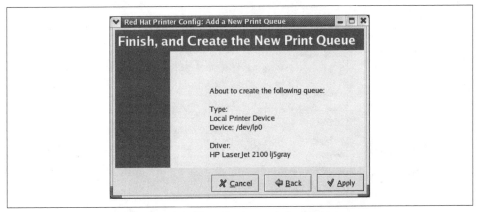

Figure 9-7. The Finish and Create the New Print Queue dialog box

sends a sample page to the printer so that you can verify correct operation. A dialog box invites you to save your configuration changes; click Yes, or your new printer configuration will be lost. The system then restarts the printer system, known as the *lpd* daemon, and informs you of the result by presenting a dialog box. This process may take several seconds. Click OK to continue. Finally, a dialog box confirms that the sample page has been sent to the printer.

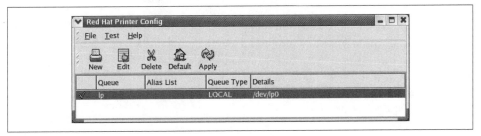

Figure 9-8. The printer configuration tool

If the sample page doesn't appear or appears incorrectly, select the printer and click Edit. Use the Edit Queue dialog box that appears, as shown in Figure 9-9, to select a different print driver or revise options associated with the current driver.

Changing the Root User Password

You can change the password associated with the *root* user account by using the Root Password tool. To do so, select System Settings → Root Password. A dialog box, shown in Figure 9-10, appears. Type the desired password twice and click OK. If the two passwords match, the password is immediately changed. Otherwise, the tool gives you another opportunity to change the password.

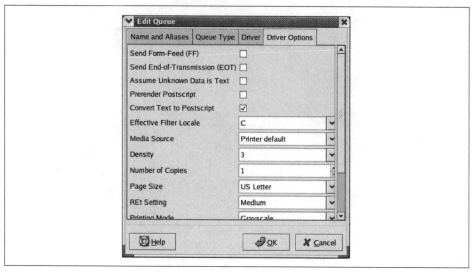

Figure 9-9. The Edit Queue dialog box

Figure 9-10. The Root Password tool

The system evaluates passwords and can determine that a password you specify is insecure. In such a case, it may prevent you from using the insecure password or, if you are the root user, it may merely inform you that the password is insecure. Unless your PC is physically secure and never connected to a network, you should choose only secure passwords.

Configuring Sound

If your system includes a sound adapter supported by Red Hat Linux, you can use the Sound Card Configuration tool to configure your adapter. If you're unsure whether your system's sound adapter is supported, check the Red Hat Linux hardware compatibility database at *http://hardware.redhat.com*. Several popular cards are not fully compatible with Red Hat Linux, so it's best to check the database before wasting time trying to configure incompatible hardware.

To configure your system's sound adapter, choose System Settings → Soundcard Detection from the GNOME or KDE menu. The Sound Card Configuration tool appears, as shown in Figure 9-11.

Figure 9-11. The Sound Card Configuration tool

The tool probes your system, seeking supported sound adapters. After a sound adapter has been identified, the tool displays the vendor and model of your sound card and the associated Linux kernel module name. If the tool was unable to find a sound adapter, it displays the text "No soundcards were detected."

If your system's sound adapter was sucessfully probed, you can click the Play test sound button to test the adapter. If you don't hear the sound, check that your speakers are plugged in and, if necessary, powered on. Otherwise, you may spend time trying to reconfigure a sound adapter that's actually working fine.

If the test sound works, but you don't hear sound at other times, check the mixer levels by choosing Sound & Video → Volume Control. If you're using KDE, you should also check Sound& Video → Sound Mixer. You may find that a volume control is set too low or a mixer setting is preventing you from hearing sounds. Be careful when adjusting volume and mixer settings. Loud noises can damage equipment, your hearing, and relationships with neighbors.

 To enable desktop sounds, choose Preferences → Sound and use the Sound Preferences (GNOME) or Sound Server KDE Control Module (KDE) to configure a sound server to start when the desktop is launched.

User and Group Administration

The Red Hat User Manager tool lets you administer users and groups. To launch the tool, select System Settings → Users and Groups from the GNOME or KDE menu. The Red Hat User Manager tool appears, as shown in Figure 9-12. The tool presents a scrollable list of user accounts (users) and displays the following information about each user account:

User Name
The login name associated with the user account.

User ID
The numeric ID associated with the user account. This ID is automatically assigned when the user account is created and is unique to each user account.

Primary Group

The name of the primary user group associated with the user account. Accounts used by people rather than by system processes generally have an associated primary group having the same name as the user account.

Full Name

The name of the person or process that owns the user account.

Login Shell

The login shell assigned to the user account. Assigning */bin/false* or */sbin/nologin* prevents the user account from logging in.

Home Directory

The home directory associated with the user account. When the user logs in, this directory is set as the current working directory.

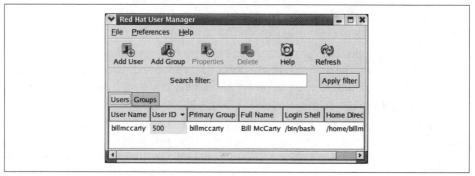

Figure 9-12. The Red Hat User Manager

When many user accounts are configured, it may be inconvenient to scroll through the list. You can use the text box labeled Search Filter to display only user accounts having names matching a specified pattern. Type the pattern in the text box and click Apply filter.

Modifying a user account

To modify a user account, click the desired account and click Properties. The User Properties dialog box, as shown in Figure 9-13, appears.

The User Data pane of the User Properties dialog box lets you view and change a variety of properties:

User Name

The login name associated with the user account.

Full Name

The name of the person or process that owns the user account.

Password

The password to be associated with the user account.

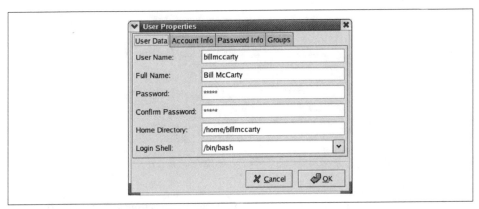

Figure 9-13. The User Properties dialog box

Confirm Password

The password to be associated with the user account. The password is specified twice in order to reduce the risk of assigning an incorrect password due to a typing error.

Home Directory

The home directory associated with the user account. When the user logs in, this directory is set as the current working directory.

Login Shell

The login shell assigned to the user account. Assigning */bin/false* or */sbin/nologin* prevents the user account from logging in.

> The Red Hat User Manager appears to be somewhat buggy. Sometimes, the Red Hat User Manager tool fails to automatically display recent changes. If, after you close the Properties dialog box, your changes aren't seen in the main window, click Refresh. Similarly, sometimes the Properties dialog box cannot be dismissed by clicking OK. In such a close, click the close icon at the top right of the dialog box. Finally, if the tool stubbornly refuses to cooperate, exit and relaunch the tool. Often, this eliminates the problem.

The Account Info pane, shown in Figure 9-14, lets you specify a date on which a user account becomes unusable. Alternatively, you can use the text box labeled User account is locked to immediately disable an account.

The Password Info pane, shown in Figure 9-15, lets you set password expiration options for the account. To do so, enable the checkbox labeled Enable password expiration. Then you can specify any of the following values:

Days before change allowed:

The number of days that must elapse before the user can change the password associated with the user account.

Figure 9-14. The Account Info pane of the User Properties dialog box

Days before change required:

> After the specified number of days, the user must change the password associated with the user account.

Days warning before change:

> This value is used in combination with the Days Before Change Required value. The user will be given advance notice of the need to change the password associated with the user account. The notification begins the specified number of days before the change must be made.

Days before account inactive:

> After the specified number of days, the user account is disabled.

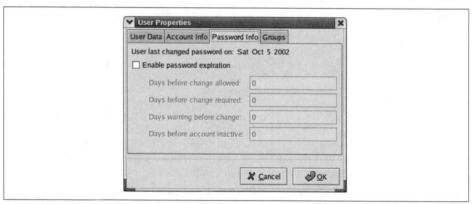

Figure 9-15. The Password Info pane of the User Properties dialog box

The Groups pane displays a series of checkboxes corresponding to user groups. To associate the user account with a group, check the box corresponding to the desired group.

Adding a new user

To create a new user account, click Add User in the Red Hat User Manager dialog box. This will launch the Create New User dialog box, shown in Figure 9-16.

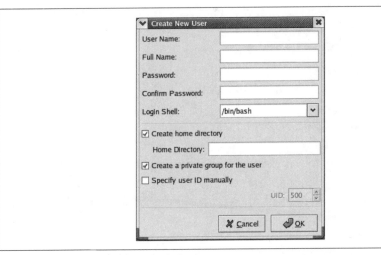

Figure 9-16. The Create New User dialog box

Choosing a Secure Password

A cracker who manages to obtain a copy of your system's */etc/shadow* file may be able to discover your password by using a utility that tries to determine your password by decrypting the encrypted password stored in the file. You can make the cracker's job more difficult by using one or more of the following techniques:

- Choose a password that is at least six characters long.
- Choose a password that is not a dictionary word. Use a made-up word or a phrase.
- Choose a password that includes uppercase and lowercase letters.
- Choose a password that includes digits as well as letters. However, don't merely follow a dictionary word by the digit 1 or use a similarly guessable scheme.
- Choose a password that includes one or more special characters, such as a dollar sign, pound sign, or underscore.

Other things being equal, the longer a password is used, the greater the likelihood that it has been compromised. One way to protect users from password crackers is to require users to change their passwords regularly.

Some overly zealous system administrators require users to change their passwords every 30 days. Unless a system contains top secret data, such a short interval is unnecessary, amounting to what's called *password fascism*. You may find that requiring users to change their passwords every six months or every year is sufficient to avoid hacker invasion of user accounts.

When you create a new user account, you can specify the following values:

User Name
> The name of the user account to be created.

Full Name
> The name of the user who will use the account.

Password
> The password to be associated with the user account.

Confirm Password
> Again, the password to be associated with the user account.

Login Shell
> The login shell associated with the account. You should generally select */bin/ bash*.

Create home directory
> You should generally check this box, so that a home directory is created.

Home Directory
> This value is used only when Create Home Directory is enabled. The default value is generally acceptable.

Create a private group for this user
> You should generally enable this checkbox, which causes automatic creation of a primary user group having the same name as the user account.

Specify user ID manually
> I recommend leaving this unchecked.

When you've specified the desired values, click OK to create the user account.

Deleting a user account

To delete a user account, click on the desired account and click Delete.

 The user account is immediately deleted; no confirmation dialog box appears. Therefore, exercise care to ensure that the correct user account is highlighted before clicking Delete.

Configuring groups

You may recall from Chapter 4 that Linux uses groups to define a set of related user accounts that can share access to a file or directory. You probably won't find it necessary to configure group definitions very often, particularly if you use your system as a desktop system rather than a server.

To view the configured groups, launch the User Manager tool and click the Groups tab. The Groups pane, as shown in Figure 9-17, appears. Groups are shown in a scrollable list, similar to the way user accounts are shown.

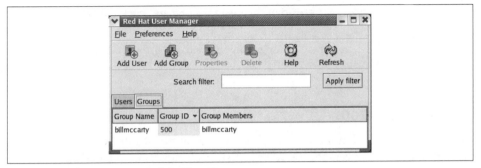

Figure 9-17. The Groups pane of the User Manager

To create a new group, click the Add Group icon. The Create New Group dialog box, as shown in Figure 9-18, appears. The dialog box lets you specify the name of the new group. When you've specified the name of the new group, click OK to create the group.

Figure 9-18. The Create New Group dialog box

To modify a group, click on the name of the group. The Group Properties dialog box, shown in Figure 9-19, appears. The Group Data pane of the dialog box lets you revise the name of the group. The Group Users pane contains a scrollable list of users; you can associate a user account with a group by enabling the checkbox adjacent to the username or dissociate a user account from a group by disabling the checkbox adjacent to the username. When you've completed your changes, click OK to make them effective.

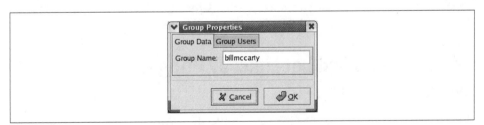

Figure 9-19. The Group Properties dialog box

To delete a group, select the group in the Groups pane and click the Delete icon.

 The selected group is immediately deleted. So, before clicking Delete, be sure the proper group is highlighted.

Switching Desktops

During the installation procedure, GNOME is automatically configured as the default desktop. You can choose KDE as the default by using the desktop switcher. To do so, select Extras → System Settings → Desktop Switching Tool from the GNOME or KDE menu. The Desktop Switcher tool, shown in Figure 9-20, appears.

Figure 9-20. The Desktop Switcher dialog box

In addition to GNOME and KDE, the Desktop Switcher lets you specify TWM (tiny window manager), a sparsely functional but highly efficient desktop. The checkbox labeled "Change only applies to current display" lets you restrict your choice of desktop to the current desktop, as indicated in the top line of the dialog box. This facility is useful if your system has been configured to allow remote users to log in via X.

To specify a desktop, click the desired radio button and click OK. A dialog box appears, informing you that you must restart X for the selected desktop to appear. To restart X, simply log out and then log in.

Administering Red Hat Linux by Using the System Tools Menu

The System Tools menu of the GNOME and KDE desktops provides access to a set of tools that help you administer Red Hat Linux. The distinction between these tools and the tools provided by the System Settings menu is rather arbitrary. That is, any given tool could as likely have been placed on one menu rather than the other. Generally, items on the System Tools menu perform an action, whereas items on the

System Settings menu let you configure a facility. But, exceptions to this rule of thumb abound.

The tools provided by the System Tools menu are:

Disk Management
> Provides access to the User Mount Tool, which lets users mount, unmount, and format filesystems

Floppy Formatter (GNOME only)
> Provides access to the Format a Floppy tool, which formats floppies

Hardware Browser
> Provides access to the Hardware Browser tool, which displays information about system hardware

Internet Configuration Wizard
> Provides access to a wizard that assists you in creating new network connections

Kickstart
> Provides access to the Kickstart Configurator tool, which lets you specify the parameters for automated installation of Red Hat Linux

Network Device Control
> Provides access to the Network Device Control tool, which lets you configure and administer network devices and connections

Red Hat Network
> Provides access to the Red Hat Update Agent, which assists Red Hat Network subscribers in updating their systems

System Logs
> Provides access to the System Logs tool, which lets you view the contents of system log files

System Monitor
> Provides access to the System Monitor tool, which lets you view system performance and resource consumption information

Terminal
> Provides access to a shell, which lets you enter commands

Traceroute
> Provides access to the My Traceroute tool, which lets you determine the network distance to a specified host

This section describes several of the tools. However, it does not explain the Floppy Formatter, since that tool appears only on the GNOME menu and since its functions are also provided by the Disk Manager. Some of the tools are described elsewhere in this book. For instance, Chapter 8 explains the Red Hat Update Agent. The Network Device Control and Traceroute tools concern network configuration and administration, which are topics considered in Chapters 10 and 11. The Kickstart tool is primarily used by enterprise system administrators and is not described in this book. And, I dispense with explanation of the Terminal tool, since its use should be self-evident.

Managing Disks

The Disk Management tool lets you mount and unmount filesystems. It also lets you format filesystems. To launch the tool, choose System Tools → Disk Management from the GNOME or KDE menu. Figure 9-21 shows the tool.

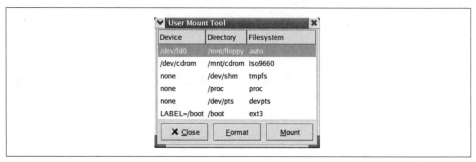

Figure 9-21. The Disk Management tool

The tool shows a list of configured filesystems, taken from */etc/fstab*. To mount a filesystem, select the filesystem and click Mount. If you mount a floppy or CD-ROM under GNOME, an icon representing the mounted filesystem appears on the desktop. Click the icon to browse the filesystem.

To unmount a mounted filesystem, select the filesystem and click Unmount. The usual restrictions apply concerning the inability to unmount a file that is in use.

To format a filesystem, select the unmounted filesystem and click Format. A dialog box appears, as shown in Figure 9-22. The dialog box lets you choose the type of filesystem to create. For floppies, you may find it convenient to use the **vfat** file system, which can be read by Linux and Windows 9x, ME, 2000, and XP. For other purposes, you should generally use the standard Linux filesystem type, **ext3**. The dialog box also lets you choose whether a low-level format should be performed. Generally, you should perform a low-level format only when formatting a floppy.

Browsing Hardware Devices

The Hardware Browser tool lets you view information describing the system's hardware devices. To launch the tool, select System Tools → Hardware Browser from the GNOME or KDE menu. Figure 9-23 shows the tool. When it starts up, the tool probes your system and may require a minute or so to complete its work. During that time, the system may become unresponsive.

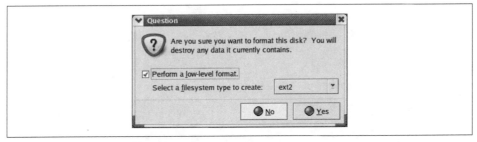

Figure 9-22. Formatting a filesystem

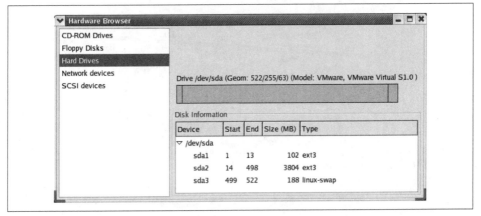

Figure 9-23. The Hardware Browser tool

To use the tool, click a device in the list at the left side of the window. A description of the device appears in the right side of the window. The tool does not let you change or configure devices. It merely lets you view information describing them.

Monitoring the System

The System Monitor tool lets you view information about system and user processes (running programs). It also lets you view CPU, memory, and disk space usage data. Essentially, the tool combines the functions performed under Windows by the Task Manager and System Information applets. To launch the tool, choose System Tools → System Monitor from the GNOME or KDE menu. Figure 9-24 shows the tool.

The display uses a tree control that displays members of a process group under their parent processes. Click the triangle next to the name of a parent process to expand or collapse the tree. To view extended information about a process, select the process and click More Info. The bottom pane of the tool is changed to show information about the selected process, as shown in Figure 9-25.

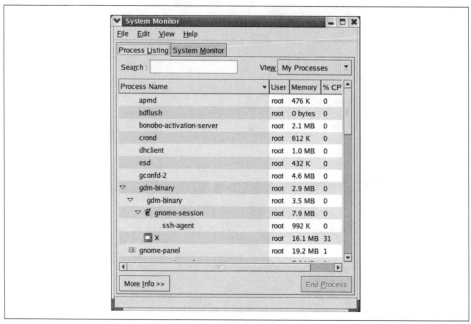

Figure 9-24. The System Monitor tool

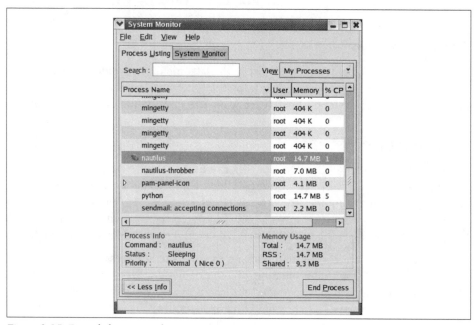

Figure 9-25. Extended process information

You can terminate a process by selecting it and clicking End Process. However, you should do so only judiciously. Terminating a necessary process or terminating a process at an unsuitable time may destabilize your system. Generally, you should terminate only processes that appear to be hung.

If the list of processes is long, you may find it convenient to use the Search box. Or, you can use the View list to view all processes, processed owned by your user account, or active processes.

Clicking the System Monitor tab displays information like that shown in Figure 9-26. The tab includes graphs that provide a running display of CPU, memory, and swap space usage. In addition, the tab includes a list box that displays the used and total space associated with mounted disk partitions.

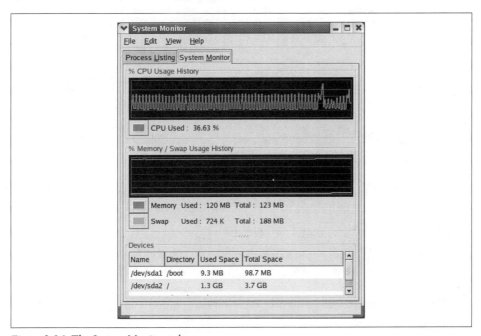

Figure 9-26. The System Monitor tab

Viewing System Logs

The System Logs tool lets you view information contained in system log files, which record information about important events. The tool is especially helpful in troubleshooting system problems, because log files may contain relevant entries that indicate or suggest the cause of the problem.

To launch the tool, choose System Tools → System Logs from the GNOME or KDE menu. Figure 9-27 shows the tool. To view log entries, select the desired log file in the left part of the window. The log entries appear in the right part of the window.

To find a particular entry or set of entries within a log file, type text into the textbox labeled "Filter for." The tool will then display only log entries containing the specified text. To disable the filter, click Reset.

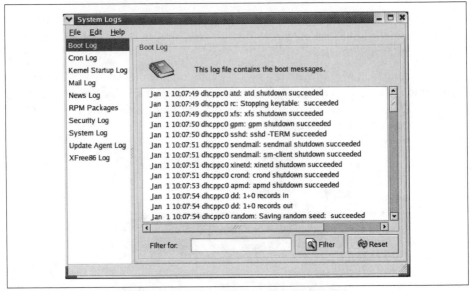

Figure 9-27. The System Logs tool

The log files available for viewing depend on which packages are installed. The standard log files are:

Boot Log
    Contains information about services started and stopped during system boot up and shutdown

Cron Log
    Contains information about the cron service, which runs tasks at scheduled times

Kernel Startup Log
    Contains information recorded during system boot up

Mail Log
    Contains information about the mail server and mail messages

News Log
    Contains information about the USENET news service

RPM Packages
    Contains information about package installations and removals

Security Log
    Contains information about logins and certain service start ups and shutdowns

System Log
> Contains general-purpose entries not sent to another log and some important entries also sent elsewhere

Update Agent Log
> Contains entries describing actions performed by the Red Hat Update Agent

XFree86 Log
> Contains entries logged by the X server

Administering Services by Using the Server Settings Menu

Services are generally processes that wait for a request to perform an operation or provide information and then do so. The Server Settings menu provides menu items that let you administer certain services. The menu also provides the Service Configuration tool that lets you start and stop services and configure which services run at various runlevels. Red Hat Linux supports seven runlevels:

0   Runlevel 0 is associated with a system shutdown.

1   Runlevel 1 is associated with the state known as single-user mode. It is generally used to troubleshoot or configure the system from a state that does not provide network services. It vaguely resembles Windows safe mode.

2   Runlevel 2 is associated with a state that provides access to the network but does not provide network services to remote hosts. Like runlevel 1, it's primarily used for troubleshooting and configuration.

3   Runlevel 3 is a normal system operating mode. It features a text-based login prompt.

4   Runlevel 4 is reserved; that is, it is not used.

5   Runlevel 5 is a normal system operating mode. It features a graphical login screen.

6   Runlevel 6 is associated with a system reboot.

Runlevels 3 and 5 are normal system operating modes. Other modes are used transiently (levels 0, 6), for troubleshooting (levels 1, 2), or not used at all (level 4). When you associate a service with a runlevel, the service is automatically started whenever the runlevel is entered. You can set the current runlevel by issuing the command:

init *n*

where *n* is the number of the desired runlevel. However, it's seldom necessary to change the runlevel of a running system. You should do so judiciously, since services may be abruptly terminated during transition from one runlevel to another.

To launch the Service Configuration tool, select Server Settings → Services from the GNOME or KDE menu. Figure 9-28 shows the appearance of the tool. Note that it reports the current runlevel. It also reports the runlevel to which changes apply, called the *editing runlevel*.

Figure 9-28. The Service Configuration tool

To learn about the function of a server, select the server's name. A description of the server may appear in the bottom pane of the Service Configuration window. Figure 9-28 features such a description. Not all services feature such descriptions.

Associating Services with Runlevels

To associate a service with a runlevel, select the runlevel by using the Edit Runlevel menu. You can edit only for runlevels 3, 4, and 5. Despite the fact that runlevel 4 is not used, it's common to associate with level 4 any services associated with level 3. However, you need not do so.

Once you've selected the desired runlevel, you can specify the services that should run when that runlevel is active. To specify that a service should run, enable the associated checkbox. To specify that a service should not run, disable the associated checkbox.

Your changes to a runlevel are not automatically saved. To save them, click the Save button on the toolbar of the Service Configuration tool.

Starting and Stopping Services

Suppose that the current runlevel is 3 and that a particular service is running. If you use the Service Configuration tool to specify that the service should no longer run in runlevel 3, the system does not immediately terminate the service. Similarly, the system does not immediately start a service newly specified to run in the current runlevel. Instead, the status of the service is changed the next time the specified run-level is entered.

However, you can use the Service Configuration to immediately start or stop a service. To do so, select the service and click the Start or Start button on the Service Configuration toolbar. You can also restart a service, which stops and then restarts the service. Restarting a service is useful when you've manually modified the service's configuration file, since restarting the service causes it to re-read the configuration file.

Hardening Your System

Many attackers target services. Therefore, a useful step in hardening a system—that is, protecting it against attack—is disabling or removing unneeded services. To disable a service, simply ensure that the service is not associated with runlevels 3 or 5. However, it's better yet to remove the service from the system. That way, an attacker will find it more difficult to enable the service.

Of course, you must not disable or remove a service that's needed on the system. So, you need to know something about a system before you tamper with it. You can discover the services for which your system is configured by examining the files in */etc/init.d*. Each service is represented by a file in that directory.

To learn about a service, first determine the name of the associated RPM package. To do so, issue the command:

    rpm -qf /etc/init.d/service

where *service* is the name of a service. For example, issuing the command:

    rpm -qf /etc/init.d/anacron

tells you that the anacron service is associated with the anacron package. Often, the name of service and the name of the associated package are the same. However, this isn't always the case.

Once you know the name of the associated package, you can learn about the service by issuing the command:

    rpm -qi package

where *package* is the name of the package.

To disable a service, you can use the Service Configuration tool. To remove a service, you can issue the command:

    rpm -e package

where *package* is the name of the package. Occasionally, it's not possible to remove a package because another package requires it. In such a case, you can remove both packages or settle for merely disabling the unremovable package.

Table 9-1 identifies several services that are seldom needed that are nevertheless installed by default in some installation configurations. Unless you have a particular need for them, you should disable or remove them from your system. Doing so is particularly important if your system is continuously connected to the Internet. However, even intermittently connected systems, such as those using dialup modems, are vulnerable to attack.

Table 9-1. Commonly unused default servers

Service	When needed
aep1000	Used with hardware cryptographic devices
bcm5820	Used with hardware cryptographic devices
httpd	The Apache web server
irda	Used with infrared devices and peripherals
isdn	Used for ISDN connections
kdcrotate	Used with Kerberos authentication
named	Used to provide DNS services (see Chapter 11)
nfs	Used with NSF (Network File Sharing)
nfslock	Used with NSF
pcmcia	Used with PCMCIA hardware, such as that common on laptops
portmap	Used with NSF and some other facilities
postfix	An alternative mail server that can be used in place of sendmail
sgi_fam	A file monitoring service (requires xinetd service)
snmpd	Used with SNMP (Simple Network Management Protocol)
snmptrapd	Used with SNMP
squid	A web and FTP proxy server
tux	A fast web server that works alongside Apache
winbind	Used with Windows file sharing
xinetd	Used to host other servers, such as sgi_fam
ypbind	Used with NIS (Network Information Services)

## CHAPTER 10

Connecting to the Internet

This chapter explains how to use Red Hat Linux to connect to the Internet via a telephone dialup, ISDN (Integrated Services Digital Network), DSL (Digital Subscriber Line), Ethernet, or wireless connection. First, it provides an overview of networking and explains how to use the Network Administration Tool, an X-based program that makes it easy to connect to the Internet via an Internet service provider (ISP). The chapter also explains how to use **wvdial**, a program that can establish a telephone dialup connection to the Internet but doesn't require X. Next, the chapter describes several popular network client applications available under Linux, including the Mozilla web browser, the Ximian Evolution email client, and a graphical FTP client. Finally, the chapter gives some tips on how to configure Linux to work with your cable or DSL modem if the Network Administration Tool is unable to do so.

Networking Overview

Most computers today handle network traffic much as the post office handles mail. Think, for example, of the steps involved in sending and receiving a letter. Your postal carrier must know where to drop off and where to pick up mail. So your home must have some kind of recognizable interface; we call this a mailbox. And whereas your postal carrier may know your neighborhood quite well, delivery in other areas will require other carriers. Mail is passed to these other carriers through a gateway; we call this the post office. Although you can think of the whole postal system as one big network, it's easier to understand if you think of it as a hierarchy of subnetworks (or subnets): the postal system is divided into states, states are divided into counties and cities with a range of Zip Codes, Zip Codes contain a number of streets, and each street contains a unique set of addresses.

Computer networking mirrors this model. Let's trace an email message from you to a coworker. You compose the message and click Send. Your computer passes the message to a network interface. This interface may be a modem by which you dial up an Internet service provider (ISP), or it may be via an Ethernet connection on a LAN.

Either way, on the other side of the interface is a gateway machine. The gateway knows how to look at the address of the recipient of the email message and interpret that message in terms of networks and subnets. Using this information, the gateway passes the message to other gateways until the message reaches the gateway for the destination machine. That gateway in turn delivers the message via a recognizable interface (such as a modem or Ethernet link) to the recipient's inbox.

If you review this story, you can easily see which parts of networking you'll need to configure on your Linux system. You'll need to know the address of your machine. Just as the town name *Sebastopol* and the Zip Code *95472* are two different names for the same location, you may have both a name, called a *hostname*, and a number, called an *IP number* or *IP address*,* that serve as the address for your machine.

To translate between these two notations, you may need to know the address of a Domain Name Server (DNS). This is a machine that matches IP addresses with hostnames. You'll also need to know the address of a gateway machine through which network traffic will be routed. Finally, you'll need to be able to bring up a network interface on your system, and you'll need to assign a route from that interface to the gateway.

While all of this can seem complex, it really isn't any more complex than the postal system, and it functions in much the same way. Fortunately, Linux comes with tools to help you automate network configuration.

Configuring an Internet Connection

The Red Hat Linux Network Administration Tool simplifies configuration of your system to access the Internet via a telephone dialup, ISDN, DSL, Ethernet, or wireless connection. The Network Administration Tool requires you to follow a three-step process:

1. Set up the hardware device associated with the connection.
2. Specify DNS settings and hostnames.
3. Activate the device, if necessary.

The following subsections explain how to perform these steps.

 The Network Administration tool supports all these methods of connecting to the Internet. However, some hardware devices are not compatible with Red Hat Linux. And, some Internet service providers insist that their customers use only Windows. In either case, you can experience difficulties in connecting to the Internet. The final section of this chapter explains some means of last resort that might help you resolve problems.

---

* IP stands for Internet Protocol.

Setting Up Hardware Devices

In the past, most computer users connected to the Internet via a POTS (plain old telephone service) dial-up modem. However, today, many means of connecting to the Internet are available. For example, many home computer users have high-speed connections using ISDN or DSL. Corporate computer users often connect to the Internet via a their local area network, using an Ethernet adapter. And wireless network adapters are becoming quite popular.

To set up a hardware device using the Network Administration Tool, login as root and choose System Settings → Network from the GNOME or KDE menu. The Network Administration Tool appears, as shown in Figure 10-1.

Figure 10-1. The Network Administration Tool

The Network Administration Tool has four tabs:

Devices
> Used to associate a physical device with a network connection

Hardware
> Used to set up a physical device

Hosts
> Used to specify names of hosts not known to a DNS server

DNS
> Used to specify DNS servers and related options

To begin setting up an Internet connection, click the Add button of the Device tab. A dialog box appears, inviting you to choose the type of your device, as shown in

Figure 10-2. Choose the appropriate device type and click Forward. Then, follow the steps in the following subsection appropriate to the type of your device.

Red Hat Linux supports two schemes used by DSL providers: PPPoE (Point-to-Point Protocol over Ethernet) and DHCP (Dynamic Host Control Protocol). If your DSL provider uses DHCP, you should configure your DSL connection as though it were an Ethernet connection. Otherwise, you should specify xDSL as the device type.

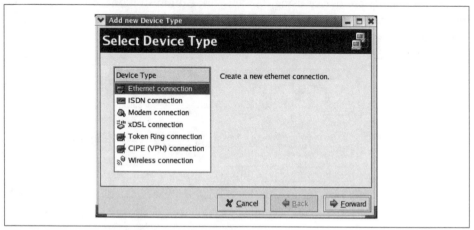

Figure 10-2. The Add new Device Type dialog box

Setting up a dialup modem

When you specify a Modem as the device type, the Network Administration Tool probes for your modem. This process may take several seconds. Once the Network Administration Tool locates the modem, it displays the Select Modem dialog box, shown in Figure 10-3, which lets you specify modem characteristics. Generally, the defaults are acceptable. However, check the documentation for your modem to be sure. If your phone line does not support touch tone dialing, de-select the Use touch tone dialing checkbox. Then, click Forward to continue.

The Select Provider dialog box appears, as shown in Figure 10-4. If your country and provider are listed, select them. Otherwise, Specify the phone number, name, login name, and password associated with your account. Then click Forward to continue.

The main Tool screen reappears. However, this time the screen includes a line identifying your modem as a ppp (Point-to-Point Protocol) device, as shown in Figure 10-5. Click Apply to save your changes.

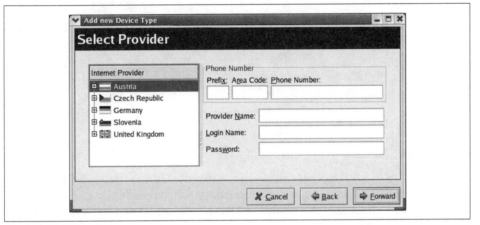

Figure 10-3. The Select Modem dialog box

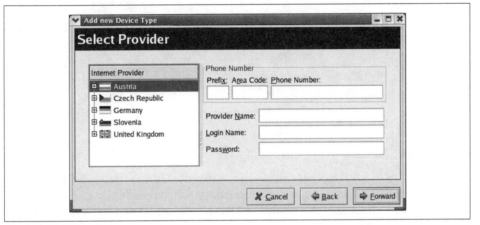

Figure 10-4. The Select Provider dialog box

If the Network Administration Tool is unable to successfully probe your modem, your modem may not be compatible with Linux. Many laptops contain incompatible modems. Some modems—so-called WinModems—are compatible only with Windows. Other modems—so-called LinModems—are supported by their manufacturer only for Windows, but have available Linux drivers. To learn more about your modem and its compatibility with Linux, see *http://www.linmodems. org* or Rob Clark's *WinModems Are Not Modems* page, *http://www. idir.net/~gromitkc winmodem.html*. If your modem is not compatible with Linux, you can often work around the problem by using an external modem. Because external modems connect via the serial port, essentially every serial modem designed for PC use is compatible with Linux.

Figure 10-5. The Network Administration Tool

Setting up an ISDN modem

When you specify an ISDN modem as the device type, the Network Administration Tool presents a list of supported ISDN modems, as shown in Figure 10-6. Specify the device characteristics and choose the D Channel Protocol used by your ISDN provider. Click Forward to continue.

The Select Provider dialog box appears, shown earlier in Figure 10-4. If your country and provider are listed, select them. Otherwise, specify the phone number, name, login name, and password associated with your account. Then, click Forward to continue. The main Tool screen reappears. However, this time the screen includes a line identifying your ISDN modem as an ippp (ISDN Point-to-Point protocol) device. Click Apply to save your changes.

Setting up an xDSL modem

Several varieties of DSL are in use, including IDSL, ADSL, and SDSL. The xDSL device type supports each variety. When you specify DSL modem, the Network Administration Tool presents the Configure DSL connection dialog box, as shown in Figure 10-7. Specify the Ethernet device associated with your DSL link and the login name and password associated with your DSL account. Click Forward to continue.

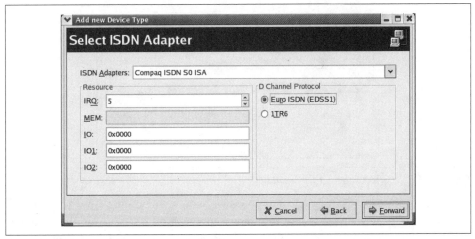

Figure 10-6. The Select ISDN Adapter dialog box

The main Tool screen reappears. However, this time the screen includes a line identifying your DSL modem as a ppp (Point-to-Point Protocol) device. Click Apply to save your changes.

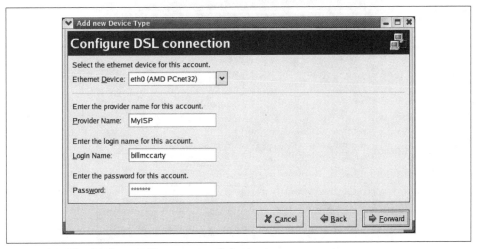

Figure 10-7. The Configure DSL connection dialog box'

Setting up an Ethernet adapter

When you select Ethernet adapter as the device type, the Network Administration Tool probes your system for supported Ethernet adapters and displays a list of the adapters it finds, as shown in Figure 10-8. Select the adapter you want to configure and click Forward.

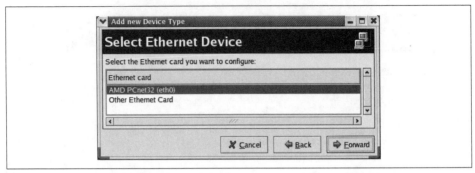

Figure 10-8. The Select Ethernet Device dialog box

The Configure Network Settings dialog box appears, as shown in Figure 10-9. If your ISP provides a DHCP server that supplies your system with its network configuration, enable the Automatically obtain IP address settings with radiobutton and choose DHCP from the drop-down list. Also, enable the Automatically obtain DNS information from provider checkbox. If your provider uses BOOTP, which is now unusual, choose BOOTP from the drop-down list.

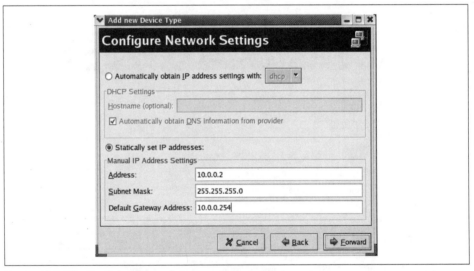

Figure 10-9. The Configure Network Settings dialog box

If your provider requires you to manually specify your system's network configuration, enable the Statically set IP address radiobutton. Then, specify the IP address, subnet mask, and default gateway address as directed by your network administrator. Click Forward to continue. The main Tool screen reappears. However, this time the screen includes a line identifying your Ethernet adapter as an eth device. Click Apply to save your changes.

Setting up a wireless adapter

When you select Wireless adapter as the device type, the Network Administration Tool probes your system for supported wireless adapters and displays a list of the adapters it finds, as shown in Figure 10-10. Select the appropriate adapter and click Forward.

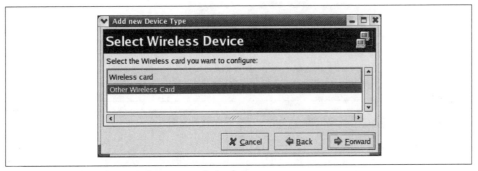

Figure 10-10. The Select Wireless Device dialog box

If the adapter is not specifically identified, choose Other Wireless Card and click Forward. The Select Ethernet Adapter dialog box appears, as shown in Figure 10-11. Choose the appropriate adapter and specify its characteristics. Click Forward to continue.

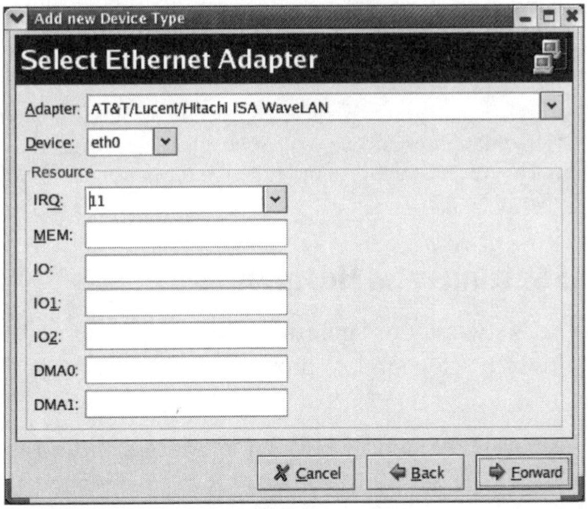

Figure 10-11. The Select Ethernet Adapter dialog box

The Configure Wireless Connection dialog box appears, as shown in Figure 10-12. Specify the mode (Managed or Ad Hoc) in which your wireless access point operates or specify Auto to configure the adapter to use whatever mode the access point uses.

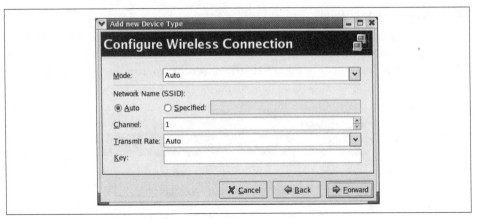

Figure 10-12. The Configure Wireless Connection dialog box

Access points using Ad Hoc mode are vulnerable to several types of attack. It's generally best to configure your access points to use Managed mode and specify Managed rather than Auto as the adapter mode.

Specify the SSID (Service Set Identifier) of your network or specify Auto if you want to connect to any available network. Then, specify the channel, transmit rate, and key (if any) associated with your network. Click Forward to continue. The main Tool screen reappears. However, this time the screen includes a line identifying your Ethernet adapter as an eth device. Click Apply to save your changes.

Many users install access points that operate using the default SSID set by the manufacturer and no key. Such users' networks are vulnerable to attack by passersby. For more information, see *http://www. wardriving.com*.

Specifying DNS Settings and Hostnames

The DNS tab of the Network Configuration Tool, shown in Figure 10-13, lets you configure DNS. However, if your ISP provides DNS information via DHCP, you don't need to do so.

Internet hosts are generally known by both an IP address and hostname. DNS translates hostnames to IP addresses and IP addresses to hostnames. Translating a hostname to an IP address is called *hostname lookup* or *address resolution*. Translating an IP address to a hostname is called *reverse lookup*. DNS is important, but not essential. For instance, without DNS, you'd have to type IP addresses rather than hostnames when browsing the Web. Doing so would be inconvenient, but workable.

Figure 10-13. The DNS tab of the Network Configuration Tool

However, you wouldn't be able to simply click hyperlinks specified using hostnames. Instead, you'd have to somehow figure out and type the proper IP address.

Using the tab, you can specify the hostname of your system, and the IP addresses of primary, secondary, and tertiary DNS servers. You can also specify one or more domain names that are automatically added to hostnames when performing hostname lookups. For example, if you frequently access hosts in the *example.com* domain, you can include *example.com* on the search path. Then, you can refer to the host *www.example.com* as simply *www*.

Activating the Device

The Network Administration Tool activates some network devices, such as Ethernet adapters, automatically. Other network devices, such as dial-up modems, must be manually activated and deactivated. To activate a device, select its name in the Devices tab of the Network Administration Tool and click Activate. If the device is a dial-up modem, it will attempt to connect to your ISP.

Once a connection is established, you should be able to access the Internet. Try to ping an Internet host by issuing a command such as **ping www.redhat.com** in a terminal window. You should see replies from the host:

```
PING www.redhat.com (66.187.232.56) from 10.0.0.2 : 56(84) bytes of data.
64 bytes from redhat.com (66.187.232.56): icmp_seq=0 ttl=239 time=94.383 msec
64 bytes from redhat.com (66.187.232.56): icmp_seq=1 ttl=239 time=92.060 msec
64 bytes from redhat.com (66.187.232.56): icmp_seq=2 ttl=239 time=91.961 msec
```

```
--- www.redhat.com ping statistics ---
3 packets transmitted, 3 packets received, 0% packet loss
round-trip min/avg/max/mdev = 91.961/92.801/94.383/1.146 ms
```

Terminate the **ping** command by typing **Ctrl-C**.

If the command doesn't work, perhaps your connection isn't working. Or perhaps your ISP's DHCP server failed to properly provide DNS information. Try pinging the IP address of a host you know to be available. For example, issue a command such as:

```
$ ping -n 66.187.232.56
```

If pinging the IP address works, simply use the DNS tab to revise your DNS configuration and you're set. Otherwise, you may have some difficulty getting the connection to work. Use the **ifconfig** and **route** commands to view your network configuration. If you can figure out the problem, again you're set. If not, you may be able to obtain help from your ISP or from participants in an Internet newsgroup, such as *linux.redhat* or *linux.redhat.misc*.

To terminate a connection, deactivate the associated device by clicking Deactivate on the Devices tab.

After setting up your hardware device, you can edit its characteristics by highlighting the line identifying it and clicking Edit.

If you use your computer in multiple locations, you can use profiles to establish multiple network connections from which you can conveniently choose. For information on doing so, see section 11.12 of *The Official Red Hat Linux Customization Guide*.

The Mozilla Web Browser

Once you've established a connection to the Internet, you can surf the Web using Mozilla, the default Red Hat Linux web browser. To launch Mozilla, choose Internet → Web Browser from the GNOME or KDE menu. Figure 10-14 shows Mozilla. Mozilla resembles its closed source ancestor, Netscape Navigator. So, if you've used Navigator, you'll feel at home in Mozilla.

The Web contains quite a bit of malicious software. You should log in as an ordinary user—that is, a user other than the root user—to surf the Web. That way, malicious software is less likely to be able to compromise your system.

When you launch Mozilla for the first time, you may see a dialog box explaining that a Mozilla profile is being created from existing Netscape 4 files. Click Convert Profile to allow Mozilla to create the profile.

Mozilla includes email and news clients that are easily configured. It also includes a web page composer and address book. To configure Mozilla email, choose Window

Figure 10-14. The Mozilla web browser

→ Mail & Newsgroups from the Mozilla menu. An Account wizard appears, asking whether you want to configure an email or newsgroup account. Select Email Account and click Next. The Identity dialog box appears, as shown in Figure 10-15. Specify your name and email address and click Next.

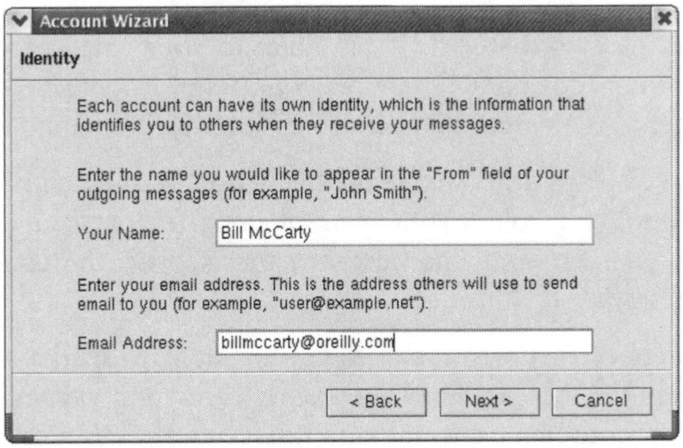

Figure 10-15. The Identity dialog box

The Server Information dialog box appears, as shown in Figure 10-16. Specify which protocol your mail server uses, POP (Post Office Protocol) or IMAP (Interim Mail Access Protocol). POP servers require you to download email. IMAP servers let you read email that resides on the server. Most up-to-date ISPs support IMAP, the newer protocol. Also specify the hostnames of your incoming and outgoing mail services. A single host may fill both roles. If you don't know this information, you can obtain it from your ISP. Click Next to continue.

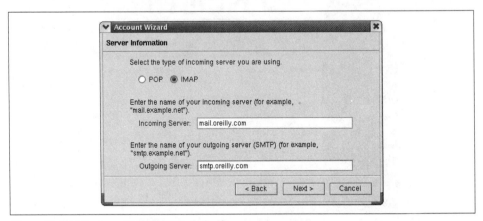

Figure 10-16. The Server Information dialog box

The User Name dialog box appears. Specify the username by which you login to your ISP's mail server. Click Next to continue. The Account Name dialog box appears. Specify a name by which to refer to your new email account so that you can distinguish it from other accounts you may create. Click Next to continue. The Congratulations! dialog box appears. Verify that the information it presents is accurate. If necessary, click Back to return to an earlier dialog box and correct the information. When you're satisfied that the information is correct, click Next to continue.

Mozilla asks your password so that it can login to your email account. Specify the password. If you want Mozilla to remember your password, enable the checkbox Use Password Manager to remember this password. Click OK to login.

Mozilla reads and displays the contents of your Inbox, as shown in Figure 10-17. The left pane of the window displays your mail folders. The top pane displays messages within the current folder. And, the bottom pane displays the contents of the currently selected message.

Mozilla's user interface is straightforward. For example, to send a message, click the Compose button in the toolbar. The best way to learn your way around Mozilla is to explore its menu and toolbar, clicking and observing the results. You'll soon be at home.

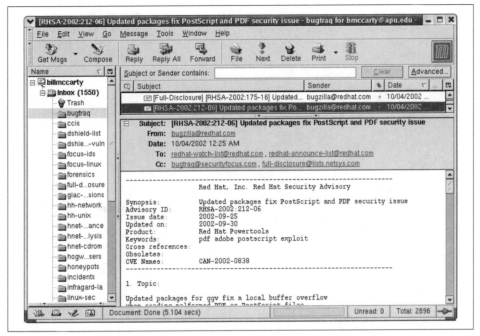

Figure 10-17. The Mozilla email screen

gFTP FTP Client

You can use your web browser to download files from an FTP server, but to upload files you need an FTP client. The gFTP client, included with Red Hat Linux, is an excellent choice, because its user interface resembles that of popular Windows FTP clients, such as WS-FTP. Figure 10-18 shows the gFTP client, which can be launched by choosing Extras → Internet → gFTP from the GNOME or KDE menu.

To connect to a remote system, specify the hostname, username, and password in the textboxes appearing on the toolbar. If the server permits anonymous logins, you can omit the username and password. To connect, click the Connect icon resembling a pair of computers at the left of gFTP's toolbar. To upload a file, click on the name of the file in the local list box at the left of the window and then click on the right-pointing arrow. To download a file, click on the name of the file in the list box at the right of the window and then click on the left-pointing arrow. When you've transferred all your files, choose Remote → Disconnect or click again on the Connect icon.

You can access an FTP server in command-line mode, if you prefer. Chapter 12 explains how to do so.

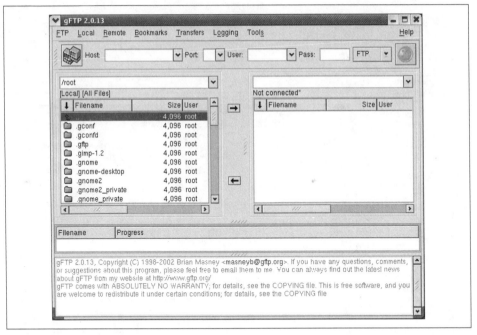

Figure 10-18. The gFTP FTP client

Using wvdial

If you have your dial-up network connection working perfectly, you may have little interest in exploring **wvdial**. However, there are two reasons you should consider learning more about **wvdial**: you can use **wvdial** even if X isn't working or isn't installed, and you can use **wvdial** in shell scripts of your own design. Chapter 13 includes an example script.

The /etc/wvdial.conf File

To configure **wvdial**, become the root user and issue the following command:

```
# wvdialconf /etc/wvdial.conf
```

This command analyzes your system and creates a template configuration file, */etc/wvdial.conf*. You must edit this file to specify the username and password your ISP expects.

The contents of the template file look something like this:

```
[Dialer Defaults]
Modem = /dev/modem
Baud = 115200
Init1 = ATZ
Init2 = ATQ0 V1 E1 S0=0 &C1 &D2 S11=55 +FCLASS=0
```

```
ISDN = 0
; Phone = <Target Phone Number>
; Username = <Your Login Name>
; Password = <Your Password>
```

Edit the last three lines of the file, deleting the leading semicolon and space and substituting the proper phone number, username, and password required to connect to your ISP. When you're done, your file should look something like this:

```
[Dialer Defaults]
Modem = /dev/modem
Baud =  115200
Init1 = ATZ
Init2 = ATQ0 V1 E1 &C1 &D2 +FCLASS=0
ISDN = 0
Phone = 15625551100
Username = bill100
Password = donttell
```

 Be sure that only the root user can read the *wvdial.conf* file. Use a file manager or the shell to change the file's permissions, if necessary. Otherwise, someone who uses your system may discover your password.

Now, you're ready to make a connection by issuing the following command:

 # wvdial &

The command generates quite a bit of output, which makes further use of this virtual terminal distracting. The simplest solution is to switch to another terminal window, or to another virtual terminal by pressing **Alt-*n***, where *n* stands for the virtual terminal (1–7). Alternatively, you can direct the output of the command to a file, by typing this command in place of the one given earlier:

 # wvdial 2>/tmp/wvdial.messages &

Of course, you'll need to consult the file if something goes wrong with **wvdial**. Do so by using the **less** command:

 # less /tmp/wvdial.messages

Once your connection is up, you can browse the Web and access other Internet services. For now, simply verify that your connection is working by issuing the command:

 # ping www.redhat.com

The **ping** command should report that echo packets were successfully received from the server. If not, check your name server configuration and other details, as described earlier in the chapter.

When you want to terminate the Internet connection, issue the command:

 # killall wvdial

Configuring Linux to Use a Cable or DSL Modem

At one time, setting up a cable or DSL modem for use with Linux was difficult. The new Network Administration Tool included in Red Hat Linux 8.0 often makes it a snap. But sometimes, the Tool fails to successfully configure the cable or DSL modem.

In such a case I recommend using a cable/DSL gateway router. Netgear and Linksys, among others, manufacture popular models. These inexpensive devices—often less than $100 retail—sit between your cable or DSL modem and your home network. Cable/DSL gateway routers generally provide a masquerading firewall and DNS proxy services. Better models have multiple ports so that you can connect several PCs without buying additional hubs or switches. Some recent models even provide a wireless LAN.

Because such devices are designed to work with as many cable and DSL configurations as possible, they work right out of the box most of the time. It's true that they generally provide no function that couldn't be provided—at least in principle—by a Linux PC. But they consume less power, occupy less space, make less noise, and require less configuration and administration than a Linux PC. I retired a quite venerable Pentium 166 Linux PC from cable modem gateway duty several years ago and have never regretted the decision.

Some useful resources when setting up Linux to access a cable or DSL modem include:

Hal Burgiss' DSL HOWTO for Linux
   http://www.tldp.org/HOWTO/DSL-HOWTO

Paul Ramey's Red Hat Linux 6.X as an Internet Gateway for a Home Network
   http://www.tldp.org/HOWTO/mini/Home-Network-mini-HOWTO.html

## CHAPTER 11

Setting Up a Networked Workstation

Linux's greatest strength is its powerful and robust networking capabilities. The good news is that everything about Linux's networking setup is open to inspection and completely configurable. Nothing is hidden from the user, and no parameters are forced on you. The challenge is to get the most out of this setup.

Basic networking principles don't differ much between Windows and Linux, and indeed the principles aren't unfamiliar. This chapter begins with an overview of networking and then looks in more detail at Linux networking on a local area network (LAN). In Chapter 12 you'll learn about setting up Internet services.

This chapter explains how to set up a LAN that includes a Linux Samba server, which lets Microsoft Windows and Unix systems access shared files and printers across the network. Samba not only lets you share files and printers, it can also be used to back up and restore files via the network. This chapter also explains how to install and configure a DHCP server that lets you manage network configurations centrally, facilitating network administration.

Configuring Hosts

Most systems attached to a network use DNS services to determine the IP address associated with a hostname. However, private hosts on your local network won't be known to your ISP's DNS and therefore can be accessed only by IP address, not by hostname. Moreover, Samba and other local area network services won't operate correctly unless they can resolve hostnames.

Fortunately, using the Network Administration Tool, you can configure your system to determine the IP address associated with a hostname even when DNS services are not available. To do so, use the Hosts tab of the Network Administration Tool, shown in Figure 11-1.

To specify host information, launch the Network Administration Tool by choosing System Settings → Network from the GNOME or KDE menu. Select the Hosts tab of

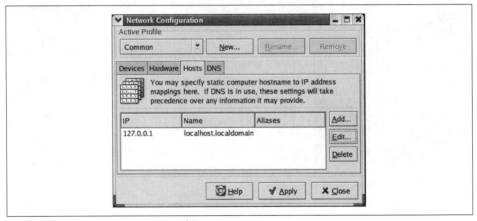

Figure 11-1. The Hosts tab of the Network Administration Tool

the Tool, click Add. The Add/Edit Hosts entry dialog box appears, as shown in Figure 11-2. Specify the IP address and name of the host. If desired, you can specify one or more aliases or abbreviated names for the host. By default, the host information includes an entry for the IP address 127.0.0.1, which is associated with the hostname *localhost*. You should not disturb this entry, which provides a way for your system to access its own network facilities.

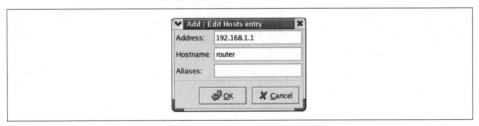

Figure 11-2. The Add/Edit Hosts entry dialog box

 Linux stores configured hostnames in the file */etc/hosts*, which you can edit by using a text editor, if you prefer. Windows has a similar file that you must revise in order for Windows hosts to interoperate with Samba and other Linux-based services. The file is named *hosts* and resides in an *etc* subdirectory of your Windows directory. Under Windows 2000, the path of the file is often *c:\windows\system32\drivers\ etc\hosts*; the location varies slightly depending on the installation options.

Each line of the file describes a single host. The left column contains the host's IP address and the right column contains the associated hostname or names. If multiple names (aliases) appear, the principal name is given first. Simply use a text editor, such as Notepad, to add the appropriate lines describing your local hosts.

Samba

Once you've configured your hostnames, you're ready to provide services to hosts on the network. To provide printer and file sharing, Windows uses a facility known as the Server Message Block (SMB). This same facility is sometimes known as the Common Internet File System (CIFS), NetBIOS, or LanManager. Thanks to Andrew Tridgell and others, Linux systems provide support for SMB via a package known as Samba. Like SMB, Samba lets you:

- Authorize users to access Samba resources
- Share printers and files among Windows, OS/2, Netware, and Unix systems
- Establish a simple name server for identifying systems on your LAN
- Back up PC files to a Linux system and restore them

Samba has proven its reliability and high performance in many organizations. According to the online survey at *http://www.samba.org/pub/samba/survey/ssstats. html*, Bank of America is using Samba in a configuration that includes about 15,000 clients, and Hewlett-Packard is using Samba in a configuration that includes about 7,000 clients.

Installing the Samba Server

If you've never installed and configured a network server, Samba is a good place to begin; its installation and configuration are generally straightforward.

The Samba server includes the *nmbd* and *smbd* programs (which run as daemons), several utility programs, manpages and other documentation, and three configuration files: */etc/samba/smbusers*, */etc/samba/smb.conf*, and */etc/samba/lmhosts*. The *smbusers* file associates several user accounts that are special to Samba with Linux user accounts; for example, it associates the Samba user IDs, *administrator* and *admin*, with *root*. Generally, you don't need to change *smbusers*. Likewise, you don't generally need to revise *lmhosts*. You'll learn how to configure the *smb.conf* file shortly.

The simplest way to install Samba is to select the Windows File Sharing package group during system installation. However, if you failed to do so, you can install Samba by using the Package Management Tool.

Whether or not you installed the Windows File Sharing package group during system installation, you should ensure that the package *samba-client*, associated with the System Tools package group, is also installed. Finally, to simplify configuration of Samba, you should install the *samba-swat* package. Unfortunately, this package does not appear on the package list provided by the Package Management Tool. To install it, mount installation CD 2, open a terminal window, and issue the following command:

```
redhat-install-packages /mnt/cdrom/RedHat/RPMS/samba-swat-*.rpm
```

Configuring Samba

The */etc/samba/smb.conf* file lets you specify a variety of options that control Samba's operation. You can edit the file by using your favorite text editor; however, the Samba Web Administration Tool (SWAT) lets you view and change options using your web browser, which is generally much easier than using a text editor. The SWAT tool verifies the values of parameters you enter and provides online help.

To use SWAT, you must first configure *xinetd* to launch SWAT when you request it. To do so, launch the Service Configuration Tool by choosing Server Settings → Services from the GNOME or KDE menu. Configure *swat* and *xinetd* to run at the current run level and save your changes. If *xinetd* is not currently running, start it by selecting the *xinetd* entry and clicking Start. The *swat* service runs under control of *xinetd*, so you don't need to start *swat*. To access SWAT, first log out of GNOME or KDE and login again, so that the menu is reloaded. Then, choose Extras → Samba Configuration from the GNOME or KDE menu. Doing so launches Mozilla, pointing the browser to port 901 of the local host using the URL *http://localhost:901/*. Your web browser will prompt you for a user account and password; specify *root* as the user account and give the appropriate password. Figure 11-3 shows *SWAT*'s main menu.

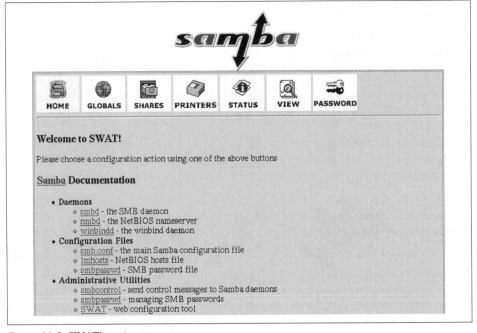

Figure 11-3. SWAT's main menu

To configure your Samba server, click the following toolbar icons:

Home
> Return to the main menu (shown in Figure 11-3). The main menu also provides convenient access to Samba documentation via the links in the body of the page.

Globals
> Configure Sambaglobal options, affecting all shares and printers.

Shares
> Configure shared files.

Printers
> Configure shared printers.

Status
> View the status of the Samba server.

View
> View Samba's configuration file, */etc/samba/smb.conf*.

Password
> Add and delete users and change user passwords.

Configuring global variables

To configure global options, click the Globals button on the toolbar. Figure 11-4 shows the Global Variables page, and Table 11-1 describes the most important options. You can access additional options by clicking Advanced View. To change an option, select or type the desired value. When you've changed all the options you want to change, click Commit Changes, and the changes take effect.

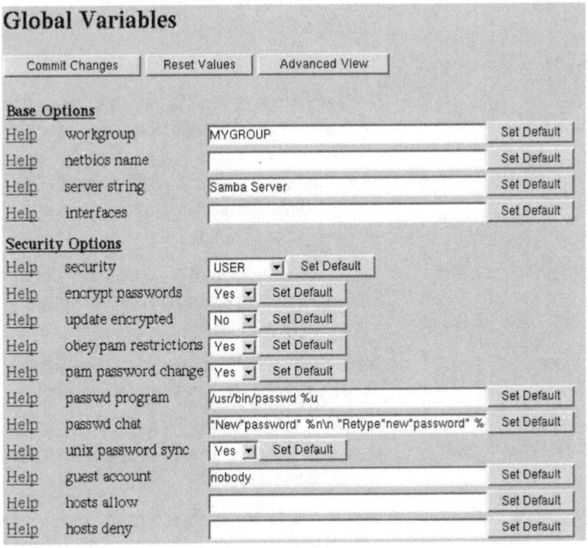

Figure 11-4. SWAT's Global Variables screen

Table 11-1. Samba's Global Variables

Option group	Option	Description
Base	workgroup	The workgroup name displayed when the server is queried by a client.
	netbios name	The NetBIOS name by which the server is known.
	server string	The text string displayed to describe the server.
	interfaces	The IP address(es) of the interface(s) through which Samba should listen. Each IP address is followed by a forward slash and a number that specifies the number of bits that pertain to the network portion of the IP address (usually 24), for example, 192.168.1.0/24. If this option is not set, Samba attempts to locate and automatically configure a primary interface. Samba lets you specify the interface name, rather than an IP address, if you prefer.
Security	security	Specifies how . Samba authenticates requests for access to shared resources. The default value, *user*, is helpful when the Samba server and its clients have many common user accounts. The value *share* can be useful when few common user accounts exist, because it allows users to access shared resources without first logging in to the server. The value *server* lets another SMB server perform authentication on behalf of the server. The value *domain* specifies that the host is integrated within a Windows NT domain; it behaves similarly to the value *user*. You should generally use the default value.
	encrypt passwords	Specifies whether Samba will negotiate encrypted passwords, which are expected by Windows NT 4.0 SP3 and later, 98, Me, 2000, and XP.
	update encrypted	Allows automatic updating of an encrypted password when a user logs on using a nonencrypted password. This option is useful when migrating to encrypted passwords and should otherwise be set to *No*. It requires that Encrypt Passwords be set to *No*.
	guest account	The Linux user account used to provide services for guest users.
	hosts allow	A list of hosts that can access the server. If not specified, all hosts are permitted access.
	hosts deny	A list of hosts that cannot access the server.
Browse	os level	Specifies the level at which Samba advertises itself for browse elections. A high number makes it more likely that Samba will be selected as the browser. The value 65 causes clients to prefer Samba to a Windows NT server. The default value is generally acceptable; inappropriately high values may cause browsing problems and may cause NT/2000 servers, and possibly XP servers, to become unstable.
	preferred master	Specifies whether Samba is the preferred master browser for its workgroup. Used with *domain master = yes* to force acceptance of the host as the master browser for its workgroup.
	local master	Specifies whether Samba will bid to become the local master browser on a subnet. Generally, the default value is acceptable.
WINS	wins server	Specifies the IP address of the WINS server with which Samba should register itself, if any. This item should be specified whenever a network includes an existing WINS server.
	wins support	Specifies that Samba should act as a WINS server. Useful when the network includes several subnets. Do not specify this option for multiple systems of a single network. Generally, the default value is acceptable.

Samba's main configuration file, */etc/samba/smb.conf*, is overwritten by SWAT. The specifications contained in the file are retained and shown as initial values; however, any comments in the file are deleted.

You probably won't need to make many changes to Samba's global variables. Setting the *workgroup* and *netbios name* is sufficient for most users. If your system has more than one network adapter card, you'll also need to set the *interfaces* variable. If your network includes Windows 98/NT/2000/XP clients, you'll need to set *encrypt passwords*.

 If your system is attached to the Internet—even intermittently—or otherwise available to untrusted users, you should specify security options that prevent unauthorized users from accessing your files or printer. For example, use the *hosts allow* option to restrict the hosts allowed to access your Samba server.

You should also place a firewall between your system and the Internet or other networks on which untrusted users reside. The inexpensive gateway routers described in Chapter 10 are ideal for this purpose.

Configuring file share parameters

To establish and maintain file shares, use the Shares button on the toolbar. Figure 11-5 shows the Share Parameters page.

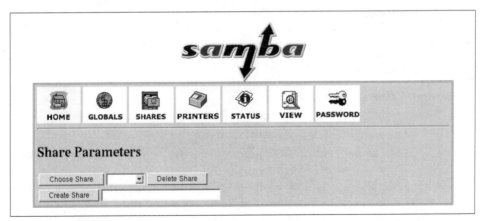

Figure 11-5. SWAT's Share Parameters screen

Red Hat Linux configures a default share, *homes*, which lets Linux users access their Linux */home* directory as a Samba share. You can create a new share by typing its name and clicking Create Share. To delete a share, choose the share name from the drop-down list and click Delete Share. To work with an existing share, choose it from the drop-down list and click Choose Share. When you click Choose Share, the page shown in Figure 11-6 appears. This page lets you view and change a variety of share options. Table 11-2 describes the principal share options. You can access additional options by clicking Advanced View. As with the global options, you may not need to change many share options. Likely candidates for change are the *comment*, *path*, and *read only* options.

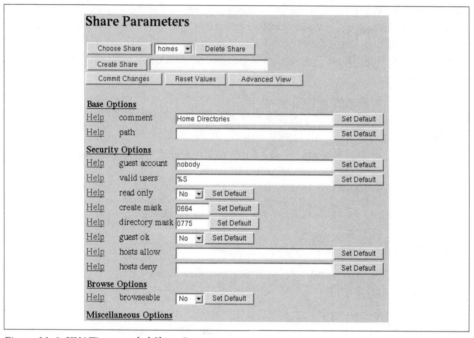

Figure 11-6. SWAT's expanded Share Parameters screen

Table 11-2. Samba file share options

Option group	Option	Description
Base	comment	The description displayed when the file share is queried by a client.
	path	The path that is shared by the server.
Security	guest account	Account under which users can connect if they are not otherwise specified. Requires that the *guest ok* be true.
	valid users	Specifies users allowed to access the share.
	read only	Specifies whether the share can be written or is read-only.
	create mask	Specifies the permissions associated with created files, as an inverse value.
	directory mask	Specifies the permissions associated with created directories, as an inverse value.
	guest ok	Specifies whether guest access (access without a password) is allowed.
	hosts allow	A list of hosts that can access the file share. If not specified, all hosts are permitted access.
	hosts deny	A list of hosts that cannot access the file share.
Browse	browseable	Specifies whether the file share is visible in the list of shares made available by the server.
Miscellaneous	available	Specifies whether the share is available; by setting this option to *No* you can prevent access to the share.

Configuring printer share parameters

You configure printer share parameters in much the same way you configure shares. Begin by clicking the Printers toolbar button. You can use the page shown in Figure 11-7 to create a new printer share, delete a printer share, or modify an existing printer share.

Figure 11-7. SWAT's Printer Parameters screen

If you select a printer from the drop-down list and click Choose Printer, the page shown in Figure 11-8 appears. Table 11-3 describes the available print share options. You can access additional options by clicking Advanced View. As with the global options and file share options, you may not need to change many printer share options. The *comment* option is the most likely to be changed.

Table 11-3. Samba print share options

Option group	Option	Description
Base	*comment*	The description displayed when the printer share is queried by a client.
	path	Temporary directory for storing files before they are printed.
Security	*guest account*	Account under which users can connect if they are not otherwise specified. Requires that *guest ok* be true.
	guest ok	Specifies whether guest access (access without a password) is allowed.
	hosts allow	A list of hosts that can access the printer share. If not specified, all hosts are permitted access.
	hosts deny	A list of hosts that cannot access the printer share.
Printing	*printable*	Specifies whether printing is permitted. If this option is set to *No*, clients may still be able to browse the printer share.
	printing	Specifies the type of printer interface used, which determines what commands Samba issues to control the printer; *lprng* is generally a good choice.

Table 11-3. Samba print share options (continued)

Option group	Option	Description
Browse	*browseable*	Specifies whether the printer share is visible in the list of shares made available by the server.
Miscellaneous	*available*	Specifies whether the printer share is available; by setting this option to *No*, you can prevent access to the printer share.

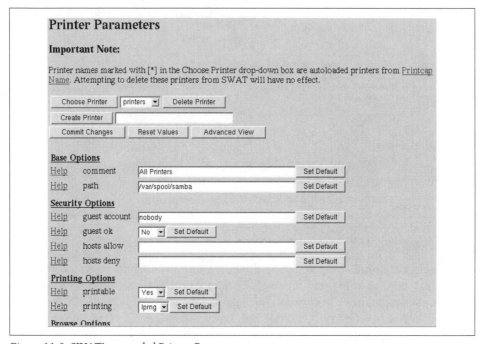

Figure 11-8. SWAT's expanded Printer Parameters screen

Viewing Samba Server Status

The Status button on SWAT's toolbar lets you view the status of the Samba server. The page shown in Figure 11-9 shows the following information about the status of your Samba server:

- The interval at which the page is refreshed, given in seconds
- The version of Samba and the status of the server daemons (*smbd* and *nmbd*)
- Any active connections
- Any active file and printer shares
- Any open files

Using the controls on the page, you can refresh the contents, set the auto refresh interval (in seconds), start and stop either daemon, and kill an active connection.

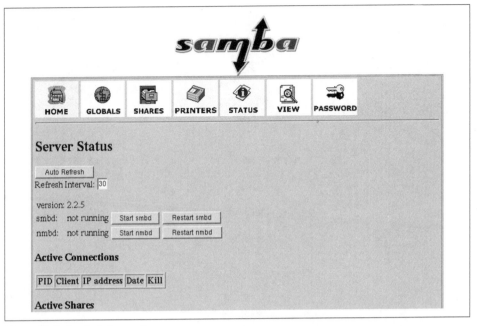

Figure 11-9. Samba's Server Status page

Viewing Samba Server Configuration

The View button on SWAT's toolbar lets you view the Samba server's main configuration file, */etc/samba/smb.conf* (shown in Figure 11-10). By default, the page shows only the basic configuration options; clicking Full View causes SWAT to display every configuration option.

Managing Users and Passwords

You can specify user accounts authorized to access Samba resources by clicking SWAT's Password toolbar button and accessing the page shown in Figure 11-11.

The Server Password Management page lets you:

- Change the password associated with a user account (by clicking the Change Password button)
- Authorize a user account to access Samba (by clicking the Add New User button)
- Delete a user account (by clicking the Delete User button)
- Disable or enable a user account (by clicking the Disable User or Enable User buttons, respectively)

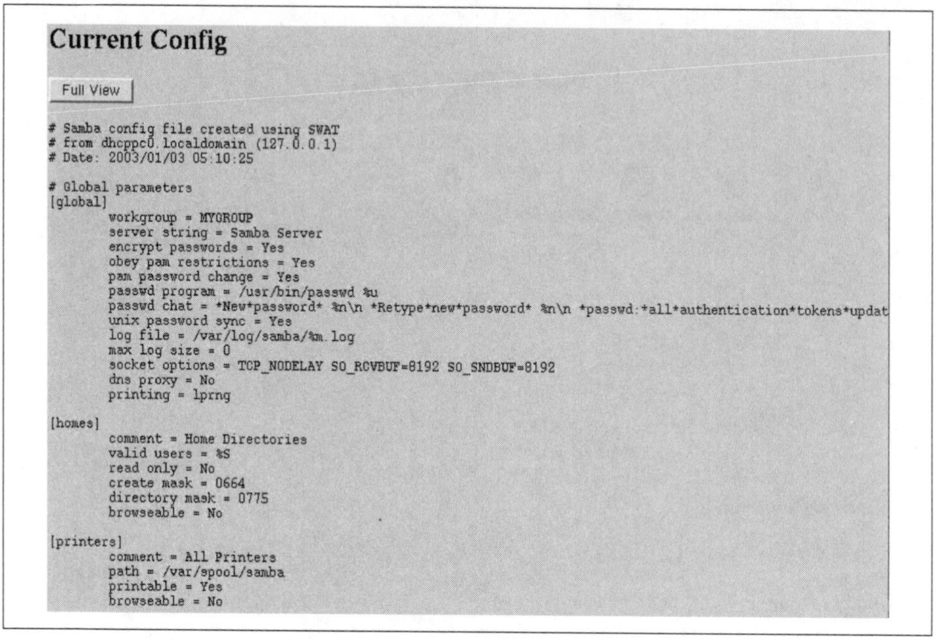
Current Config
Full View
Samba config file created using SWAT
from dhcppc0.localdomain (127.0.0.1)
Date: 2003/01/03 05:10:25
Global parameters
[global]
workgroup = MYGROUP
server string = Samba Server
encrypt passwords = Yes
obey pam restrictions = Yes
pam password change = Yes
passwd program = /usr/bin/passwd %u
passwd chat = *New*password* %n\n *Retype*new*password* %n\n *passwd:*all*authentication*tokens*updat
unix password sync = Yes
log file = /var/log/samba/%m.log
max log size = 0
socket options = TCP_NODELAY SO_RCVBUF=8192 SO_SNDBUF=8192
dns proxy = No
printing = lprng
[homes]
comment = Home Directories
valid users = %S
read only = No
create mask = 0664
directory mask = 0775
browseable = No
[printers]
comment = All Printers
path = /var/spool/samba
printable = Yes
browseable = No

Figure 11-10. SWAT's Current Config screen

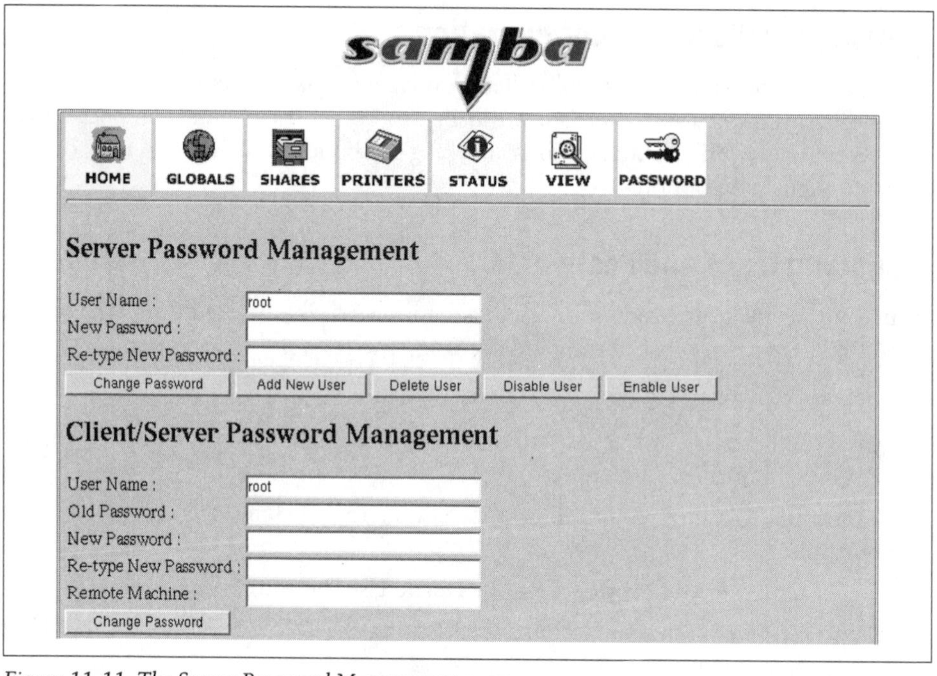
samba
HOME
GLOBALS
SHARES
PRINTERS
STATUS
VIEW
PASSWORD
Server Password Management
User Name :
root
New Password :
Re-type New Password :
Change Password
Add New User
Delete User
Disable User
Enable User
Client/Server Password Management
User Name :
root
Old Password :
New Password :
Re-type New Password :
Remote Machine :
Change Password

Figure 11-11. The Server Password Management page

The user accounts that you specify on the Server Password Management page are those that your Samba server recognizes as authorized to access its resources.

The bottom part of the page, titled Client/Server Password Management, lets you change the password associated with a user account on a remote system running Samba or SMB. Changing a password by using Client/Server Password Management is often more convenient than logging in to the remote host and using its password change facility.

Starting and Stopping Samba

If you've reconfigured Samba, you should restart the *smb* service so that the changes take effect. To do so, highlight the Service Configuration Tool's entry for the *smb* service and click Restart.

If you want Samba to start automatically when you boot your system, use the Service Configuration Tool to associate the *smb* service with the current runlevel.

To stop Samba, highlight the Service Configuration Tool's entry for the *smb* service and click Stop.

Troubleshooting Samba

To verify that Samba is working, use the Share Parameters screen to create a publicly accessible, read-only share. Then, use the Server Password Management screen to authorize a Linux user account to access the share. Restart the *smb* service to make your changes effective.

On the Windows host, launch the Explorer and choose Tools → Map Network Drive. The Map Network Drive dialog box appears. Click Connect using a different username and specify a username and password that you configured Samba to accept. Click OK to return to the Map Network Drive dialog box. Specify the hostname and share name in the Folder textbox by using the Windows convention, *server**share*, where *system* is the hostname of your Samba system and *share* is the name of a share you created. You'll find more information on using Samba shares in the next section.

If you can't access the share, consider the following likely reasons:

- Your host firewall is blocking access.
- You specified the wrong username or password.
- The username and password are not the same on the Samba and Windows hosts.
- You haven't authorized the user to access Samba.
- Networking isn't properly configured on the Samba or Windows host.

If your host firewall is blocking access, use the Security Level Tool to customize your firewall, allowing the following ports and protocols:

```
137:tcp,138:tcp,139:tcp,445:tcp,137:udp,138:udp,139:udp
```

If you're unable to find the problem, consult the documentation that accompanies Samba. In particular, peruse the file *DIAGNOSIS.txt*, which resides in the */usr/share/doc/samba-*/docs/textdocs* directory or its equivalent on your system. This file includes a step-by-step procedure for verifying the operation of your Samba server. When a step fails, you can consult the file to determine the likely causes and how to go about fixing the problem. Chances are, you'll be able to administer Samba without outside help, but if not, you'll find the participants in the *comp.protocols.smb* newsgroup to be helpful. Another resource is O'Reilly's *Using Samba*, by Robert Eckstein, David Collier-Brown, and Peter Kelly. Since the book was published under the Open Publication License (OPL), *Using Samba* is also available online in electronic form at *http://www.oreilly.com/catalog/samba/*.

Like any network server, Samba provides a wealth of options and facilities. If you thoroughly explore these facilities, you're likely to break your server. To avoid problems, you should keep a backup copy of your */etc/samba/smb.conf* file. Doing so can be as easy as issuing the following command after Samba is up and running:

```
# cp /etc/samba/smb.conf /etc/samba/smb.conf.bak
```

Then, if your server ceases to work, you can restore your old configuration by issuing the command:

```
# cp /etc/samba/smb.conf.bak /etc/samba/smb.conf
```

You'll also need to restart the *smb* service.

Samba Client Configuration and Use

Once you've got your Samba server up and running, you can access it via Windows and Linux. This section shows you how to access the Samba server and also how to use your Samba server to create backups of important datafiles on client systems.

SMB clients are also available for most popular operating systems, including OS/2 and Mac OS (including Mac OS X). You shouldn't expect to have trouble getting them to work with Samba. If your client seems not to work, simply follow the procedure given earlier in "Troubleshooting Samba."

Windows client

Windows 3.11, 9*x*, Me, and NT—including Windows 2000 and XP, which are updated releases of Windows NT—have built-in support for the SMB protocol, so systems running these operating systems can easily access your Samba server's resources. Under Windows 9*x*/NT, you can access Samba resources by using the Windows Explorer. Log on with a user account that's authorized to access Samba resources, then click Network Neighborhood, and you should see a subtree that corresponds to your workgroup. Click that subtree, and you should see a subtree that corresponds to your Samba server. By expanding the subtree, you can see the browseable file and printer shares that are available. You can easily drag and drop files to and from a shared directory, assuming your user account is permitted the necessary access.

To use a shared printer, click Start → Settings → Printers and then double-click Add Printer. The wizard will guide you through the setup procedure. Simply choose the Network Printer option and browse to select the desired printer. If you configured the printer share without the browseable option, you cannot browse and therefore must type the name of the printer share. To do so, type two backward slashes, followed by the name of your Samba server, followed by a single backslash, followed by the name of the printer share. For example, if you want to access a printer share named *lp* on the Samba server known as *SERVER*, you'd type **\\SERVER\lp**.

You can map a file share to a drive letter by using the Tools → Map Network Drive menu item of the Windows Explorer. Simply select an available drive letter and type the name of the file share, which consists of two backward slashes, followed by the name of your Samba server, followed by a single backslash, followed by the name of the file share. For example, if you want to access a file share named *db* on the Samba server known as *SERVER*, you'd type **\\SERVER\db**.

If you have difficulty connecting to your Samba server, follow the procedure given earlier in "Troubleshooting Samba."

Linux client

The Samba package includes a simple SMB client that can access your Samba server and other SMB servers accessible to your system. To demonstrate that your client and server are working, log on using a user account that has Samba authorization and issue the following command:

```
$ smbclient -L localhost
```

You should see a list of the browseable shares available on your server. To query a different SMB server, issue the following command:

```
$ smbclient -L server
```

where *server* is the name of the SMB server you want to contact. Rather than logging on using an authorized user account, you can explicitly specify a user account by using this command form:

```
$ smbclient -L server -U userid
```

To actually access resources via SMB, use the following command form:

```
$ smbclient 'service' -U userid
```

where *service* specifies the name of the SMB host and share and *userid* specifies the user account to be used. The name of the SMB host should be preceded by two backward slashes and followed by one backward slash; for example:

```
$ smbclient //server/myshare -U billmccarty
```

If the SMB server accepts your request, the client displays a special prompt:

```
smb: dir>
```

where *dir* indicates the current working directory on the SMB server. To download a file from the server, issue the command:

```
get file
```

where *file* specifies the name of the file to be downloaded. To upload a file to the server, issue the command:

```
put file
```

where *file* specifies the name of the file. To list the contents of the current directory, issue the command:

```
dir
```

To enter a subdirectory, issue the following command, where *dir* specifies the name of the subdirectory:

```
cd dir
```

You can return to the parent directory by issuing the command:

```
cd ..
```

You can obtain a list of commands by issuing the command **help** or, to obtain help on a particular command, by issuing the command:

```
help command
```

where *command* specifies the command that you need help with. To exit the SMB client, issue the command **exit**.

You can use the *smbprint* script included in the Samba package to print Linux files by using a printer share. However, you'll probably have to do some tweaking of configuration files and adjusting of shell scripts to get *smbprint* to work.

Using the Linux Samba client for file backup and recovery

One of the most practical uses of the Linux SMB client is creating backup copies of files stored on a Windows system. To do so, simply share the drive or directory containing the files you want to back up. Using the Windows Explorer, right-click the drive or directory, click Properties, click the Sharing tab, and select the desired share options. Then, access the share from Linux using *smbclient*. Once you have the SMB prompt, move to the directory you want to back up and issue the SMB **tar** command:

```
tar c backup.tar
```

The syntax of the SMB **tar** command resembles that of the **tar** command, though it supports only a handful of options. When you issue the SMB **tar** command with the **c** option, the files of the current directory and all its subdirectories will be backed up and stored in the file *backup.tar* on your Linux system. Of course, you can specify a filename other than *backup.tar* if you wish (although the *.tar* extension is required). Once you've created the backup file, you can write it to a tape, a writable CD-ROM, or other media. If your backup requirements are meager, it may be sufficient merely to have a copy of the file on both your Windows and Linux systems.

To restore a backup, move to the directory where you want the files restored and issue the SMB **tar** command:

```
tar x backup.tar
```

The SMB client restores each file from the *backup.tar* file. Of course, you must have write access to the shared directory in order to be able to restore files.

Setting Up a DHCP Server

Managing the network configurations of the hosts on even a small network can be tedious. Administrators of large networks, including ISPs, have long used the DHCP service to centrally manage network configurations. Red Hat Linux includes a DHCP server that you can install in order to facilitate the management of your network. Hosts configured with DHCP clients can load their network configurations from the DHCP server at boot time, including such configuration items as:

- Hostname
- Domain name
- IP address
- Netmask
- Broadcast IP address
- Gateway IP address
- DNS server address

Installing the DHCP Server

Before installing the DHCP server, you should check whether your system's network adapter is properly configured to support DHCP. To do so, issue the **ifconfig** command as root:

```
# ifconfig -a
eth0      Link encap:Ethernet  HWaddr 00:A0:CC:25:8A:EC
          inet addr:192.168.0.5  Bcast:192.168.255.255
            Mask:255.255.0.0
          UP BROADCAST RUNNING MULTICAST  MTU:1500  Metric:1
          RX packets:71910 errors:0 dropped:0 overruns:0
```

```
            frame:0
      TX packets:108334 errors:0 dropped:0 overruns:0
            carrier:0
      collisions:89 txqueuelen:100
      Interrupt:11 Base address:0x6000
```

If your system's network adapter is properly configured to support DHCP, the output of the **ifconfig** command will indicate that the adapter supports BROADCAST. If the output doesn't include this specifications, you must reconfigure or replace the network adapter. Fortunately, it's rare that an adapter lacks these capabilities.

To set up a DHCP server, use the Package Management Tool to install the *dhcp* package, which is part of the Network Servers package group. In doing so, be sure to disable the checkboxes associated with any unwanted services. Then, configure the service as explained in the following section.

Configuring the DHCP Service

To configure the DHCP service, you must create the DHCP configuration file, */etc/ dhcpd.conf*. Here's a simple configuration that you can use as a starting point:

```
ddns-update-style ad-hoc;
default-lease-time 64800;
max-lease-time     64800;
option domain-name-servers 192.168.0.1;
option domain-name        "oreilly.com";
subnet 192.168.0.0 netmask 255.255.255.0
{
  option subnet-mask        255.255.255.0;
  option broadcast-address  192.168.0.255;
  option routers            192.168.0.1;
  server-identifier 192.168.0.5;
  host sara
  {
    hardware ethernet  00:50:04:d2:3f:15;
    fixed-address       192.168.0.33;
    default-lease-time 86400;
  }
  range 192.168.0.50 192.168.0.254;
}
```

When a DHCP client obtains a network configuration from the server, it doesn't generally obtain the configuration permanently. Instead, a DHCP client is said to *lease* a configuration. The two lines at the top of the configuration file specify the default and maximum lease duration, in seconds. The figure 64800 (seconds) is equivalent to 18 hours. By choosing a relatively long lease time, a client will not generally need to renew its leased network configuration during a workday. You can choose a shorter or longer duration, as you prefer.

The next two lines specify information transmitted to clients as part of their network configurations:

domain-name-servers
> The DNS server IP address. More than one server can be specified. Each server is separated from its neighbor by a comma.

domain-name
> The domain name.

Next comes a group of lines—delimited with paired curly braces—that define a network or subnetwork. In this case, the network defined has the IP address 192.168.0.0 with a netmask of 255.255.255.0. This means that the range of network addresses is from 192.168.0.0 to 192.168.0.255.

Hosts in this network share three parameters:

subnet-mask
> The network mask, which indicates by 1-bits the bit positions of the IP address associated with the network, rather than the host. Often, the network mask has the value 255.255.255.0.

broadcast-address
> The IP address of the network, with all 1-bits in the bit positions associated with the host address. Often, this means that the first three members of the dotted quad IP address appear, followed by the value 255.

routers
> The default gateway IP address.

The next set of lines define the network configuration for a particular host, named *sara*:

```
host sara
  {
     hardware ethernet  00:50:04:d2:3f:15;
     fixed-address      192.168.0.33;
     default-lease-time 86400;
  }
```

The host's network adapter has an Ethernet MAC address of 00:50:04:d2:3f: 15. The Ethernet address is a unique code, assigned by the adapter's manufacturer, that serves to identify the adapter. When it queries the DHCP server, this adapter will be leased the IP address 192.168.0.33; the lease will have a duration of 24 hours (86400 seconds). This adapter will always receive this IP address, which is also known as a static IP address.

The next line defines a range of IP addresses:

```
range 192.168.0.50 192.168.0.254;
```

Hosts not assigned a static IP address will be leased an address within the specified range. Such an IP address is termed a *dynamic IP address*.

For more information about the *dhcpd.conf* file, see the associated manpage.

Starting the DHCP Service

To start the DHCP service, launch the Service Configuration Tool by choosing Server Settings → Services from the GNOME or KDE menu. Select the list entry associated the DHCP service, named *dhcpd*, and click Start.

To verify that the DHCP service has started, issue the following command to view recent system log entries:

```
$ tail -40 /var/log/messages
```

You should see something like the following:

```
Nov  3 11:35:39 localhost dhcpd: Internet Software Consortium DHCP Server V3.0pl1
Nov  3 11:35:39 localhost dhcpd: Copyright 1995-2001 Internet Software Consortium.
Nov  3 11:35:39 localhost dhcpd: All rights reserved.
Nov  3 11:35:39 localhost dhcpd: For info, please visit http://www.isc.org/products/
DHCP
Nov  3 11:35:39 localhost dhcpd: Wrote 0 deleted host decls to leases file.
Nov  3 11:35:39 localhost dhcpd: Wrote 0 new dynamic host decls to leases file.
Nov  3 11:35:39 localhost dhcpd: Wrote 0 leases to leases file.
Nov  3 11:35:39 localhost dhcpd:
Nov  3 11:35:39 localhost dhcpd: Listening on LPF/eth0/00:50:da:76:59:fd/192.168.0.0/
24
Nov  3 11:35:39 localhost dhcpd: Sending on   LPF/eth0/00:50:da:76:59:fd/192.168.0.0/
24
Nov  3 11:35:39 localhost dhcpd: Sending on   Socket/fallback/fallback-net
Nov  3 11:35:39 localhost dhcpd: dhcpd startup succeeded
```

Now, boot a client configured to obtain its network configuration via DHCP. If you need help configuring a client to use DHCP, consult the next section. If the DHCP client and server are working, you should see system log messages that resemble the following:

```
Nov  3 11:59:40 localhost dhcpd: DHCPREQUEST for
   192.168.0.4 from 00:50:04:d2:3f:15 via eth0
Nov  3 11:59:40 localhost dhcpd: DHCPACK on 192.168.0.4 to
   00:50:04:d2:3f:15 via eth0
```

If you find that the DHCP server is not working, consult the file */usr/share/doc/dhcp- */README*.

 What often appears to be a problem with a DHCP server is most likely a problem with the DHCP client. If you have difficulty getting the DHCP service to work properly, configure the client as explained in the next section. Another common problem is configuring multiple DHCP servers on the same network. In order to avoid conflicts between servers, you should generally operate only a single DHCP server on your network.

If you want the DHCP service to start automatically when you boot your system, use the Service Configuration Tool to associate the service with the desired runlevel or runlevels.

Configuring DHCP Clients

To configure a Windows 9x client to use DHCP, select Start → Settings → Control Panel → Network → Configuration to open the TCP/IP Properties dialog box. Select the TCP/IP network component associated with the network adapter you want to configure and click Properties. Select the IP Address tab and choose Obtain an IP address automatically. Then select the DNS tab and choose Disable DNS. This setting does not actually disable DNS; it merely configures the system to rely on DHCP to provide the IP address of the DNS server.

Next, select the Gateway tab and remove any installed gateways. Click OK to dismiss the TCP/IP Properties dialog box, and click OK again to dismiss the Network Properties dialog box. You can use a similar procedure to configure Windows NT/ 2000 clients.

Windows 9x lets you view leased network configuration information. To do so, run the program *winipcfg* and select the proper adapter. The program shows the Ethernet address, IP address, subnet mask, and default gateway associated with the client, if any. Click More to view additional information, such as hostname, DNS server IP address, and the lease expiration time. You can manually release or renew a lease by clicking Release or Renew.

Under Windows 2000 and XP, you can view similar information describing the network configuration by issuing the command:

```
$ ipconfig /all
```

To configure a Linux client to use DHCP, launch the Network Administration Tool. Select the Devices tab and click the interface you want to configure. Click Edit to view the Ethernet Device dialog box. Finally, enable the checkbox labelled Automatically obtain IP address settings with, choose DHCP from the drop-down box, and click OK. To determine the status of a DHCP lease held by a Linux client, you can search the system log for relevant messages.

CHAPTER 12

Setting Up Internet Services

In the preceding chapters, you learned how to connect your Linux system to a local area network (LAN) or to the Internet via an Internet service provider (ISP). By doing so, you were able to access a plethora of services provided by others, including file transfers via FTP (File Transfer Protocol), web pages, email, and Telnet. This chapter explains how to set up several Linux Internet servers, including an FTP server, an Apache web server, and a DNS server. These applications let you and others access data on your Linux system via the Internet. These applications will be most useful if your system is connected to the Internet 24/7. But, even if your connection is intermittent, you and others can access the services these applications provide whenever the connection is active. The chapter also explains how to implement a basic firewall to help protect your systems from unauthorized access via the Internet. Finally, the chapter explains how to use Nmap to test your firewall. Most Internet services are configurable only by the root user. So, most of the operations in this chapter require that you be logged in as root, or possess temporary root privileges as indicated by the keys icon.

 If you configured a medium- or high-security firewall during system installation or thereafter, remote hosts will not be able to connect to Internet services offered by your host. To permit remote hosts to access services, you must disable or customize your firewall, as described in the section "Implementing a Basic Firewall."

Running an FTP Server

An FTP server lets you transfer files from one system to another via a network. When two computers are connected to the Internet, you can use FTP to transfer files from one to the other even though the computers are not directly connected.

An FTP server attempts to authenticate users that ask to use it. You can configure your FTP server to accept requests only from users who have an account on the system running the FTP server, or you can configure it to accept requests from anyone, via a facility known as *anonymous FTP*.

 FTP carries significant risk. FTP sends login passwords over the network as clear text. Anyone using a packet sniffer can discover passwords entered during an FTP session and use them to breach security. A more secure alternative is the Secure Shell (SSH) *scp* utility, described later in this chapter. However, servers providing public access to downloadable files must use FTP rather than SSH.

Installing and Starting the FTP Server

To install the FTP Server package group, use the Package Management Tool. After installing the package group, you must tell *xinetd* to respond to FTP clients. To do so, use the Service Settings Tool to associate the *xinetd* and *vsftpd* services with the current runlevel. Also, restart *xinetd* so that it's aware that it knows to respond to requests for the *vsftpd* service.

Testing the FTP Server

To test your FTP server, start an FTP client by issuing the following command:

    ftp localhost

The FTP server should prompt you for a login user account name and password. To log in anonymously, specify the username *anonymous* and use an email address, such as *user@example.com*, as the password. If you correctly supply the username and password, you should see the FTP prompt that lets you know the FTP server is ready to execute FTP subsystem commands. Type **quit** and press **Enter** to exit the FTP client.

 By default, FTP does not allow the root user to log in. You could modify this behavior, but doing so could compromise system security because FTP sends passwords across the network in an insecure manner.

Once your FTP server is working, try contacting it from a remote system. If you have a Windows machine, you can contact your server by using the built-in Windows FTP client that works similarly to the Linux FTP client, interpreting the same FTP subsystem commands. Open an MS-DOS Prompt window and type the command:

    ftp server

where *server* specifies the hostname or IP address of your Linux server. Generally, once the FTP subsystem prompt is available, you should immediately issue the **binary** (or **bin**) command. This command specifies that files will be transferred verbatim; without it, executable files, documents, and other files that contain binary data will be scrambled when transferred. Generally, transferring text files and other non-binary files in binary mode will not damage them.

 If your FTP server fails to respond, check your host firewall configuration. The firewall may be blocking FTP traffic. See the section "Implementing a Basic Firewall."

When you're ready to actually transfer some files, use the FTP commands described in Table 12-1. Here's a typical FTP session that you can use as a model:

```
# ftp localhost
C:\>ftp 192.168.0.2
Connected to 192.168.0.2.
220 ready, dude (vsFTPd 1.1.0: beat me, break me)
Name (localhost:root): billmccarty
331 Please specify the password.
Password:
230 Login successful. Have fun.
ftp> bin
200 Binary it is, then.
ftp> ls
200 PORT command successful. Consider using PASV.
150 Here comes the directory listing.
-rw-r--r--    1 500      500            33 Jan 04 17:06 file-for-download.txt
226 Directory send OK.
ftp: 79 bytes received in 0.00Seconds 79000.00Kbytes/sec.
ftp> get 3c90x-1.0.0e.tar.gz
200 PORT command successful. Consider using PASV.
150 Opening BINARY mode data connection for file-for-download.txt (33 bytes).
226 File send OK.
ftp: 33 bytes received in 0.00Seconds 33000.00Kbytes/sec.
ftp> quit
221 Goodbye.
```

Table 12-1. Important FTP commands

Command	Function
!command	Invokes a shell on the local system. For example, to obtain a listing of the current directory on the local system, issue the !ls command for a Unix system, or !dir for a Microsoft system.
ascii	Specifies that files will be transferred in ASCII mode.
binary bin	Specifies that files will be transferred in binary mode, which performs no translation.
cd directory	Changes to the specified directory of the remote system.
delete file	Deletes the specified file from the remote system.
dir	Displays the contents of the current directory of the remote system.
get file	Retrieves the specified file from the remote system.
hash	Prints a series of hash marks (#) during file transfer (upload or download).
help	Displays command help information.

Table 12-1. Important FTP commands (continued)

Command	Function
lcd *directory*	Changes to the specified directory of the local system.
mkdir *directory*	Creates the specified directory on the remote system.
put *file*	Stores the specified local file on the remote system.
pwd	Displays the current working directory on the remote system.
quit	Exits the FTP session and returns you to the shell prompt.
rmdir *directory*	Removes the specified directory from the remote system.
status	Shows the status of the FTP session.

Securing Your FTP Server

If your computer is connected to the Internet or another potentially hostile network, you should revise the FTP configuration to improve security. Two measures are generally recommended.

First, if you don't need to provide FTP to anonymous users, disable anonymous FTP. To do so, edit the file */etc/vsftpd.conf*, replacing the line:

```
anonymous_enable=YES
```

with the line:

```
anonymous_enable=NO
```

Second, if your users only download files, never upload them, you should disable FTP writes. To do so, edit the file */etc/vsftpd.conf*, replacing the line:

```
write_enable=YES
```

with the line:

```
write_enable=NO
```

 The *vsftpd* FTP server does not allow anonymous users to upload files. If you require this capability, you can remove *vsftpd* and replace it with the Washington University FTP server, contained in the package *wu-ftpd*. However, permitting anonymous users to upload files may make you site more vulnerable to attack.

Running Apache

Installing and configuring the Apache web server is not much more difficult than installing an FTP server. Moreover, web servers tend to be more secure than FTP servers, so a web server may be a better way for you to publish files. Once your web server is up and running, other Internet users can view and download documents within the web-enabled directories on your Linux system. This section explains the installation and configuration of Apache, the most popular web server on the Internet.

The Tux Web Server

Red Hat 8.0 ships with Tux, a web server developed by Red Hat. Tux may be the fastest web server available. The secret of Tux's speed is that it is integrated with the Linux kernel, so the overhead involved in serving a web page is minimal.

However, don't toss Apache overboard just yet. Tux can serve only static HTML pages. It can't be used with server-side includes, PHP, or other popular methods of serving web pages whose content is determined when they're served. When Tux is asked to serve a dynamic page, it can hand off the request to Apache, so Tux and Apache can work together to rapidly serve static web pages yet provide the full power and flexibility of Apache.

Unless you're planning to establish a high-traffic web site, you won't need to be concerned with Tux, which is somewhat complicated to configure. To learn more about Tux, which Red Hat calls *Red Hat Content Accelerator*, see *http://www.redhat.com/docs/manuals/tux/TUX-2.2-Manual/*.

Installing Apache

Use the Package Management Tool to install the Web Server package group, which contains the Apache web server.

Configuring Apache

Configuring a web server can be as easy or as difficult as you choose. Like other web servers, Apache provides seemingly countless options. As distributed with Red Hat Linux, Apache has a default configuration that generally requires only a little tweaking before use. Apache's configuration files reside in the directory */etc/httpd/conf*. For historical reasons that no longer apply, Apache has three configuration files:

- *access.conf*
- *httpd.conf*
- *srm.conf*

However, the only configuration file that's currently used is *httpd.conf*. The easiest way to perform a basic configuration of Apache is with the Apache Configuration Tool. To configure Apache, choose Server Settings → HTTP Server from the GNOME or KDE menu. The main configuration screen, shown in Figure 12-1, appears.

Figure 12-1. The Apache Configuration Tool

The Configuration Tool contains four tabs: Main, Virtual Hosts, Server, and Performance Tuning. The Main tab lets you specify the following:

Server Name
> This is the hostname of your system. Often, this will be *www.domain.com*, where *domain.com* is the name of your domain.

Webmaster email address
> Any messages concerning the web server will be sent to this address.

Available Addresses
> This is the IP address (or addresses) on which the web server listens.

You should specify the Server Name and Webmaster email address. Unless your system has multiple network adapters or you want to run the web server on a nonstandard port (that is, a port other than 80), you don't need to modify the Available Addresses configuration item.

The Virtual Hosts tab, shown in Figure 12-2, lets you specify virtual hosts. Virtual hosting is a feature that lets you host multiple web sites with a single IP address. For example, both *www.myfirstsite.com* and *www.myothersite.com* could be hosted on the same system using a single IP address. However, virtual hosting is not compatible with HTTP 1.0 browsers.

The Server tab, shown in Figure 12-3, lets you specify the location of important files and directories and the user account and group used by Apache. You should not generally alter these configuration items.

The Performance Tuning tab, shown in Figure 12-4, provides access to configuration items that let you optimize Apache's performance. Unless your web server will see very heavy service, you should reduce the maximum number of connections. A value of 15 is more than appropriate for a personal web server.

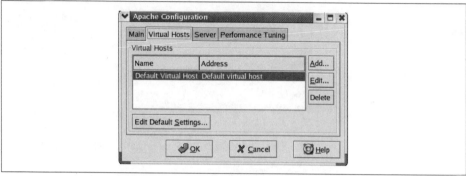

Figure 12-2. The Virtual Hosts tab

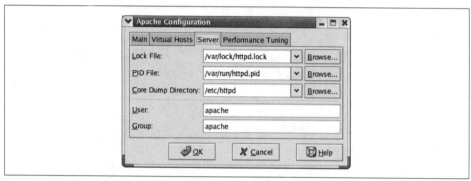

Figure 12-3. The Server tab

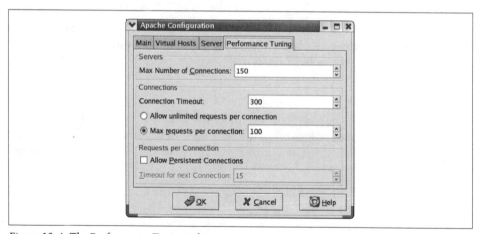

Figure 12-4. The Performance Tuning tab

If you're interested in exploring the many other configuration options provided by Apache, see the Apache manual, which resides in */var/www/manual*. You can view the file with Links or another HTML browser. Also, see the Apache web site (*http://www.apache.org*), which includes a tutorial on Apache configuration.

Starting and Stopping Apache

Once you've configured your web server, you can start, stop, and restart it by using the Service Configuration Tool. You can also associate the *httpd* service with one or more runlevels, so that it starts automatically when your system boots. You can use Mozilla to test your web server by pointing Mozilla to the URL *http://localhost/*.

You should see a screen that resembles Figure 12-5.

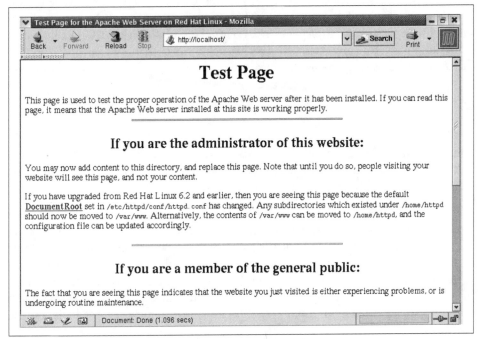

Figure 12-5. The Apache start page as viewed with Mozilla

Once you can access your web server locally, try accessing it from a remote computer. This should be as simple as forming a URL that includes the fully qualified hostname or IP address of your system (that is, the host and domain names), for example, *http://mysystem.mydomain*. However, bear in mind that you can reference your system by hostname only if its IP address is known to the DNS server or contained in the client's */etc/hosts* file.

If you change Apache's configuration, you must restart the server so that the server reads the revised configuration file. You can do so by using the Service Configuration Tool.

Creating Web Pages

You can create HTML pages in */var/www/html*, owned by the *root* user account. These pages are accessible via the URL *http://www.domain.com*, where *domain.com* is the name of the host.

Alternatively, users can create a *public_html* subdirectory within their home directory, for example, */home/joepublic/public_html*. There, they can publish files that are web-accessible. To access such files, use a special URL that consists of a tilde (~) followed by the name of the user account. For example, *http:// www.domain.com/~joepublic* refers to the user *joepublic*'s web directory. However, support for user publishing of web pages is not enabled by default. To enable it, edit the file */etc/ httpd/conf/httpd.conf*, changing the line:

```
UserDir disable
```

to:

```
UserDir enable all
```

Then, restart the *httpd* service. If you want to permit only specified users to publish web pages, replace the keyword *all* with a list of usernames, separating each from the next with one or more spaces:

```
UserDir enable billmccarty andyoram
```

You must also change the permissions of files and directories you want to be accessible via the Web. For the user *joepublic*'s web pages to be web-accessible, the *apache* user account or group must have execute access to the directories */home*, */home/ joepublic*, and */home/joepublic/public_html*. Moreover, if automatic directory indexes are desired, the *apache* user account or group must have read access to the directory */home/joepublic/public_html*. The files themselves must be readable by the *apache* user.

> The rule of thumb is to give the */home/joepublic* directory permissions 711 and the */home* and */home/joepublic/public_html* directory permissions 755. Within */home/joepublic/public_html*, directories should have permissions 755 and files should have permissions 644. However, your particular needs may dictate that other permissions should be used.

If you have trouble accessing web pages on your server, check Apache's log files, which you can view via the System Logs Tool. The log files may provide valuable clues to help you understand what's going wrong.

The Secure Shell

The Secure Shell (SSH) lets you connect to a system from another system via TCP/IP and obtain a shell prompt, from which you can issue commands and view output in

---

a secure fashion. SSH works similarly to Telnet, but differs in that conversations between SSH and its clients are sent in encrypted form so hackers cannot easily discover private information, including user account names and passwords.

Installing SSH

The installation procedure automatically installs an SSH client and server and associates the *sshd* service with runlevels 3–5. You can start, stop, and restart the *sshd* service and changes its associations with runlevels by using the Service Configuration Tool. The service must be running in order to respond to clients.

 The SSH service has several configuration files, residing in */etc/ssh*. You don't have to modify them to get SSH running. If you're curious about them, view the *sshd* manpage.

Using SSH

To verify that the SSH server is properly running, you can access it via a client on the local system by issuing the following command:

```
$ ssh localhost
```

The client will attempt to log you on to the local system using your current user account and will prompt you for your password. If you supply the correct password, you should see a shell prompt, indicating that the client and server are functioning correctly. Type **exit** and press **Enter** to exit SSH.

To log on to a remote system, simply specify the hostname or IP address of the remote system in place of *localhost*. If you want to log in to a user account other than one named identically to the account you're using on the local system, issue the command:

```
$ ssh userid@host
```

where *host* is the hostname or IP address of the remote host and *userid* is the name of the user account you want to use. For example:

```
$ ssh billmccarty@gonzo.apu.edu
```

You can use the SSH client's **scp** command to transfer files to or from a remote system running an SSH server. To transfer a file to a remote system, issue a command such as this one:

```
$ scp file userid@host:destination
```

where *file* is the path of the file to be transferred, *host* is the hostname or IP address of the remote host, *destination* is the directory to which the file should be transferred, and *userid* is your user account on the remote system. If given as a relative path, the destination path is understood as being relative to the home directory of the specified user. For example:

```
$ scp rhbook_rev.txt billmccarty@gonzo.apu.edu: files
```

To transfer files to your home directory on the remote system, omit the *path* argument; however, retain the colon or the command will be misinterpreted.

You can specify multiple files to be transferred if you like. You can use shell metacharacters to specify a set of files to be transferred. You can also specify the -**r** flag, which specifies that **scp** should recursively copy a directory. For example, the following command copies an entire directory to the remote system:

```
$ scp -r Desktop billmccarty@gonzo.apu.edu: files
```

To transfer files from a remote system, issue a command based on this pattern:

```
$ scp userid@host:file path
```

where *host* is the hostname or IP address of the remote system, *file* is the path of the file to be transferred, *path* is the destination path of the file, and *userid* is your user account on the remote system. For example:

```
$ scp billmccarty@author.ora.com:/out/ch12.doc files
```

This command would log in the user *billmccarty* to *author.ora.com/out*, retrieve the *ch12.doc* file, and place it in his *files* directory.

SSH also provides the **sftp** command, which lets you transfer files in much the same way the **ftp** command does. The command has the following form:

```
$ sftp user@host
```

The command will prompt for the password associated with the specified user account. For example, to transfer files to and from the host *author.ora.com*, you could issue the following command:

```
$ sftp billmccarty@author.ora.com
```

After establishing a connection to the specified host, the **sftp** command presents a prompt that lets you enter commands similar to those supported by the **ftp** command. Use the **help** command to learn more about the supported commands.

Using a Windows SSH Client

To log on to your Linux system from a remote system via SSH, you must install an SSH client on the remote system. A suitable client for Windows is Simon Tatham's *PuTTY*, available at *http://www.chiark.greenend.org.uk/~sgtatham/putty*. Simply download *PuTTY* to any convenient directory (the *windows* directory is a good choice). The program doesn't have a setup script; you can run it by selecting Start → Run and typing **putty**; if the directory in which *PuTTY* resides is not on the execution path, you must type the drive, path, and filename. Alternatively, you can create a shortcut that spares you the trouble. Figure 12-6 shows *PuTTY*'s main screen.

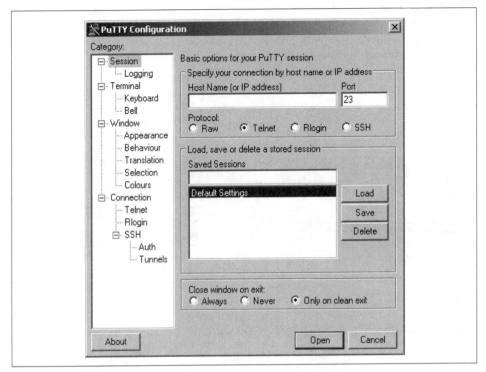

Figure 12-6. PuTTY's screen

To use *PuTTY* to connect to a host, specify the following information:

Hostname
> The hostname or IP address of the SSH server.

Protocol
> You should select SSH. This causes *PuTTY* to automatically select port 22, the default SSH port. If the SSH server listens on a different port, specify the non-standard port by using the Port text box.

Click Open to make the connection to the specified host.

The left pane of *PuTTY*'s screen provides access to several configuration options, such as:

- Key mappings
- Character translations
- Selection, copy, and paste options
- Screen colors

Like most Telnet or FTP clients, *PuTTY* lets you save configurations so you can quickly connect to often-used hosts. Use the Load, Save, and Delete buttons to manage your list of hosts and associated configurations.

For best results when using *PuTTY* to view screens that include color, enable the option Use background color to erase screen, found in the Terminal settings.

Another useful Windows SSH tool is WinSCP, which provides a user interface resembling that of a graphical FTP client. Figure 12-7 shows a WinSCP session. To learn more about WinSCP or obtain the program, visit *http://winscp.vse.cz/eng/*.

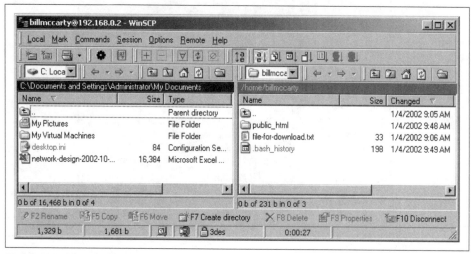

Figure 12-7. The WinSCP SSH client

Protocol Tunneling

SSH lets you establish a network connection that you can use as a *Virtual Private Network* (VPN), so called because traffic flowing over the connection is encrypted and therefore secure from eavesdroppers. This facility is known as *protocol tunneling* because the data that flows via the connection need not use the standard TCP/IP protocol; for example, the data might be encoded using Novell's IPX protocol.

Configuring and troubleshooting a VPN is not a task for a Linux newbie. However, if your Linux skills are growing and you desire a challenge, see *The Official Red Hat Linux Security Guide*, available at *http://www.redhat.com/docs/manuals/linux/RHL-8.0-Manual/security-guide/*. Also see *Virtual Private Networks*, by Charlie Scott, Paul Wolfe, and Mike Erwin (O'Reilly & Associates, Inc.).

Configuring DNS

DNS maps hostnames to IP addresses and vice versa. Configuring DNS can be somewhat difficult. However, you can easily configure your Linux system as a *caching name server*. A caching name server remembers mappings it has recently fetched and can supply them to clients. Accessing a local or nearby caching name server is much faster than accessing a remote name server.

The Linux program that performs name resolution is the Berkeley Internet Name Daemon (BIND). BIND is sometimes referred to as *named* (pronounced *name dee*), an abbreviation for *name daemon*. So, the same facility is variously referred to as DNS, BIND, or *named*. Some Linux/Unix systems are configured to use a name server other than BIND; however, BIND is the most popular name server on the Internet.

To install BIND and configure it as a caching name server, use the Package Mangement Tool to install the DNS Name Server package group and the extra package *caching-nameserver*.

To start the *named* service, use the Service Configuration Tool. You can also use the Tool to associate the service with one or more runlevels.

To use the *named* server, you must specify its IP address in the resolver configuration. To do so, launch the Network Administration Tool. Make a record of the existing specification and then specify 127.0.0.1 as the IP address of the primary name server. Test your name server by pinging an Internet host:

```
ping www.ora.com
```

A series of replies confirms that the name server is working. Press **Ctrl-C** to halt the pinging.

Implementing a Basic Firewall

Sometimes you may want a host to provide certain services to only local clients or clients on other hosts of a network that you control. If your network is connected to the Internet, you can use a *firewall* to prevent undesired access to services. A Linux firewall depends on certain kernel facilities to examine incoming and outgoing packets. Packets that fail to pass specified rules can be rejected, preventing undesired access to private services.

A related facility, known as *IP masquerading*, lets hosts on a network connect to the Internet via a host known as the *masquerading host*. All packets from the network seem to the outside host to have come from the masquerading host. IP masquerading lets you:

- Prevent outside access to services offered on a private network
- Hide the structure of private networks
- Conserve IP addresses by assigning freely usable reserved IP addresses to masqueraded hosts

Configuring the Firewall

At installation time, Red Hat Linux lets you configure a firewall for your system; however, you can reconfigure the firewall after installation. For a firewall to be secure and flexible, customization is almost always required. However, customizing a firewall requires an understanding of the ports and protocols used by each running service, an expertise that generally requires considerable time to achieve. To learn more about services, ports, and protocols, see the resources described at the end of this chapter.

To configure a firewall, launch the Security Level Tool by choosing System Settings → Security Level from the GNOME or KDE menu.

The Security Level Tool, as shown in Figure 12-8, appears.

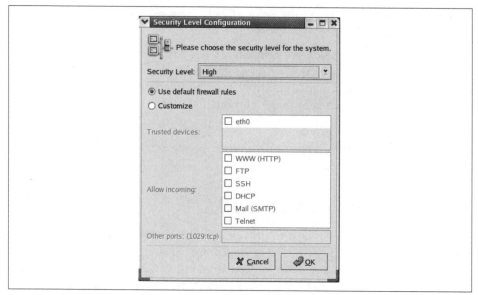

Figure 12-8. The Firewall Configuration dialog box

The Firewall Configuration dialog box lets you select the desired security level:

High
> The firewall admits only DNS and DHCP replies, which are generally necessary for normal system operation. The firewall prohibits active-mode FTP, Internet Relay Chat (IRC) file transfers, Real Audio playback, and Remote X clients. In addition, outside access to services is blocked, unless you use the Customize dialog box to make them available.

Medium
> The firewall blocks access to privileged ports (ports 0–1023), used by protocols such as FTP, SSH, SMTP (*sendmail*), and HTTP (Apache). In addition, it blocks

the NFS server port (2049). It blocks access to the local X Window System display and font server port by remote clients.

No Firewall

The firewall is disabled; remote clients can freely access services on your host.

To customize the access permitted to remote clients, click on Customize. You can use the Allow Incoming checkboxes to allow access to services that would otherwise be blocked by the medium or high security levels. If you want to allow access to a service other than one of the six listed, you can use the Other ports text box. There, you can list the number (or name) of the port, followed by a colon and the port type (*tcp* or *udp*). The file */etc/services* lists the commonly agreed-upon port numbers and the associated services. For example, the IMAP mail service is associated with port 143 and both TCP and UDP port types. To permit access to IMAP, you could place the specification 143:tcp,143:udp in the Other ports text box.

You can list as many ports as you like, separating each from its neighbor by a comma. It is possible to list ports by name, but since the names acceptable to the dialog box are not documented, it's better to use port numbers.

You can use the Trusted devices checkbox to specify that packets originating from the specified device will not be blocked by the firewall. This facility is useful when a host has two network adapters: one associated with a public network, such as the Internet, and another associated with a private network. By specifying the network adapter associated with the private network as a trusted device, you permit clients on the private network free access to services, while blocking clients on the public network from access other than that permitted by the firewall configuration.

Controlling the Firewall

To start, stop, or restart the firewall, you can use the Service Configuration Tool, which identifies the firewall as the *iptables* service. Generally, you should use the Tool to associate the *iptables* service with runlevels 2–5, so that your system is protected when networking is active.

Configuring IP Masquerading

To configure IP masquerading, properly configure and start your firewall. Then, issue a command of the following form:

```
# iptables -t nat -A POSTROUTING -o eth0 -s xxx.xxx.xxx.xxx -j MASQUERADE
```

where eth0 is the network adapter that connects to the Internet, and xxx.xxx.xxx.xxx is the IP address of the host to be masqueraded. If more than one host is to be masqueraded, the command can be repeated as necessary.

For example, to masquerade the hosts 192.168.0.1 and 192.168.0.2, routing to the Internet via the adapter eth0, issue the commands:

```
# iptables -t nat -A POSTROUTING -o eth0 -s 192.168.0.1 -j MASQUERADE
# iptables -t nat -A POSTROUTING -o eth0 -s 192.168.0.2 -j MASQUERADE
```

Then, save the current firewall status by issuing the command:

```
# service ipchains save
```

Checking Your Security by Using Nmap

Many users have misconfigured firewalls such that they are all but useless in defending against attacks. You can determine the state of your firewall by using the same tool hackers use to find its weaknesses, Nmap. To install Nmap, use the Package Management Tool to install the System Tools package group, and the extra packages *nmap* and *nmap-frontend*.

Unfortunately, Nmap doesn't have a place on the GNOME or KDE menus. You can launch Nmap by issuing the command:

```
# xnmap &
```

from a terminal window. The Nmap screen should appear shortly thereafter, as shown in Figure 12-9.

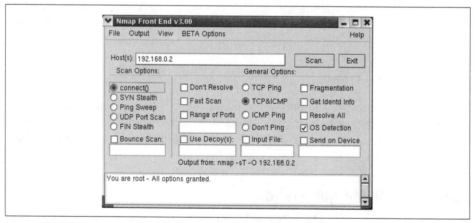

Figure 12-9. Nmap

Nmap has enough features to be the topic of a book. You can learn more about Nmap from its author's web site, *http://www.insecure.org/*. A vanilla use of Nmap involves configuring it to send TCP or UDP packets to every important port of a specified system. The target system's responses reveal whether it has services listening on scanned ports.

To configure Nmap to perform a TCP port scan, specify the IP address of the host, the connect() Scan Option, and the TCP & ICMP General Option. Then, commence scanning by clicking Scan. After a few minutes, you'll see a report like that shown in Figure 12-10. The report shown in the figure indicates that the target host is listening on eight TCP ports. To scan UDP ports, specify the UDP Port Scan Scan Option. UDP port scans are slower than TCP port scans and may take several minutes to complete.

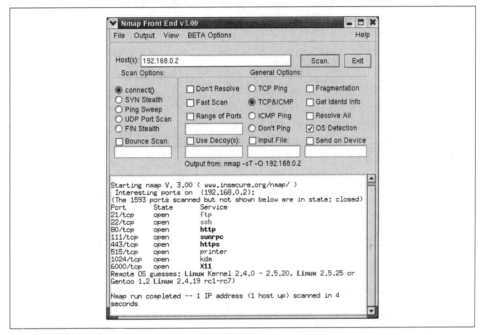

Figure 12-10. An Nmap report

Some ports listed in Nmap's report may not be remotely accessible. Therefore, to accurately determine the state of a system, you must scan it remotely. If a remote scan of your system discloses unexpected open ports, you should check your firewall and service configurations to determine whether anything is amiss.

Open ports above port 1023 that come and go with successive scans are not generally cause for concern. Usually, these are associated with established connections and are not really open. However, they can also be an early indication of the presence of a Trojan horse installed by an attacker. It's good practice to scan your hosts after you configure them so that you can later distinguish normal from abnormal behavior.

Don't scan someone else's system without permission. In some jurisdictions, it's a crime to do so. Even when scanning is legal, it may violate your ISP's terms of use. And, even if your ISP doesn't object, the scanned host's administrator may believe that the host is under attack, diverting his or her attention from other business. So, it's best to scan only systems on your local network, under your direct administrative control.

Network Security Tips

Anyone who administers a system connected to the Internet needs to know something about network security. It's not uncommon for systems connected to the Internet to be probed by would-be hackers several times daily. If a would-be hacker manages to detect a vulnerability, the hacker can often exploit it in a matter of seconds. Therefore, it's almost certain that a system administrator ignorant of network security will eventually suffer a system break-in.

Network security is a large and sophisticated topic that can be only cursorily surveyed in a book such as this. Concerned readers should consult books such as *Building Internet Firewalls*, by Elizabeth D. Zwicky, Simon Cooper, and D. Brent Chapman (O'Reilly & Associates, Inc.); *Computer Security Basics*, by Deborah Russell and G.T. Gangemi, Sr. (O'Reilly); and *Practical Unix & Internet Security*, by Simson Garfinkel and Gene Spafford (O'Reilly).

If a sufficiently skilled hacker is intent on compromising a system you administer, the hacker will probably succeed. However, here are some tips that can help you avoid falling victim to amateur hackers:

- Establish a firewall that prevents outsiders from accessing services you don't need to make publicly available.

- Monitor security web sites and mailing lists so that you're aware of recent threats and the associated countermeasures. The CERT Coordination Center, *http:// www.cert.org*, provides many useful resources.

- Apply bug fixes promptly, particularly those related to security. See Red Hat's errata page, *http://www.redhat.com/support/errata/rh8-errata.html*, for applicable fixes. To be informed of Red Hat Linux fixes when they're released, subscribe to Red Hat Network or the *redhat-watch-list* email list. To subscribe to Red Hat Network, visit *http://rhn.redhat.com*. To subscribe to the email list, visit *https://listman.redhat.com/mailman/listinfo/*.

## CHAPTER 13

Advanced Shell Usage
and Shell Scripts

Like an MS-DOS prompt window, the Unix shell is a command interpreter that lets you issue and execute commands. By means of the shell, you use and control your system. If you're accustomed to the point-and-click world of graphical user interfaces, you may question the value of learning to use the Linux shell. Many users initially find the shell cumbersome, and some retreat to the familiar comfort of the graphical user interface (GUI), avoiding the shell whenever possible. However, as this chapter explains, the shell unlocks the true power of Linux.

The Power of the Unix Shell

While it's true that the shell is an older style of interacting with a computer than the GUI, the graphical user interface is actually the more primitive interface. The GUI is easy to learn and widely used, but the shell is vastly more sophisticated. Using a GUI is somewhat like communicating in American Indian sign language. If your message is a simple one, like "We come in peace," you can communicate it by using a few gestures. However, if you attempted to give Lincoln's Gettysburg address—a notably short public discourse—you'd find your task quite formidable.[*]

The designer of a program that provides a GUI must anticipate all the possible ways in which the user will interact with the program and provide ways to trigger the appropriate program responses by means of pointing and clicking. Consequently, the user is constrained to working only in predicted ways. The user is therefore unable to adapt the GUI program to accommodate unforeseen tasks and circumstances. In a nutshell, that's why many system administration tasks are performed using the shell: system administrators, in fulfilling their responsibility to keep a system up and running, must continually deal with and overcome the unforeseen.

---

[*] American Sign Language, used to communicate with those who have a hearing impairment, is a much richer language than American Indian sign language. Unfortunately, programmers have not yet risen to the challenge of creating graphical user interfaces that are equally sophisticated.

The shell reflects the underlying philosophy of Unix, which provides a wide variety of small, simple tools (that is, programs), each performing a single task. When a complex operation is needed, the tools work together to accomplish the complex operation as a series of simple operations, one step at a time. Many Unix tools manipulate text, and since Unix stores its configuration data in text form rather than in binary form, the tools are ideally suited for manipulating Unix itself. The shell's ability to freely combine tools in novel ways is what makes Unix powerful and sophisticated. Moreover, as you'll learn, the shell is extensible: you can create *shell scripts* that let you store a series of commands for later execution, saving you the future tedium of typing or pointing and clicking to recall them.

The contrary philosophy is seen in operating systems such as Microsoft Windows, which employ elaborate, monolithic programs that provide menus, submenus, and dialog boxes. Such programs have no way to cooperate with one another to accomplish complex operations that weren't anticipated when the programs were designed. They're easy to use so long as you remain on the beaten path, but once you step off the trail, you find yourself in a confusing wilderness.

Of course, not everyone shares this perspective. The Usenet newsgroups, for example, are filled with postings debating the relative merits of GUIs. Some see the Unix shell as an arcane and intimidating monstrosity. But, even if they're correct, it's inarguable that when you learn to use the shell, you begin to see Unix as it was intended (whether that's for better or for worse).

When you are performing common, routine operations, a GUI that minimizes typing can be a relief, but when faced with a complex, unstructured problem that requires a creative solution, the shell is more often the tool of choice. Creating solutions in the form of shell scripts allows solutions to be stored for subsequent reuse. Perhaps even more important, shell scripts can be studied to quickly bone up on forgotten details, expediting the solution of related problems.

Filename Globbing

Before the shell passes arguments to an external command or interprets a built-in command, it scans the command line for certain special characters and performs an operation known as *filename globbing*. Filename globbing resembles the processing of wildcards used in MS-DOS commands, but it's much more sophisticated. Table 13-1 describes the special characters, known as filename metacharacters, used in filename globbing.

Table 13-1. Filename metacharacters

Metacharacter	Function
*	Matches a string of zero or more characters
?	Matches exactly one character

Table 13-1. Filename metacharacters (continued)

Metacharacter	Function
[abc...]	Matches any of the characters specified
[a-z]	Matches any character in the specified range
[!abc...]	Matches any character other than those specified
[!a-z]	Matches any character not in the specified range
~	The home directory of the current user
~userid	The home directory of the specified user
~+	The current working directory
~-	The previous working directory

In filename globbing, just as in MS-DOS wildcarding, the shell attempts to replace metacharacters appearing in arguments in such a way that arguments specify filenames. Filename globbing makes it easier to specify names of files and sets of files.

For example, suppose the current working directory contains the files *file1*, *file2*, *file3*, and *file04*. Suppose you want to know the size of each file. The following command reports that information:

```
ls -l file1 file2 file3 file04
```

However, the following command reports the same information and is much easier to type:

```
ls -l file*
```

As Table 13-1 shows, the * filename metacharacter can match any string of characters. Suppose you issued the following command:

```
ls -l file?
```

The ? filename metacharacter can match only a single character. Therefore, *file04* would not appear in the output of the command.

Similarly, the command:

```
ls -l file[2-3]
```

would report only *file2* and *file3*, because only these files have names that match the specified pattern, which requires that the last character of the filename be in the range 2–3.

You can use more than one metacharacter in a single argument. For example, consider the following command:

```
ls -l file??
```

This command will list *file04*, because each metacharacter matches exactly one filename character.

Most commands let you specify multiple arguments. If no files match a given argument, the command ignores the argument. Here's another command that reports all four files:

```
ls -l file0* file[1-3]
```

 Suppose that a command has one or more arguments that include one or more metacharacters. If none of the arguments matches any filenames, the shell passes the arguments to the program with the metacharacters intact. When the program expects a valid filename, an unexpected error may result.

The tilde (~) metacharacter lets you easily refer to your home directory. For example, the following command:

```
ls ~
```

would list the files in your home directory.

Filename metacharacters don't merely save you typing. They let you write scripts that selectively process files by name. You'll see how that works later in this chapter.

Shell Aliases

Shell aliases make it easier to use commands by letting you establish abbreviated command names and by letting you pre-specify common options and arguments for a command. To establish a command alias, issue a command of the form:

```
alias name='command'
```

where *command* specifies the command for which you want to create an alias and *name* specifies the name of the alias. For example, suppose you frequently type the MS-DOS command **dir** when you intend to type the Linux command **ls -l**. You can establish an alias for the **ls -l** command by issuing this command:

```
alias dir='ls -l'
```

Once the alias is established, if you mistakenly type **dir**, you'll get the directory listing you wanted instead of the default output of the **dir** command, which resembles **ls** rather than **ls -l**. If you like, you can establish similar aliases for other commands.

Your default Linux configuration probably defines several aliases on your behalf. To see what they are, issue the command:

```
alias
```

If you're logged in as *root*, you may see the following aliases:

```
alias cp='cp -i'
alias dir='ls -l'
alias ls='ls --color'
alias mv='mv -i'
alias rm='rm -i'
```

Notice how several commands are self-aliased. For example, the command **rm -i** is aliased as **rm**. The effect is that the -i option appears whenever you issue the **rm** command, whether or not you type the option. The -i option specifies that the shell will prompt for confirmation before deleting files. This helps avoid accidental deletion of files, which can be particularly hazardous when you're logged in as *root*. The alias ensures that you're prompted for confirmation even if you don't ask to be prompted. If you don't want to be prompted, you can issue a command like:

    `rm -f files`

where *files* specifies the files to be deleted. The -f option has an effect opposite that of the -i option; it forces deletion of files without prompting for confirmation. Because the command is aliased, the command actually executed is:

    `rm -i -f files`

The -f option takes precedence over the -i option, because it occurs later in the command line.

If you want to remove a command alias, you can issue the **unalias** command:

    `unalias alias`

where *alias* specifies the alias you want to remove. Aliases last only for the duration of a login session, so you needn't bother to remove them before logging off. If you want an alias to be effective each time you log in, you can use a shell script, which we'll discuss later in the chapter.

Using Virtual Consoles

You can use a terminal window to issue shell commands. However, you can issue shell commands even when X is not running or available. To do so, you use the Linux virtual console feature.

Linux provides six virtual consoles for interactive use; a seventh virtual console is associated with the graphical user interface. You can use special keystrokes to switch between virtual consoles. The keystroke **Alt-F***n*, where *n* is the number of a virtual console (1–6), causes Linux to display virtual console *n*. For example, you can display virtual console 2 by typing **Alt-F2**. You can view only a single console at a time, but you can switch rapidly between consoles by using the appropriate keystroke. The keystroke **Alt-F7** causes Linux to enter graphical mode using virtual console 7.

Virtual consoles also have a screensaver feature like that found on Windows. If a virtual console is inactive for an extended period of time, Linux blanks the monitor. To restore the screen without disturbing its contents, simply press the **Shift** key.

Logging In

To log in using a virtual console, type your user ID and press **Enter**. The system prompts you for the password associated with your account. Type the proper password and press **Enter**. To prevent anyone nearby from learning your password, Linux does not display your password as your enter it. If you suspect you've typed it incorrectly, you can either hit the **Backspace** key a number of times sufficient to delete the characters you've entered and type the password again or simply press **Enter** and start over. If you type the user ID or password incorrectly, Linux displays the message "login incorrect" and prompts you to try again.

When you've successfully logged in, you'll see a command prompt that looks something like this:

```
[bill@home bill]$
```

If you logged in as the root user, you'll see a prompt that contains a hash mark (#); if you've logged in as an ordinary user, you'll see a dollar sign ($). The prompt tells you that the Linux *bash* shell is ready to accept your commands.

Logging Out

When you're done using a virtual console, you should log out by typing the command **exit** and pressing **Enter**. When you log out, the system frees memory and other resources that were allocated when you logged in, making those resources available to other users.

When the system logs you out, it immediately displays a login prompt. If you change your mind and want to access the system, you can log in simply by supplying your username and password.

X and the Shell

You can configure your system to boot into nongraphical mode, if you prefer. If your video adapter is not compatible with X, you have no alternative but to do so. However, some Linux users prefer to configure their system to boot into nongraphical mode. A simple command lets such users launch an X session whenever they wish.

Configuring a Nongraphical Login

Linux provides several runlevels. Each runlevel has an associated set of services. For instance, runlevel 3 is associated with a text-based login and run level 5 is associated with an X-based, graphical login. Changing runlevels automatically starts and stops services associated with the old and new run levels.

You can determine the current runlevel by issuing the following command:

```
$ runlevel
```

The output of the command shows the previous and current runlevels. For example, the output:

```
3 5
```

indicates that the current run level is 5 and that the previous run level was 3.

To change the current runlevel, issue the **init** command. For example, to enter runlevel 3, issue the following command while logged in as *root*:

```
# init 3
```

In response to this command, the system will start and stop services as required to enter runlevel 3.

The */etc/inittab* file specifies the default runlevel, which the system enters when booted. By changing the default run level to 3, you can configure your system to provide a nongraphical login when it boots. To do so, log in as *root* and load the */etc/inittab* file into the *pico* editor by issuing the command:

```
# pico /etc/inittab
```

Find the line that reads:

```
id:5:initdefault:
```

Change the 5 to a 3:

```
id:3:initdefault:
```

Save the file and exit *pico*. The next time you boot your system, it will automatically enter runlevel 3 and provide a nongraphical login screen.

Starting and Stopping X from a Text-Based Login

To start X from a text-based login, type the command:

```
$ startx
```

Your system's screen should briefly go blank and then you should see X's graphical desktop.

 If the screen is garbled or remains blank for more than about 30 seconds, your X configuration may be faulty. Immediately turn off your monitor or terminate X by pressing **Ctrl-Alt-Backspace**.

To quit X, press **Ctrl-Alt-Backspace**. This is a somewhat abrupt way of exiting X. Depending on the X configuration, you may be able to right-click the desktop and select Exit from the pop-up menu. This method is less abrupt than pressing **Ctrl-Alt-Backspace**, but it still falls short of ideal.

Shell Scripts

A shell script is simply a file that contains a set of commands to be run by the shell when invoked. By storing commands as a shell script, you make it easy to execute them again and again. As an example, consider a file named *deleter*, which contains the following lines:

```
echo -n Deleting the temporary files...
rm -f *.tmp
echo Done.
```

The **echo** commands simply print text on the console. The **-n** option of the first **echo** command causes omission of the trailing newline character normally written by the **echo** command, so both **echo** commands write their text on a single line. The **rm** command removes all files having names ending in *.tmp* from the current working directory.

You can execute this script by issuing the **sh** command, as follows:

```
$ sh deleter
```

 If you invoke the **sh** command without an argument specifying a script file, a new interactive shell is launched. To exit the new shell and return to your previous session, issue the **exit** command.

If the *deleter* file were in a directory other than the current working directory, you'd have to type an absolute path, for example:

```
$ sh /home/bill/deleter
```

You can make it a bit easier to execute the script by changing its access mode to include execute access. To do so, issue the following command:

```
$ chmod 555 deleter
```

This gives you, members of your group, and everyone else the ability to execute the file. To do so, simply type the absolute path of the file, for example:

```
$ /home/bill/deleter
```

If the file is in the current directory, you can issue the following command:

```
$ ./deleter
```

You may wonder why you can't simply issue the command:

```
$ deleter
```

In fact, this still simpler form of the command will work, so long as *deleter* resides in a directory on your search path. You'll learn about the search path later.

Linux includes several standard scripts that are run at various times. Table 13-2 identifies these and gives the time when each is run. You can modify these scripts to operate differently. For example, if you want to establish command aliases that are available whenever you log in, you can use a text editor to add the appropriate lines to the *.profile* file that resides in your */home* directory. Since the name of this file begins with a dot (.), the **ls** command won't normally show the file. You must specify the **-a** option in order to see this and other hidden files.

Table 13-2. Special shell scripts

Script	Function
/etc/profile	Executes when the user logs in
~/.bash_profile	Executes when the user logs in
~/.bashrc	Executes when *bash* is launched
~/.bash_logout	Executes when the user logs out

 If you want to modify one of the standard scripts that should reside in your home directory but find that your */home* directory does not contain the indicated file, simply create the file. The next time you log in, log out, or launch *bash* (as appropriate) the shell will execute your script.

Input/Output Redirection and Piping

The shell provides three standard data streams:

stdin   The standard input stream
stdout   The standard output stream
stderr   The standard error stream

By default, most programs read their input from *stdin* and write their output to *stdout*. Because both streams are normally associated with a console, programs behave as you generally want, reading input data from the console keyboard and writing output to the console screen. When a well-behaved program writes an error message, it writes the message to the *stderr* stream, which is also associated with the console by default. Having separate streams for output and error messages presents an important opportunity, as you'll see in a moment.

Although the shell associates the three standard input/output streams with the console by default, you can specify input/output redirectors that, for example, associate an input or output stream with a file. Table 13-3 summarizes the most important input/output redirectors.

Table 13-3. Input/output redirectors

Redirector	Function
>file	Redirects standard output stream to specified file
2>file	Redirects standard error stream to specified file
>>file	Redirects standard output stream to specified file, appending output to the file if the file already exists

Table 13-3. Input/output redirectors (continued)

Redirector	Function
2>>file	Redirects standard error stream to specified file, appending output to the file if the file already exists
&>file	Redirects standard output and error streams to the specified file
2>&1	Combines the standard error stream with the standard output stream
<file	Redirects standard input stream from the specified file
<<text	Reads standard input until a line matching text is found, at which point end-of-file is posted
cmd1 | cmd2	Takes the standard input of cmd2 from the standard output of cmd1 (also known as the pipe redirector)

To see how redirection works, consider the **wc** command. This command takes a series of filenames as arguments and prints the total number of lines, words, and characters present in the specified files. For example, the command:

```
$ wc /etc/passwd
```

might produce the output:

```
22      26      790 /etc/passwd
```

which indicates that the file */etc/passwd* contains 22 lines, 26 words, and 790 characters. Generally, the output of the command appears on your console. But consider the following command, which includes an output redirector:

```
$ wc /etc/passwd > total
```

If you issue this command, you won't see any console output, because the output is redirected to the file *total*, which the command creates (or overwrites, if the file already exists). If you execute the following commands:

```
$ wc /etc/passwd > total
$ cat total
```

you will see the output of the **wc** command on the console.

Perhaps you can now see the reason for having the separate output streams *stdout* and *stderr*. If the shell provided a single output stream, error messages and output would be mingled. Therefore, if you redirected the output of a program to a file, any error messages would also be redirected to the file. This might make it difficult to notice an error that occurred during program execution. Instead, because the streams are separate, you can choose to redirect only *stdout* to a file. When you do so, error messages sent to *stderr* appear on the console in the usual way. Of course, if you prefer, you can redirect both *stdout* and *stderr* to the same file or redirect them to different files. As usual in the Unix world, you can have it your own way.

A simple way of avoiding annoying output is to redirect it to the null device file, */dev/null*. If you redirect the *stderr* stream of a command to */dev/null*, you won't see any error messages the command produces. For example, the **grep** command prints an error message if you invoke it on a directory. So, if you invoke the **grep** command on the current directory (*) and the current directory contains subdirectories, you'll see unhelpful error messages. To avoid them, use a command like this one, which searches for files containing the text "localhost":

```
$ grep localhost * 2>/dev/null
```

Just as you can direct the standard output or error stream of a command to a file, you can also redirect a command's standard input stream to a file so the command reads from the file instead of the console. For example, if you issue the **wc** command without arguments, the command reads its input from *stdin*. Type some words and then type the end-of-file character (**Ctrl-D**), and **wc** will report the number of lines, words, and characters you entered. You can tell **wc** to read from a file, rather than the console, by issuing a command like:

```
$ wc </etc/passwd
```

Of course, this isn't the usual way of invoking **wc**. The author of **wc** helpfully provided a command-line argument that lets you specify the file from which **wc** reads. However, by using a redirector, you could read from any desired file even if the author had been less helpful.

 Some programs are written to ignore redirectors. For example, when invoked without special options, the **passwd** command expects to read the new password only from the console, not from a file. You can compel such programs to read from a file, but doing so requires techniques more advanced than redirectors.

When you specify no command-line arguments, many Unix programs read their input from *stdin* and write their output to *stdout*. Such programs are called *filters*. Filters can be easily fitted together to perform a series of related operations. The tool for combining filters is the *pipe*, which connects the output of one program to the input of another. For example, consider this command:

```
$ ls ~ | wc -l
```

The command consists of two commands, joined by the pipe redirector (|). The first command lists the names of the nonhidden files in the user's home directory, one file per line. The second command invokes **wc** by using the -l option, which causes **wc** to print only the total number of lines, rather than printing the total number of lines, words, and characters. The pipe redirector sends the output of the **ls** command to the **wc** command, which counts and prints the number of lines in its input, which happens to be the number of files in the user's home directory.

This is a simple example of the power and sophistication of the Unix shell. Unix doesn't include a command that counts the files in the user's home directory and doesn't need to do so. Should the need to count the files arise, a knowledgeable Unix user can prepare a simple script that computes the desired result by using general-purpose Unix commands.

Shell Variables

If you've studied programming, you know that programming languages resemble algebra. Both programming languages and algebra let you refer to a value by a name. And both programming languages and algebra include elaborate mechanisms for manipulating named values.

The shell is a programming language in its own right, letting you refer to variables known as *shell* or *environment variables*. To assign a value to a shell variable, you use a command that has the following form:

```
$ variable=value
```

For example, the command:

```
$ DifficultyLevel=1
```

assigns the value 1 to the shell variable named DifficultyLevel. Unlike algebraic variable, shell variables can have nonnumeric values. For example, the command:

```
$ Difficulty=medium
```

assigns the value medium to the shell variable named Difficulty.

Shell variables are widely used within Unix, because they provide a convenient way of transferring values from one command to another. Programs can obtain the value of a shell variable and use the value to modify their operation, in much the same way they use the value of command-line arguments.

You can see a list of shell variables by issuing the **set** command. Usually, the command produces more than a single screen of output. So, you can use a pipe redirector and the **less** command to view the output one screen at a time:

```
$ set | less
```

Press the spacebar to see each successive page of output. You'll probably see several of the shell variables described in Table 13-4 among those printed by the **set** command. The values of these shell variables are generally set by one or another of the startup scripts described earlier in this chapter.

Table 13-4. Important environment variables

Variable	Function
DISPLAY	The X display to be used; for example, localhost:0
HOME	The absolute path of the user's home directory
HOSTNAME	The Internet name of the host
LOGNAME	The user's login name
MAIL	The absolute path of the user's mail file
PATH	The search path (see the upcoming section "The Search Path")
SHELL	The absolute path of the current shell

Table 13-4. Important environment variables (continued)

Variable	Function
TERM	The terminal type
USER	The user's current username; may differ from the login name if the user executes the **su** command

You can use the value of a shell variable in a command by preceding the name of the shell variable by a dollar sign ($). To avoid confusion with surrounding text, you can enclose the name of the shell variable within curly braces ({ }); it's good practice (though not necessary) to do so consistently. For example, you can change the current working directory to your */home* directory by issuing the command:

```
$ cd ${HOME}
```

Of course, issuing the **cd** command with no argument causes the same result. However, suppose you want to change to the */work* subdirectory of your home directory. The following command accomplishes exactly that:

```
$ cd ${HOME}/work
```

An easy way to see the value of a shell variable is to specify the variable as the argument of the **echo** command. For example, to see the value of the HOME shell variable, issue the command:

```
$ echo ${HOME}
```

To make the value of a shell variable available not just to the shell, but to programs invoked by using the shell, you must export the shell variable. To do so, use the **export** command, which has the form:

```
$ export variable
```

where *variable* specifies the name of the variable to be exported. A shorthand form of the command lets you assign a value to a shell variable and export the variable in a single command:

```
$ export variable=value
```

You can remove the value associated with a shell variable by giving the variable an empty value:

```
$ variable=
```

However, a shell variable with an empty value remains a shell variable and appears in the output of the **set** command. To dispense with a shell variable, you can issue the **unset** command:

```
$ unset variable
```

Once you unset the value of a variable, the variable no longer appears in the output of the **set** command.

The Search Path

The special shell variable PATH holds a series of paths known collectively as the *search path*. Whenever you issue an external command, the shell searches the paths that comprise the search path, seeking the program file that corresponds to the command. The startup scripts establish the initial value of the PATH shell variable, but you can modify its value to include any desired series of paths. You must use a colon (:) to separate each path of the search path. For example, suppose that PATH has the following value:

```
/usr/bin:/bin:/usr/local/bin:/usr/bin/X11:/usr/X11R6/bin
```

You can add a new search directory, say */home/bill*, by issuing the following command:

```
$ PATH=${PATH}:/home/bill
```

Now, the shell will look for external programs in */home/bill* as well as in the default directories. However, the problem is that the shell will look there last. If you prefer to check */home/bill* first, issue the following command instead:

```
$ PATH=/home/bill:${PATH}
```

The **which** command helps you work with the PATH shell variable. It checks the search path for the file specified as its argument and prints the name of the matching path, if any. For example, suppose you want to know where the program file for the **wc** command resides. Issuing the command:

```
$ which wc
```

will tell you that the program file is */usr/bin/wc* (or whatever other path is correct for your system).

Quoted Strings

Sometimes the shell may misinterpret a command you've written, globbing a filename or expanding a reference to a shell variable that you hadn't intended. Of course, it's actually your interpretation that's mistaken, not the shell's. Therefore, it's up to you to rewrite your command so the shell's interpretation is congruent with what you intended.

Quote characters, described in Table 13-5, can help you by controlling the operation of the shell. For example, by enclosing a command argument within single quotes, you can prevent the shell from globbing the argument or substituting the argument with the value of a shell variable.

Table 13-5. Quote characters

Character	Function
' (single quote)	Characters within a pair of single quotes are interpreted literally; that is, their metacharacter meanings (if any) are ignored. Similarly, the shell does not replace references to shell or environment variables with the value of the referenced variable.

Table 13-5. Quote characters (continued)

Character	Function
" (double quote)	Characters within a pair of double quotes are interpreted literally; that is, their metacharacter meanings (if any) are ignored. However, the shell does replace references to shell or environment variables with the value of the referenced variable.
´ (backquote)	Text within a pair of backquotes is interpreted as a command, which the shell executes before executing the rest of the command line. The output of the command replaces the original backquoted text.
\ (backslash)	The following character is interpreted literally; that is, its metacharacter meaning (if any) is ignored. The backslash character has a special use as a line continuation character. When a line ends with a backslash, the line and the following line are considered part of a single line.

To see quoted characters in action, consider how you might cause the **echo** command to produce the output $PATH. If you simply issue the command:

```
$ echo $PATH
```

the **echo** command prints the value of the PATH shell variable. However, by enclosing the argument within single quotes, you obtain the desired result:

```
$ echo '$PATH'
```

Double quotes have a similar effect. They prevent the shell from globbing a filename but permit the expansion of shell variables.

Backquotes operate differently; they let you execute a command and use its output as an argument of another command. For example, the command:

```
$ echo My home directory contains ´ls ~ | wc -l´ files.
```

prints a message that gives the number of files in the user's */home* directory. The command works by first executing the command contained within backquotes:

```
$ ls ~ | wc -l
```

This command, as explained earlier, computes and prints the number of files in the user's directory. Because the command is enclosed in backquotes, its output is not printed; instead the output replaces the original backquoted text.

The resulting command becomes:

```
echo My home directory contains 22 files.
```

When executed, this command prints the output:

```
My home directory contains 22 files.
```

You may now begin to appreciate the power of the Linux shell: by including command aliases in your *bashrc* script, you can extend the command repertoire of the shell. And, by using filename completion and the history list, you can reduce the amount of typing it takes to enter frequently used commands. Once you grasp how to use it properly, the Linux shell is a powerful, fast, and easy-to-use interface that avoids the limitations and monotony of the more familiar point-and-click graphical interface.

But the shell has additional features that extend its capabilities even further. As you'll see in the next section, the Linux shell includes a powerful programming language that provides argument processing, conditional logic, and loops.

Understanding Shell Scripts

This section explains how more advanced shell scripts work. The information is also adequate to equip you to write many of your own useful shell scripts. The section begins by showing how to process a script's arguments. Then it shows how to perform conditional and iterative operations.

Processing Arguments

You can easily write scripts that process arguments, because a set of special shell variables holds the values of arguments specified when your script is invoked. Table 13-6 describes the most popular such shell variables.

Table 13-6. Special shell variables used in scripts

Variable	Meaning
$#	The number of arguments
$0	The command name
$1, $2, ... ,$9	The individual arguments of the command
$*	The entire list of arguments, treated as a single word
$@	The entire list of arguments, treated as a series of words
$?	The exit status of the previous command; a value of 0 denotes a successful completion
$$	The ID of the current process

For example, here's a simple one-line script that prints the value of its second argument:

```
echo My second argument has the value $2.
```

Suppose you store this script in the file *second*, change its access mode to permit execution, and invoke it as follows:

```
$ ./second a b c
```

The script will print the output:

```
My second argument has the value b.
```

Notice that the shell provides variables for accessing only nine arguments. Nevertheless, you can access more than nine arguments. The key to doing so is the **shift** command, which discards the value of the first argument and shifts the remaining values down one position. Thus, after executing the **shift** command, the shell variable $9 contains the value of the 10th argument. To access the 11th and subsequent arguments, you simply execute the **shift** command the appropriate number of times.

Exit Codes

The shell variable $? holds the numeric exit status of the most recently completed command. By convention, an exit status of zero denotes successful completion; other values denote error conditions of various sorts. You can set the error code in a script by issuing the **exit** command, which terminates the script and posts the specified exit status. The format of the command is:

```
$ exit status
```

where *status* is a nonnegative integer that specifies the exit status.

Conditional Logic

A shell script can employ conditional logic, which lets the script take different action based on the values of arguments, shell variables, or other conditions. The **test** command lets you specify a condition, which can be either true or false. Conditional commands (including the **if**, **case**, **while**, and **until** commands) use the **test** command to evaluate conditions.

The test command

Table 13-7 describes some argument forms commonly used with the **test** command. The **test** command evaluates its arguments and sets the exit status to zero, which indicates that the specified condition was true, or a nonzero value, which indicates that the specified condition was false.

Table 13-7. Commonly used argument forms of the test command

Form	Function
-d *file*	The specified file exists and is a directory.
-e *file*	The specified file exists.
-r *file*	The specified file exists and is readable.
-s *file*	The specified file exists and has nonzero size.
-w *file*	The specified file exists and is writable.
-x *file*	The specified file exists and is executable.
-L *file*	The specified file exists and is a symbolic link.
f1 -nt *f2*	File *f1* is newer than file *f2*.
f1 -ot *f2*	File *f1* is older than file *f2*.
-n *s1*	String *s1* has nonzero length.
-z *s1*	String *s1* has zero length.
s1 = *s2*	String *s1* is the same as string *s2*.
s1 != *s2*	String *s1* is not the same as string *s2*.
n1 -eq *n2*	Integer *n1* is equal to integer *n2*.
n1 -ge *n2*	Integer *n1* is greater than or equal to integer *n2*.

Table 13-7. Commonly used argument forms of the test command (continued)

Form	Function
n1 -gt *n2*	Integer *n1* is greater than integer *n2*.
n1 -le *n2*	Integer *n1* is less than or equal to integer *n2*.
n1 -lt *n2*	Integer *n1* is less than integer *n2*.
n1 -ne *n2*	Integer *n1* is not equal to integer *n2*.
!	The NOT operator, which reverses the value of the following condition.
-a	The AND operator, which joins two conditions. Both conditions must be true for the overall result to be true.
-o	The OR operator, which joins two conditions. If either condition is true, the overall result is true.
\(... \)	You can group expressions within the test command by enclosing them within \(and \).

To see the **test** command in action, consider the following script:

```
test -d $1
echo $?
```

This script tests whether its first argument specifies a directory and displays the resulting exit status, a zero or a nonzero value that reflects the result of the test.

If the script was stored in the file *tester*, which permitted execute access, executing the script might yield results similar to the following:

```
$ ./tester /
0
$ ./tester /missing
1
```

These results indicate that the root directory (/) exists and that the /missing directory does not.

The if command

The **test** command is not of much use by itself, but combined with commands such as the **if** command, it is useful indeed. The **if** command has the following form:

```
if command
then
 commands
else
 commands
fi
```

The command that usually follows **if** is a **test** command. However, this need not be so. The **if** command merely executes the specified command and tests its exit status. If the exit status is zero, the first set of commands is executed; otherwise, the second set of commands is executed. An abbreviated form of the **if** command does nothing if the specified condition is false:

```
if command
then
 commands
fi
```

When you type an **if** command, it occupies several lines; nevertheless, it's considered a single command. To underscore this, the shell provides a special prompt, called the *secondary prompt*, after you enter each line. You won't see the secondary prompt when entering a script using a text editor, or any other shell prompt for that matter.

As an example, suppose you want to delete a file, *file1*, if it's older than another file, *file2*. The following command would accomplish the desired result:

```
if test file1 -ot file2
then
  rm file1
fi
```

You could incorporate this command in a script that accepts arguments specifying the filenames:

```
if test $1 -ot $2
then
  rm $1
  echo Deleted the old file.
fi
```

If you name the script *riddance* and invoke it as follows:

```
$ riddance thursday wednesday
```

the script will delete the *thursday* file if that file is older than the *wednesday* file.

The case command

The **case** command provides a more sophisticated form of conditional processing:

```
case value in
  pattern1) commands ;;
  pattern2) commands ;;
  ...
esac
```

The **case** command attempts to match the specified value against a series of patterns. The commands associated with the first matching pattern, if any, are executed. Patterns are built using characters and metacharacters, such as those used to specify command arguments. As an example, here's a **case** command that interprets the value of the first argument of its script:

```
case $1 in
  -r) echo Force deletion without confirmation ;;
  -i) echo Confirm before deleting ;;
   *) echo Unknown argument ;;
esac
```

The command echoes a different line of text, depending on the value of the script's first argument. As done here, it's good practice to include a final pattern that matches any value.

The while command

The **while** command lets you execute a series of commands iteratively (that is, repeatedly) so long as a condition tests true:

```
while command
do
  commands
done
```

Here's a script that uses a **while** command to print its arguments on successive lines:

```
echo $1
while shift 2> /dev/null
do
  echo $1
done
```

Notice how the 2> operator is used to direct error messages to the device */dev/null*, which prevents them from being seen. You can omit this operator if you prefer.

The commands that comprise the **do** part of a **while** (or any other loop command) can include **if**, **case**, and even other **while** commands. However, scripts rapidly become difficult to understand when this occurs often. You should include conditional commands within other conditional commands only with due consideration for the clarity of the result. Don't forget to include comments in your scripts (with each commented line beginning with a #) to clarify difficult constructs.

The until command

The **until** command lets you execute a series of commands iteratively (that is, repeatedly) so long as a condition tests false:

```
until command
do
  commands
done
```

Here's a script that uses an **until** command to print its arguments on successive lines, until it encounters an argument that has the value *red*:

```
until test $1 = red
do
  echo $1
  shift
done
```

For example, if the script were named *stopandgo* and stored in the current working directory, the command:

```
$ ./stopandgo green yellow red blue
```

would print the lines:

```
green
yellow
```

The for command

The **for** command iterates over the elements of a specified list:

```
for variable in list
do
 commands
done
```

Within the commands, you can reference the current element of the list by means of the shell variable *$variable*, where *variable* is the name specified following the **for**. The list typically takes the form of a series of arguments, which can incorporate metacharacters. For example, the following **for** command:

```
for i in 2 4 6 8
do
   echo $i
done
```

prints the numbers 2, 4, 6, and 8 on successive lines.

A special form of the **for** command iterates over the arguments of a script:

```
for variable
do
 commands
done
```

For example, the following script prints its arguments on successive lines:

```
for i
do
   echo $i
done
```

The break and continue commands

The **break** and **continue** commands are simple commands that take no arguments. When the shell encounters a **break** command, it immediately exits the body of the enclosing loop (**while**, **until**, or **for**) command. When the shell encounters a **continue** command, it immediately discontinues the current iteration of the loop. If the loop condition permits, other iterations may occur; otherwise the loop is exited.

Periscope: A Useful Networking Script

Suppose you have a free email account such as that provided by Yahoo! You're traveling and find yourself in a remote location with web access. However, you're unable to access files on your home machine or check email that has arrived there. This is a common circumstance, especially if your business requires that you travel.

If your home computer runs Windows, you're pretty much out of luck. You'll find it extraordinarily difficult to access your home computer from afar. However, if your home computer runs Linux, gaining access is practically a piece of cake.

In order to show the power of shell scripts, this subsection explains a more complex shell script, *periscope*. At an appointed time each day, *periscope* causes your computer (which you must leave powered on) to establish a PPP connection to your ISP, which is maintained for about one hour. This provides you enough time to connect to an ISP from your hotel room or other remote location and then connect via the Internet with your home Linux system, avoiding long-distance charges. Once connected, you have about an hour to view or download mail and perform other work. Then, *periscope* breaks its PPP connection, which it will reestablish at the appointed time the next day.

The following code shows the *periscope* script file, which is considerably larger than any script you've so far encountered in this chapter. Therefore, we'll disassemble the script, explaining it line by line. As you'll see, each line is fairly simple in itself, and the lines work together in a straightforward fashion.

```
1   route del default
2   wvdial &
3   sleep 1m
4   ifconfig | mail username@mail.com
5   sleep 1h
6   killall wvdial
7   sleep 2s
8   killall -9 wvdial
9   killall pppd
10  sleep 2s
11  killall -9 pppd
12  echo "/root/periscope" | at 10:00
```

Here's the line-by-line analysis of the *periscope* script:

1. route del default

   This line is perhaps the most complex line of the entire script. The **route** command is normally issued by the system administrator. You've probably never issued the command yourself, because **neat** or another network configuration program has issued it on your behalf. The effect of the command is to delete the default network route, if any. The default route is the one along which TCP/IP sends packets when it knows no specific route to their specified destination. It's necessary to delete the default route because the **wvdial** program, which the script uses to establish its PPP connection, will not override an existing default route.

2. wvdial &

   This line launches the **wvdial** program. As specified by the ampersand (&), the program will run in the background, so the script continues executing while **wvdial** starts up and runs.

3. sleep 1m

   This line pauses the script for one minute, giving **wvdial** time to establish the PPP connection.

4. `ifconfig | mail username@mail.com`

   This line runs the **ifconfig** command and mails its output to the specified user (you must replace *username@mail.com* with your own email address, which you can access remotely).

   The **ifconfig** command produces output that looks something like this:

   ```
   ppp0   Link encap:Point-Point Protocol
          inet addr:10.144.153.105  P-t-P:10.144.153.52 Mask:255.255.255.0
          UP POINTOPOINT RUNNING  MTU:552  Metric:1
          RX packets:0 errors:0 dropped:0 overruns:0
          TX packets:0 errors:0 dropped:0 overruns:0
   ```

   You'll probably see other sections in the output that describe your Ethernet interface (eth0) and a loopback device (lo). The `inet addr` given in the command output (`10.144.153.105`) is the IP address of your computer. By mailing the output to yourself, you provide a simple way to discover your computer's IP address, which is likely to be different each time it connects to your ISP.

5. `sleep 1h`

   This line causes the script to pause for an interval of one hour. You can easily change this interval to something more appropriate to your own needs.

6. `killall wvdial`

   Now that the connection interval has elapsed, the last line terminates all executing instances of the **wvdial** program.

    Appendix D briefly describes the **killall** command and other possibly unfamiliar commands employed in this script.

7. `sleep 2s`

   The script then pauses for two seconds, to ensure that **wvdial** has completely terminated.

8. `killall -9 wvdial`

   Under some circumstances, a program will ignore a termination request. This line deals with this possibility by sending a special code that compels a reluctant program to terminate without further delay.

9. `killall pppd`

   Behind the scenes, **wvdial** launches a program known as **pppd**, which actually establishes and manages the PPP connection. Another **killall** command is designed to terminate **pppd** if **wvdial** has failed to do so.

10. `sleep 2s`

    Again, the script pauses for a few seconds. This time, it does so to ensure that **pppd** has completely terminated.

11. `killall -9 pppd`

And, again, the script uses the **-9** option to specify that any remaining instances of **pppd** should terminate immediately.

12. `echo "/root/periscope" | at 10:00`

Finally, the script uses the **at** command to schedule itself for execution at 10:00 tomorrow. The **at** command reads one or more commands from its standard input and executes them at the time specified as an argument.

To try the script for yourself, you must have installed the *wvdial* program, as explained in Chapter 10. Place the script in the file */root/periscope*. Of course, you'll probably want to customize the script to specify an appointment time and duration of your own choosing. To start *periscope*, log in as *root* and issue the command:

```
# (echo "/root/periscope" | at 10:00)&
```

The parentheses cause the **&** operator to apply to the entire command, not just the **at**. When 10:00 a.m. (or any other time you specify) comes around, your Linux system should obediently dial your ISP and maintain the connection for the specified interval of time.

Using Periscope

At the appointed time, fire up your computer and access your email account. You should find a mail message that contains the **ifconfig** output giving your computer's current IP address. Now you can use *telnet* or an *ssh* client—your choice corresponds to the server you're running on your Linux system—to contact your computer and work for the remainder of the specified connection time. At the end of the connection time, your Linux system will sever its PPP connection and begin counting down until it's again time to connect.

Linux Directory Tree

Table A-1 describes the directories in the Linux directory tree.

Table A-1. The Linux directory tree

Directory	Description
/bin	User programs and scripts essential to system startup
/boot	Boot information, including the kernel
/dev	Device files
/etc	Host-specific configuration files
/etc/sysconfig	Stores configuration files specific to Red Hat Linux
/home	Users' home directories
/initrd	Used during boot process as a mount point for a directory containing special device drivers
/lib	Libraries, modules, and other object files
/lib/modules	Loadable kernel modules
/lost+found	Recovered data from bad clusters
/mnt	Temporarily mounted filesystems
/opt	Used to store large applications
/proc	Kernel pseudo-directory that provides access to kernel information and configuration items
/root	System administrator's home directory
/sbin	System administration programs and scripts essential to system startup
/tmp	Temporary files, which are automatically deleted by Red Hat Linux
/usr	Files needed for system operation but not needed to boot system (can be mounted read-only, except when being changed by root user)
/usr/bin	Programs and scripts not essential to system startup
/usr/dict	System dictionaries for spell checking
/usr/etc	Configuration files
/usr/games	Game files
/usr/include	C/C++ header files

Directory	Description
/usr/kerberos	Kerberos files
/usr/lib	Libraries and kernel modules
/usr/libexec	Libraries stored in alternate formats
/usr/local	Locally defined directory tree (structure is similar to that of /usr)
/usr/sbin	System administration programs and scripts not essential to system start up
/usr/share	Shared files
/usr/share/doc	Documentation (formerly residing in /usr/doc)
/usr/share/man	Manpages
/usr/src	Source files
/usr/src/linux	Linux kernel source
/usr/X11R6	X-related files
/var	Dynamic files, such as log files and spool files
/var/arpwatch	Data used by arpwatch
/var/cache	Application cache data
/var/ftp	Data used by the FTP server
/var/gdm	Data used by the GNOME display manager
/var/kerberos	Data used by Kerberos
/var/lib	Variable state information
/var/lib/rpm	Files related to RPM
/var/local	Locally defined data
/var/lock	Lock files
/var/log	Log files and directories
/var/named	Data used by BIND (named)
/var/opt	Data used by applications in /opt
/var/run	Process IDs of running processes
/var/spool	Application spool data
/var/spool/anacron	Anacron's spool data
/var/spool/at	At's spool data
/var/spool/cron	Cron's spool data
/var/spool/fax	Fax's spool data
/var/spool/lpd	Printer queues
/var/spool/mail	Mail boxes
/var/spool/mqueue	Mail queue
/var/spool/news	USENET News spool data
/var/spool/rwho	Rwho spool data
/var/spool/samba	Samba spool data

Table A-1. The Linux directory tree (continued)

Directory	Description
/var/spool/slrnpull	Slrnpull spool data
/var/spool/squid	Squid spool data
/var/spool/uucp	UUCP spool data
/var/spool/uucpublic	Public UUCP spool data
/var/spool/up2date	Files used by Red Hat Update Agent
/var/tmp	Temporary files preserved between system reboots
/var/tux	Files used by Tux
/var/www	Files used by Apache
/var/yp	Files used by NIS

For more information on the Linux directory tree, see the current version of the Linux Filesystem Hierarchy Standard (*http://www.pathname.com/fhs*). Red Hat Linux generally complies with that standard.

Principal Linux Files

Table B-1 describes the principal Linux files. You can use it, for example, to help you locate configuration files quickly.

Table B-1. Principal Linux files

File(s)	Description
/boot/grub/grub.conf	GRUB configuration file
/boot/module-info-*	Module information for the Linux kernel
/boot/System.map-*	Map of the Linux kernel
/boot/vmlinuz-*	Linux kernel
/etc/aliases	Mail aliases
/etc/at.deny	User IDs of users forbidden to use the **at** command
/etc/auto.master	Configuration file for the *autofs* daemon, which automatically mounts filesystems
/etc/auto.misc	Automounter map file
/etc/bashrc	Systemwide functions and aliases for the *bash* shell
/etc/cron.daily/*	Daily *cron* jobs
/etc/cron.hourly/*	Hourly *cron* jobs
/etc/cron.monthly/*	Monthly *cron* jobs
/etc/cron.weekly/*	Weekly *cron* jobs
/etc/crontab	System *cron* file
/etc/csh.cshrc	C shell initialization file
/etc/csh.login	C shell login file
/etc/default/useradd	Defaults for the **useradd** command
/etc/DIR_COLORS	Directory listing colors
/etc/exports	NFS exported directories
/etc/filesystems	Supported filesystem types
/etc/fstab	Filesystems mounted or available for mounting
/etc/group	System group definitions

Table B-1. Principal Linux files (continued)

File(s)	Description
/etc/host.conf	Resolver configuration file
/etc/hosts	Map of IP numbers to hostnames
/etc/hosts.allow	Hosts allowed to access Internet services
/etc/hosts.deny	Hosts forbidden to access Internet services
/etc/httpd/conf/*	Apache configuration files
/etc/httpd/httpd.conf	Web server configuration file
/etc/initlog.conf	Logging configuration file
/etc/inittab	Configuration for the *init* daemon, which controls executing processes
/etc/issue	Linux kernel and distribution version
/etc/ld.so.conf	Shared library configuration file
/etc/login.defs	Options for **useradd** and related commands
/etc/logrotate.conf	Log rotation configuration file
/etc/logrotate.d/*	Scripts to rotate logs
/etc/lpd.conf	Printer configuration file
/etc/lpd.perms	Printer spooler permissions file
/etc/mail/*	Mail server configuration files
/etc/mailcap	*metamail* MIME information
/etc/man.config	*man* configuration file
/etc/mime.types	MIME types
/etc/mime-magic*	Magic numbers for MIME data
/etc/minicom.users	User IDs allowed to use *minicom*
/etc/modules.conf	Aliases and options for loadable kernel modules
/etc/motd	Message of the day
/etc/mtab	Mounted filesystems
/etc/named.conf	BIND configuration file
/etc/nscd.conf	BIND cache configuration file
/etc/nsswitch.conf	Resolver configuration file
/etc/openldap/*	Open LDAP configuration files
/etc/pam.d/*	PAM configuration files
/etc/paper.config	Paper sizes
/etc/passwd	User account information
/etc/ppp/*	PPP configuration
/etc/printcap	Printer options and capabilities
/etc/profile	Default environment for users of the *bash* shell
/etc/profile.d/*	Shell initialization
/etc/protocols	Protocol names and numbers

Table B-1. Principal Linux files (continued)

File(s)	Description
/etc/pwdb.conf	*pwdb* library configuration
/etc/rc	Scripts for system and process startup and shutdown
/etc/init.d/*	SysV initialization scripts
/etc/rc.local	Local startup script
/etc/rc.sysinit	System initialization file
/etc/rc?.d/*	Service start/stop scripts
/etc/rndc.conf	BIND control configuration
/etc/rpc	RPC program number database
/etc/rpm/*	RPM database and configuration files
/etc/samba/*	Samba configuration files
/etc/securetty	Secure tty configuration
/etc/security/*	PAM configuration files
/etc/sensors.conf	*libsensors* configuration file
/etc/services	Standard service names and numbers
/etc/shadow	Secure user account information
/etc/skel	Skeleton files used to establish new user accounts
/etc/ssh/*	SSH configuration files
/etc/sysconfig/*	System configuration files
/etc/sysconfig/network-scripts/*	Network adapter configuration files
/etc/sysctl.conf	*sysctl* configuration file
/etc/syslog.conf	System logging process configuration
/etc/termcap	Terminal capabilities and options
/etc/tux.mime.types	MIME types for Tux web server
/etc/updatedb.conf	*updatedb*/*locate* configuration file
/etc/vsftpd*	FTP configuration files
/etc/wvdial.conf	GNOME dialer configuration file
/etc/X11/applnk/*	X application shortcuts
/etc/X11/fs/config	X font server configuration
/etc/X11/gdm/*	GNOME display manager configuration
/etc/X11/prefdm	Display manager configuration file
/etc/X11/xdm/*	X display manager configuration file
/etc/X11/XF86Config	X configuration file
/etc/X11/xinit/Xclients	Default script for *xinit*
/etc/X11/xinit/xinitrc	X session initialization file
/etc/X11/Xmodmap	Key mappings used by *xdm* and *xinit*
/etc/xinetd.conf	General *xinetd* configuration file

Table B-1. Principal Linux files (continued)

File(s)	Description
/etc/xinetd.d/*	*xinetd* configuration files for specific servers
/etc/yp.conf	Yellow Pages (NIS) configuration file
/home/*/public_html	User web pages
/root/.bash_history	*bash* command history for system administrator
/root/.bash_logout	*bash* logout script for system administrator
/root/.bash_profile	*bash* initialization script for system administrator
/root/.bashrc	*bash* options for system administrator
/root/.Xresources	X resources for system administrator
/usr/share/config/*	Miscellaneous configuration files
/usr/share/fonts/*	Fonts
/usr/share/ssl/openssl.cnf	SSL certificate configuration
/usr/X11R6/lib/X11/app-defaults/*	X application defaults
/usr/X11R6/lib/X11/fonts/*	X fonts
/var/ftp/*	FTP files
/var/log/cron	Log of *cron* activity
/var/log/httpd/access_log	Log of web server access
/var/log/httpd/error_log	Log of web server errors
/var/log/lastlog	Last login log
/var/log/boot.log	Boot messages
/var/log/cron	*Cron* log
/var/log/dmesg	Kernel message log
/var/log/maillog	Mail transfer log
/var/log/messages	System log
/var/log/rpmpkgs	RPM package installation log
/var/log/samba/*	Samba logs
/var/log/secure	System security log
/var/log/up2date	Up2date log
/var/named/*	BIND configuration
/var/www/cgi-bin	CGI scripts
/var/www/html/*	Web pages
/var/yp/*	Yellow Pages (NIS) configuration files

Managing the Boot Process

In this appendix, you'll learn more about how to boot a Linux system; in particular, you'll learn more about configuring your computer system to boot any of several operating systems. The appendix focuses on GNU GRUB, the Grand Unified Boot-loader, the most popular utility for booting Linux systems.

Booting Linux

When you boot a PC, you cause it to execute a small program known as a *boot loader*. The purpose of the boot loader is to locate and read into memory the first stage of an operating system and transfer control to it. The operating system then locates and reads its remaining components as needed.

The simplest way to boot Linux is by using a floppy diskette. By doing so, you're able to leave the boot information on your hard drive untouched, ensuring that you can still boot Microsoft Windows or another operating system stored on the same hard drive. Moreover, some operating systems and virus protection programs prevent modification of the boot information on your hard drive. By booting from a floppy diskette, you avoid several potential problems.

However, many users find booting from a floppy disk slow or inconvenient. You don't have to boot Linux from a floppy diskette; you can boot it in any of several other ways. The most popular method is by using GRUB, which replaces the boot loader stored on your hard drive.

This appendix cannot describe the entire range of issues involved in booting Linux. Much of the information here is taken from several Linux HOWTOs that contain additional useful information on booting Linux:

- BootPrompt-HOWTO
- CD-Writing-HOWTO
- CDROM-HOWTO

- Ethernet-HOWTO
- Ftape-HOWTO
- Hardware-HOWTO
- Multi-Disk-HOWTO
- PCI-HOWTO
- PCMCIA-HOWTO

Boot Floppies

Even if you don't want to boot Linux from a floppy diskette, you should create and keep on hand a Linux boot floppy. If something goes wrong with your system, preventing you from booting in the normal way, you may be able to boot your system by using the floppy. Then, you can diagnose and repair the problem and get back to business as usual.

Creating a Boot Floppy

The Red Hat install program gives you the option of creating a boot diskette when you install Linux. You should exercise this option each time you install Linux, so that you have a fresh boot floppy containing software consistent with that stored on your hard drive.

However, you can easily create a boot diskette after the installation is complete. To do so, insert a blank floppy diskette into your system's floppy drive. Log on as *root* and issue the following command:

```
# /sbin/mkbootdisk version
```

For *version*, supply the version number of your kernel. If you don't recall the version, execute the following command, which reports it:

```
# uname -a
```

The version number resembles the version number of an RPM package. For example, a typical kernel version number is 2.4.18-14.

The **mkbootdisk** command creates a boot floppy that uses the same kernel running when the command is issued. It also configures the boot floppy to load any necessary SCSI modules, so that your SCSI drives will be accessible after booting from the floppy.

Using a Boot Floppy

Insert the boot floppy into your system's floppy drive. If your system is turned off, power up your system. If your system is turned on, first shut down the active operating system in the proper manner, then restart the system. Linux should then boot from the floppy.

 To use your boot floppy, your system's CMOS must be configured to allow booting from the floppy drive. If your system boots from its hard drive even when the boot floppy is present, you must change your system's CMOS configuration. The relevant option is generally named Boot Sequence, Boot Order, or something similar. The value you want is generally labeled *A:*, *C:*, or something similar. Consult your system's documentation for further information.

The GRUB Loader

Most PCs can be booted from a floppy drive or hard drive; most recently manufactured computers can be booted from a CD-ROM drive. The first sector of a disk, diskette, or partition is known as the *boot sector*. The boot sector associated with a disk or diskette (the first sector of the disk or diskette) is known as the *Master Boot Record* (MBR). In order for a diskette or disk to be bootable, it must contain a boot loader, which can reside in:

- The boot sector of the floppy diskette
- The MBR of the first hard disk or the first CD-ROM drive, if the PC supports booting from a CD-ROM
- The boot sector of a Linux filesystem partition on the first hard disk
- The boot sector of an extended partition on the first hard disk

GRUB is a sophisticated boot loader that can load Linux, Microsoft Windows 3.*x* and 9*x*, NT, 2000, XP, and other popular operating systems. Most users install GRUB on the MBR of their system's first hard disk. That way, when the system is started, it boots GRUB, which can be used to load Linux, Microsoft Windows, or another operating system.

Unless you direct otherwise, the Red Hat Linux installation procedure automatically installs GRUB. So you don't need to install GRUB; you just need to configure it.

Similarly, when you boot by using GRUB, you can also boot parameters to control the boot process; you can specify GRUB's boot parameters by selecting an operating system from GRUB's menu and pressing **e**. In response, GRUB displays an editor screen that shows the commands associated with the selected operating system, as shown in Figure C-1.

Commands that can be used in the editor screen are listed in Table C-1.

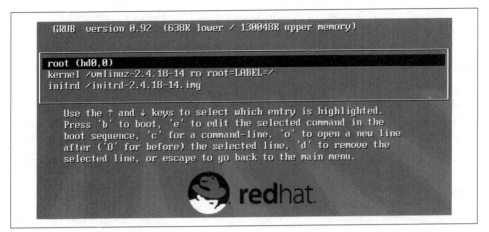

Figure C-1. The GRUB editor screen

Table C-1. GRUB editor commands

Command	Meaning
b	Boot the currently selected operating system.
e	Edit the currently selected GRUB command.
c	Open a screen for interactively entering and executing GRUB commands.
o	Enter a new command after the currently selected command.
O	Enter a new command before the currently selected command.
d	Delete the currently selected command.
Esc	Return to the main GRUB menu.

The principal GRUB commands are:

chainloader
> Used to load a Microsoft operating system, including DOS, Windows 3.*x*, 9*x*, NT, or 2000.

initrd
> Specifies the file containing an initial RAM disk used in loading Linux. This command is necessary, for instance, when booting Linux from a SCSI drive.

kernel
> Specifies the file containing the Linux kernel to be booted.

root
rootnoverify
> Specifies the partition to be mounted as the root partition. The **root** command causes the filesystem to be verified before the partition is mounted.

GRUB refers to hard disks using the syntax (hdn), where n specifies the device number assigned by the system BIOS. For example, (hd0) refers to the first hard drive.

Partitions are designated by the related syntax (hd*n,m*), where *m* is the number of the partition. For example, (hd1,0) refers to the first partition of the second hard drive.

GRUB can refer to the disk blocks that comprise a file by using a special syntax known as a *blocklist*. A blocklist consists of a comma-separated list of block ranges, each of which consists of a starting block number, followed by a plus sign (+), followed by the number of blocks in the range. For example, the blocklist 0+1,10+20 refers to a block range beginning at block 0 and including 1 block and a block range beginning at block 10 and including 20 blocks.

If the starting block number of a block range is omitted, the block range is implied to begin with block 0. For example, the block range +1 begins at block 0 and includes 1 block.

A blocklist can appear after a reference to a partition; if no partition is identified, the partition identified by the preceding **root** command is implied. For example, in:

```
root (hd0,0)
chainlist +1
```

the blocklist +1 is implicitly associated with (hd0,0) and is equivalent to the blocklist (hd0,0)+1.

A typical GRUB entry for booting Linux resembles the following:

```
root (hd0,0)
kernel /boot/vmlinuz-2.4.18-14 root=LABEL=/
initrd /initrd-2.4.18-14.img
```

This entry boots the specified kernel residing on partition 0 of the first hard drive, mounting the partition labelled "/" as the root partition. Linux boot parameters, such as those described in the upcoming section "Boot Parameters," can be specified by using the **kernel** command.

If the kernel requires access to special drivers residing on a RAM disk, a RAM disk can be identified as in this entry:

```
root (hd0,0)
kernel /boot/vmlinuz-2.4.18-14 ro root=LABEL=/
initrd /initrd-2.4.18-14.img
```

Notice that the name of the RAM disk file is specified as though the file resides in the root directory, whereas it actually resides in the */boot* directory. This is necessary because GRUB initially mounts the */boot* filesystem, as specified in the preceding **root** command. The mounted filesystem is treated by GRUB as its root filesystem.

A typical GRUB entry for booting a Microsoft operating system has this form:

```
rootnoverify (hd0,0)
chainloader +1
```

This entry boots the Microsoft operating system residing on partition 0 of the first hard drive. The blocklist +1 points to the first block of the root partition. Microsoft operating systems place their boot file at this location.

To boot your system, GRUB uses your system's BIOS, which may not be able to load a Linux kernel (or other program) stored beyond cylinder 1023 of your hard drive. Booting a kernel stored beyond cylinder 1023 requires a motherboard that supports *logical byte addressing* (LBA). Most motherboards manufactured in the last several years are supposed to support LBA. Unfortunately, some motherboards that claim to support LBA do not. If you're installing Linux on a preexisting hard drive, you may not be able to place your Linux kernel in an appropriate location. In that case, you won't be able to use GRUB to boot your system.

To learn more about GRUB, see the following resources:

- The manpage for GRUB
- The GRUB home page, *http://www.gnu.org/software/grub*
- The Multiboot-with-GRUB mini HOWTO, *http://www.redhat.com/mirrors/LDP/ HOWTO/mini/Multiboot-with-GRUB.html*

Boot Parameters

Boot parameters are specified using a three-part directive that includes the name of the parameter and an optional list of options, which consists of an equal sign (=) followed by a comma-separated list of option values

No spaces may appear in the directive. As an example, the following directive specifies the identity of the Linux root partition:

```
root=/dev/hda1
```

The installation program generally refers to partitions by using labels, so that you can boot a system even if you move the partitions around. A root directive referring to a label looks like this:

```
root=LABEL=/usr
```

You can specify multiple directives by separating them with a space. For example, the following specifies the identity of the Linux root partition and that the root partition is initially mounted read-only, so that a thorough check of its filesystem can be performed:

```
root=/dev/hda1 ro
```

Most directives are interpreted by the kernel, though GRUB is also capable of processing directives. If you specify a directive that neither the kernel nor GRUB understands (assuming you're using GRUB), a directive that includes an equal sign is passed to the *init* process as an environment variable. You learned about environment variables in Chapter 7. A nonkernel directive that doesn't include an equal sign is passed to the *init* process. An example of this usage is specifying the directive `single`, which causes *init* to start your system in single-user mode:

```
root=/dev/hda1 ro single
```

General Boot Arguments

Table C-2 describes some of the most popular and useful boot arguments. These arguments apply to your system as a whole; in subsequent sections, you'll learn about other boot arguments that apply to specific devices or functions. In addition to boot arguments previously introduced, the table describes the reserve argument, which is helpful in avoiding system memory conflicts.

Table C-2. Selected general boot arguments

Argument	Description and options
init=	Specifies arguments passed by the kernel to the init process.
mem=	Specifies the amount of physical memory available to Linux; lets you instruct Linux to avoid high memory areas used by some systems for BIOS or caching. You can specify the amount as a hexadecimal number or as a decimal number followed by k or M, denoting kilobytes or megabytes, respectively.
reserve=	Specifies I/O ports that must not be probed. The port number is specified by using a hexadecimal number, and the range is specified by using a decimal number. For example, reserve=0x320,32 specifies that I/O ports 320-33f must not be probed.
ro	Initially mounts the root filesystem in read-only mode, so that a more effective filesystem check can be done.
root=	Identifies the root filesystem:
	/dev/fdn
	Floppy disk *n* (0 or 1)
	/dev/hdxn
	Partition *n* of IDE drive *x* (a to d)
	/dev/sdxn
	Partition *n* of SCSI drive *x* (a to e)
rw	Initially mounts the root filesystem in read/write mode; does not perform a filesystem check.
vga=	Specifies the default display mode set before booting. Specifying vga=ask will cause *lilo* to list the available video modes. You can then specify the desired mode in place of ask. (This argument is interpreted by *lilo* and will have no effect if another loader is used.)

RAM Disk Boot Arguments

Table C-3 describes four boot arguments used in working with RAM disks. You won't likely need to specify any of these, but knowing about them may help you understand boot specifications written by others, including those used by Red Hat Linux.

Table C-3. Selected RAM disk arguments

Argument	Description and options
load_ramdisk=	Specifies that a RAM disk is not to be loaded (0) or is to be loaded (1).
prompt_ramdisk=	Specifies whether to provide a prompt instructing the user to insert a floppy containing a RAM disk (1) or provide no such prompt (0).
ramdisk_size=	Specifies the amount of RAM to be allocated to a RAM disk. If not specified, the default is 4 MB.
ramdisk_start=	Specifies the offset (in disk blocks from the start of the boot media) of the RAM disk data; lets a kernel and RAM disk data occupy the same floppy disk.

SCSI Host Adapter Boot Arguments

Table C-4 describes the most often used boot arguments related to SCSI host adapters. Table C-5 describes the options used by the SCSI host adapter boot arguments and other boot arguments.

Table C-4. Selected SCSI host adapter arguments

Argument	Description and options
advansys=	Advansys SCSI host adapter: `iobase,[iobase,[iobase,[iobase]]]`
aha152x=	Adaptec aha151x, ada152x, aic6260, aic6360, and SB16-SCSI SCSI host adapters: `iobase[,irq[,scsi_id[,reconnect[,parity]]]]`
aha1542=	Adaptec aha154x SCSI host adapter: `iobase[,buson,busoff[,dmaspeed]]`
aic7xxx=	Adaptec aha274x, aha284x, aic7xxx SCSI host adapters: `extended,no_reset`
AM53C974=	AMD AM53C974-based SCSI host adapters: `scsi-id,dev_id,dmaspeed,offset` See the file *linux/drivers/scsi/README.AM53C974*.
buslogic=	BusLogic SCSI controller. Many options are available. See the BootPrompt-HOWTO.
eata=	EATA SCSI host adapter: `iobase,[iobase,[iobase,[iobase]]]`
fdomain=	Future Domain SCSI controller: `iobase,irq[,scsi_id]`
in2000=	Always SCSI host adapter. The driver for the Always SCSI controller accepts options in somewhat different format than other drivers. See the Boot Prompt-HOWTO.
max-scsi-luns=	Specifies the maximum number of SCSI logical units to be probed; lets you avoid probing devices that might lock up the SCSI bus.

ncr5380=	NCR 5380-based SCSI host adapters:
	`iobase,irq,dma`
	`membase,irq,dma`

ncr53c400=	NCR 53c400-based SCSI host adapters:
	`iobase,irq,pio`
	`membase,irq,pio`

ncr53c406a=	NCR 53c406a-based SCSI host adapters:
	`iobase,irq,pio`
	`membase,irq,pio`

pas16=	Pro Audio Spectrum SCSI host adapter: `iobase,irq`
ppa=	Iomega parallel port SCSI adapter for ZIP drive: `iobase,speed_high,speed_low,nybble`
st0x=	Seagate ST-0x SCSI host adapter: `membase,irq`

Table C-4. Selected SCSI host adapter arguments (continued)

Argument	Description and options
t128=	Trantor T128 SCSI host adapter: `membase,irq`
tmc8xx=	Future Domain TMC-8xx and TMC-950 SCSI host adapters: `membase,irq`
u14-34f=	Ultrastor SCSI host adapter: `iobase,[iobase,[iobase,[iobase]]]`
wd7000=	Western Digital WD7000 SCSI host adapter: `irq,dma,iobase`

For example, from Table C-4 you can learn that Adaptec aha154x SCSI host adapters use a boot argument having the form:

```
iobase[,buson,busoff[,dmaspeed]]
```

Table C-5 helps you understand the form of the *iobase* option and the other italicized options. The *iobase* option, for example, lets you specify the I/O port associated with the SCSI host adapter. For example, you can specify a boot argument for an Adaptec aha154x SCSI host adapter by writing only an *iobase* option; the remaining options are optional. However, as indicated by the square brackets, if you include a *buson* option, you must include a *busoff* option. Similarly, to include the *dmaspeed* option, you must include each of the other options. Here's an example of a complete boot argument:

```
aha1542=0x300,11,4
```

Table C-5. Selected boot prompt options

Option	Description and options
busoff	The interval (number of microseconds) during which the device will relinquish the ISA bus, specified as a decimal integer, for example, 4.
buson	The interval (number of microseconds) during which the device will dominate the ISA bus, specified as a decimal integer, for example, 11.
ctl	The I/O port used for control, specified as a hexadecimal number, for example, 0x300.
cyl,head,sect	The geometry of the storage device, specified as three integers denoting the number of cylinders, heads, and sectors, respectively.
dev_id	A SCSI device with which the host adapter communicates, specified as a decimal integer, for example, 2.
dma	The DMA (direct memory access) channel by used by the device, specified as a decimal integer, for example, 3.
dmaspeed	The rate (in MB/sec.) at which DMA transfers are performed, specified as a decimal integer, for example, 5.
extended	Whether extended translation for large disks is enabled (1) or not (0).

Table C-5. Selected boot prompt options (continued)

Option	Description and options
`magic_number`	Whether the driver attempts to work, even if the firmware version is unknown (79); other values are ignored.
`no_reset`	Whether the driver should reset the SCSI bus when setting up the host adapter at boot (1) or not (0).
`iobase`	An I/O port, specified as a hexadecimal number, for example, 0x300.
`irq`	A hardware interrupt number, specified as a decimal integer, for example, 5.
`is_pas_card`	Whether a Pro Audio Spectrum (PAS) card is used; otherwise, do not specify this option.
`membase`	The base address of a memory region used for memory-mapped I/O, specified as a hexadecimal number, for example, 0x2000.
`parity`	Whether the SCSI host adapter uses parity (1) or does not use parity (0).
`pio`	Whether `insl` and `outsl` multibyte instructions (1) or `inb` and `outb` single-byte instructions (0) are used.
`reconnect`	Whether the SCSI host adapter is allowed to disconnect and reconnect (1) or holds a connection until the operation is complete (0).
`scsi_id`	The ID by which the SCSI host adapter identifies itself, specified as a decimal integer, for example, 7.

To determine a proper value for options described in Table C-5, you must often know something about the hardware structure of your system. The procedures described in Chapter 2 will help you.

IDE Hard Drive and CD-ROM Boot Arguments

Table C-6 describes the most commonly used boot arguments associated with IDE hard drives and CD-ROM drives. Refer to Table C-5 to determine the form of the italicized options.

Table C-6. Selected IDE hard drive arguments

Argument	Description and options
`hdx=`	IDE hard drive or CD-ROM (x denotes the physical device and must be a letter from a to h):
	autotune Specifies that the driver should attempt to tune the interface to the fastest possible mode and speed
	cdrom Specifies that the drive is a CD-ROM drive
	cyl,head,sect Specifies the geometry of the drive
	none Specifies that the drive is not present—do not probe
	noprobe Specifies that the driver should not probe for the device
	nowerr Specifies that the `WRERR_STAT` bit should be ignored on this drive

Table C-6. Selected IDE hard drive arguments (continued)

Argument	Description and options
ide0=	IDE hard drive or CD-ROM:
	ali14xx Probe for and support the alil4xx interface
	cmd640_vlb Probe for and support the cmd640 chip (required for controllers using a VLB interface)
	dtc2278 Probe for and support the dtc2278 interface
	ht6560b Probe for and support the ht6560b interface
	qd6580 Probe for and support the qd6580 interface
	umc8672 Probe for and support the umc8672 interface
idex=	IDE hard drive or CD-ROM (*x* specifies the physical device and must be a digit from 0 to 3):
	autotune Specifies that the driver should attempt to tune the interface to the fastest possible mode and speed
	iobase Specifies the I/O port used by the drive
	iobase,ctl Specifies the I/O port and control port used by the drive
	iobase,ctl,irq Specifies the I/O port, control port, and IRQ used by the drive
	noautotune Specifies that the driver should not attempt to tune the interface for fastest mode and speed
	noprobe Specifies that the driver should not probe for the device
	serialize Specifies that I/O operations should not be overlapped

Non-IDE CD-ROM Drive Boot Arguments

Table C-7 describes the most common boot arguments for non-IDE CD-ROM drives. Refer to Table C-5 to determine the form of the italicized options.

Table C-7. Selected CD-ROM arguments

Argument	Description and options
aztcd=	Aztech CD-ROM: `iobase[,magic_number]`[a]
cdu31a=	Sony CDU-31A or CDU-33A CD-ROM: `iobase,[irq[,is_pas_card]`
sonycd535=	Sony CDU-535 CD-ROM: `iobase[,irq]`

Table C-7. Selected CD-ROM arguments (continued)

Argument	Description and options
gscd=	Goldstar CD-ROM: *iobase*
isp16=	ISP16 CD-ROM: *[port[,irq[,dma]]][[,]drive_type]*
mcd=	Mitsumi CD-ROM: *iobase,[irq[,wait_value]]*
optcd=	Optical Storage CD-ROM: *iobase*
cm206=	Phillips CD206 CD-ROM: *[iobase][,irq]*
sjcd=	Sanyo CD-ROM: *iobase[,irq[,dma_channel]]*
sbpcd=	SoundBlaster Pro CD-ROM: *iobase,type*

a Don't include the square brackets in your boot argument; they merely indicate which options must be present.

Floppy Drive Boot Arguments

A few systems require special boot arguments to best use their floppy drives. Table C-7 describes the most common boot arguments related to floppy drives. Floppy drives that are not well behaved may malfunction if you specify the daring option, which you should use only with care. For additional boot arguments related to floppy drives, see */usr/src/linux/Documentation/floppy.txt*.

Table C-8. Selected floppy disk arguments and options

Argument and option	Description
floppy=asus_pci	Specifies that only units 0 and 1 are allowed, to work around problem with BIOS of certain ASUS motherboards.
floppy=daring	Specifies that the floppy controller is well behaved, allowing more efficient operation.
floppy=0,daring	Specifies that the floppy controller may not be well behaved (default).
floppy=thinkpad	Specifies that the system is an IBM ThinkPad.
floppy=no_ unexpected_ interrupts or floppy=L40SX	Specifies that a message should be printed when an unexpected interrupt is received. This is required by IBM L40SX laptops in certain video modes.

Bus Mouse Boot Arguments

Two boot arguments provide bus mouse support. The first supports the Microsoft bus mouse:

    msmouse=irq

The second supports any non-Microsoft bus mouse:

```
bmouse=irq
```

Each argument accepts a single option specifying the IRQ associated with the mouse.

Parallel Port Printer Boot Arguments

The Linux printer driver claims all available parallel ports. If you want to access a device other than a printer attached to a parallel port, you must instruct the printer driver to reserve only the ports associated with printers. To do so, use the lp boot argument, which takes as its options a list of ports and IRQs used to support printers. For example, the following boot argument specifies two printers:

```
lp=0x3bc,0,0x378,7
```

The first printer is on port 0x3bc and the second is on port 0x378. The first printer uses a special IRQ-less mode known as polling, so its IRQ is specified as 0. The second printer uses IRQ 7.

To disable all printers, specify lp=0.

Loadable Ethernet Drivers

Early versions of Linux used a so-called monolithic kernel. At that time, Linux distributions typically included several kernels, offering support for a variety of devices that might be needed to boot and install a Linux system. Devices not needed to boot and install a system—so-called special devices—had second-class status. To access special devices, users had to compile customized kernels that included support for those devices. When adding a device to a system, users often had to compile a new kernel, which was something of an inconvenience.

More recent versions of Linux feature a modular kernel, which allows drivers to be dynamically loaded on command. This makes it much easier than before to configure your Linux system to support Ethernet cards and other special devices. Red Hat Linux is generally able to configure your primary Ethernet card automatically, by probing for it during installation of Linux.

However, the autoprobe doesn't always succeed. Moreover, if you have more than one Ethernet card, the installation program sets up only the first card it finds. To set up additional cards, you need to know a bit about Linux's loadable modules.

Dynamically Loading a Modular Driver

To dynamically load a modular driver, issue the following command:

```
# modprobe driver
```

where *driver* specifies the module to be loaded. As an example, the command:

```
# modprobe ne2k-pci
```

loads the modular driver for the PCI-based NE2000 Ethernet card.

To find out what network adapters are supported by Red Hat Linux or to find out what driver to use with a particular adapter, see the Red Hat Linux Hardware Compatibility List, *http://hardware.redhat.com*.

When a driver is loaded, it generally probes to locate the supported device. In case an autoprobe fails, most drivers let you specify the I/O port and IRQ by using a command like the following:

```
# modprobe ne2k=pci io=0x280 irq=11
```

Some cards support additional options; these are documented in the file */usr/src/linux/Documentation/networking/net-modules.txt*.

Loading Modular Drivers at Boot Time

The Linux kernel automatically loads modules specified in the module configuration file, */etc/modules.conf*. So, once you've determined the proper module and options required by your Ethernet card, you can add a line or two to the module configuration file so that your card will be made ready to operate each time you boot your system.

The **alias** directive associates a logical module name with an actual module. Logical module names specify types of devices; for example, *eth0* specifies the first Ethernet card in a system, and *eth1* specifies the second Ethernet card in a system. Suppose your system includes two Ethernet cards: a non-PCI-based NE2000 and an SMC EtherPower, which is based on DEC's TULIP chip. You could use the following directives to automatically load these modules at boot time:

```
alias eth0 ne
alias eth1 tulip
```

If a driver requires options, you can specify them by using an options directive, which has the following form:

```
options driver argument=value[,value,...] argument=value[,value,...] ...
```

For example, you might specify the I/O port and IRQ used by the NE2000 card like this:

```
options ne io=0x280 irq=12
```

Most ISA modules accept parameters like io=0x340 and irq=12 on the **insmod** command line. You should supply these parameters to avoid probing for the card. Unlike PCI and EISA devices, ISA devices sometimes cannot be safely autoprobed.

Administering Modular Drivers

The **lsmod** command, which takes no arguments, lists the loaded modular drivers. To unload a modular driver, specify the driver as the argument of the **modprobe** command and specify the -r argument. For example, to remove the ne driver, issue the command:

```
# modprobe -r ne
```

To unload every unused module—that is, every module not associated with an operational device—invoke the **rmmod** command and specify the -a argument:

```
# rmmod -a
```

You can't remove a module that's in use; therefore, you must shut down the device before removing it. To shut down an Ethernet device, you can use Neat. Or you can issue the following command:

```
# ifconfig ethn down
```

where ethn specifies the logical device (for example, eth0 or eth1).

Linux Command Quick Reference

The following list describes some of the most useful and popular Linux commands. Consult the manpage for each command to learn about additional arguments and details of operation.

adduser *userid*

Creates a new *userid*, prompting for necessary information (requires root privileges).

alias name=*'command'*

Defines name as an alias for the specified command.

apropos *keyword*

Searches the manual pages for occurrences of the specified keyword and prints short descriptions from the beginning of matching manual pages.

at *time*

at -f *file time*

Executes commands entered via STDIN (or by using the alternative form, the specified file) at the specified time. The time can be specified in a variety of ways; for example, in hour and minute format (*hh:mm)* or in hour, minute, month, day, and year format (*hh:mm mm/dd/yy).*

atq

Displays descriptions of jobs pending via the **at** command.

atrm *job*

Cancels execution of a job scheduled via the **at** command. Use the **atq** command to discover the identities of scheduled jobs.

bg

bg *jobs*

Places the current *job* (or by using the alternative form, the specified jobs) in the background, suspending its execution so that a new user prompt appears immediately. Use the **jobs** command to discover the identities of background jobs.

cal *month year*

    Displays a calendar for the specified month of the specified year.

cat *files*

    Displays the contents of the specified files.

cd

cd *directory*

    Changes the current working directory to the user's home directory or the specified directory.

chgrp *group files*

chgrp -R *group files*

    Changes the group of the specified files to the specified group. The alternative form of the command operates recursively, changing the group of subdirectories and files beneath a specified directory. The group must be named in the */etc/ groups* file, maintained by the **newgroup** command.

chmod *mode files*

chmod -R *mode files*

    Changes the access mode of the specified files to the specified mode. The alternative form of the command operates recursively, changing the mode of subdirectories and files beneath a specified directory.

chown *userid files*

chown -R *userid files*

    Changes the owner of the specified files to the specified *userid*. The alternative form of the command operates recursively, changing the owner of subdirectories and files beneath a specified directory

clear

    Clears the terminal screen.

cmp *file1 file2*

    Compares two files, reporting all discrepancies. Unlike the **diff** command, **cmp** can compare multiple files and binary files.

cp *file1 file2*

cp *files directory*

cp -R *files directory*

    Copies a file to another file or directory or copies a subdirectory and all its files to another directory.

date

date *date*

    Displays the current date and time or changes the system date and time to the specified value, of the form *MMddhhmmyy* or *MMddhhmmyyyy*.

df

    Displays the amount of free disk space on each mounted filesystem.

diff *file1 file2*
> Compares two files, reporting all discrepancies. Similar to the **cmp** command, though the output format differs.

dmesg
> Displays the messages resulting from the most recent system boot.

du
du *directories*
> Displays the amount of disk space used by the current directory (or the specified directories) and its (their) subdirectories.

echo *string*
echo -n *string*
> Displays the specified text on the standard output stream. The -**n** option causes omission of the trailing newline character.

fdformat *device*
> Formats the media inserted in the specified floppy disk drive. The command performs a low-level format only; it does not create a filesystem. To create a filesystem, issue the **mkfs** command after formatting the media.

fdisk *device*
> Edits the partition table of the specified hard disk.

fg
fg *jobs*
> Brings the current job (or the specified jobs) to the foreground.

file *files*
> Determines and prints a description of the type of each specified file.

find *path* -**name** *pattern* -**print**
> Searches the specified path for files with names matching the specified pattern (usually enclosed in single quotes) and prints their names. The **find** command has many other arguments and functions; see the online documentation.

finger *users*
> Displays descriptions of the specified users.

free
> Displays the amount of used and free system memory.

ftp *hostname*
> Opens an FTP connection to the specified host, allowing files to be transferred. The FTP program provides subcommands for accomplishing file transfers; see the online documentation.

grep *pattern files*
grep -i *pattern files*
grep -n *pattern files*
grep -v *pattern files*

> Searches the specified files for text matching the specified pattern (usually enclosed in single quotes) and prints matching lines. The **-i** option specifies that matching is performed without regard to case. The **-n** option specifies that each line of output is preceded by the filename and line number. The **-v** option reverses the matching, causing nonmatched lines to be printed.

gzip *files*
gunzip *files*

> Expands or compresses the specified files. Generally, a compressed file has the same name as the original file, followed by *.gz*.

head *files*

> Displays the first several lines of each specified file.

hostname
hostname *name*

> Displays (or sets) the name of the host.

info

> Launches the GNU Texinfo help system.

init *runlevel*

> Changes the system runlevel to the specified value (requires *root* privileges).

insmod *module*

> Dynamically loads the specified module (requires *root* privileges).

ispell *files*

> Checks the spelling of the contents of the specified files.

jobs

> Displays all background jobs.

kill *process_ids*
kill -l
kill -signal *process_ids*

> Kills the specified processes, prints a list of available signals, or sends the specified processes the specified signal (given as a number or name).

killall *program*
killall -signal *program*

> Kills all processes that are instances of the specified program or sends the specified signal to all processes that are instances of the specified program.

less *file*

> Lets the user peruse a file too large to be displayed as a single screen (page) of output. The **less** command, which is more powerful than the **more** command,

provides many subcommands that let the user navigate the file. For example, the spacebar moves forward one page, the **b** key moves back one page, and the **q** key exits the program.

links *URL*
> Views the specified web page.

ln *old new*
ln -s *old new*
> Creates a hard (or soft) link associating a new name with an existing file or directory.

locate *pattern*
> Locates files with names containing the specified pattern. Uses the database maintained by the **updatedb** command.

lpq
> Displays the entries of the print queue.

lpr *files*
> Displays the specified files.

lprm *job*
> Cancels printing of the specified print queue entries. Use **lpq** to determine the contents of the print queue.

ls
ls *files*
ls -a *files*
ls -l *files*
ls -lR *files*
> Lists (nonhidden) files in the current directory or the specified files or directories. The **-a** option lists hidden files as well as nonhidden files. The **-l** option causes the list to include descriptive information, such as file size and modification date. The **-R** option recursively lists the subdirectories of the specified directories.

mail
> Launches a simple mail client that permits sending and receiving email messages.

man *title*
man *section title*
> Displays the specified manpage.

mkdir *directories*
mkdir -p *directories*
> Creates the specified directories. The **-p** option causes creation of any parent directories needed to create a specified directory.

mkfs -t *type device*
> Creates a filesystem of the specified type (such as *ext3* or *msdos*) on the specified *device* (requires *root* privileges).

mkswap *device*

Creates a Linux swap space on the specified hard disk partition (requires *root* privileges).

more *file*

Lets the user peruse a file too large to be displayed as a single screen (page) of output. The **more** command provides many subcommands that let the user navigate the file. For example, the spacebar moves forward one page, the **b** key moves back one page, and the **q** key exits the program.

mount

mount *device directory*

mount -o *option* **-t** *type device directory*

Displays the mounted devices or mounts the specified device at the specified mount point (generally a subdirectory of */mnt*). The mount command consults */etc/fstab* to determine standard options associated with a device. The command generally requires *root* privileges. The -o option allows specification of a variety of options, for example, **ro** for read-only access. The -t option allows specification of the filesystem type (for example, *ext3*, *msdos*, or *iso9660*, the filesystem type generally used for CD-ROMs).

mv *paths target*

Moves the specified files or directories to the specified target.

newgroup *group*

Creates the specified group.

passwd

passwd *user*

Changes the current user's password or that of the specified user (requires *root* privileges). The command prompts for the new password.

pico

pico *file*

Launch **pico** to edit the specified file, if any.

ping -n *ip_address*

ping *host*

Sends an echo request via TCP/IP to the specified host. A response confirms that the host is operational.

pr *files*

Formats the specified files for printing, by inserting page breaks and so on. The command provides many arguments and functions.

ps

ps -aux

Displays the processes associated with the current *userid* or displays a description of each process.

pwd

Displays the absolute path corresponding to the current working directory.

reboot

Reboots the system (requires *root* privileges).

reset

Clears the terminal screen and resets the terminal status.

rm *files*
rm -f *files*
rm -i *files*
rm -if *files*
rm -rf *files*

Deletes the specified files or (when the **-r** option is specified) recursively deletes all subdirectories of the specified files and directories. The **-f** option suppresses confirmation; the **-i** option causes the command to prompt for confirmation. Because deleted files cannot generally be recovered, the **-f** option should be used only with extreme care, particularly when used by the *root* user.

rmdir *directories*
rmdir -p *directories*

Deletes the specified empty directories or (when the **-p** option is specified) the empty directories along the specified path.

scp *host1:file host2:*

Copies *file* from *host1* to *host2*, via SSH.

shutdown *minutes*
shutdown -h *minutes*
shutdown -r *minutes*

Shuts down the system after the specified number of minutes elapses (requires *root* privileges). The **-r** option causes the system to be rebooted once it has shut down. If the **-r** option is absent, the system is halted and powered off; the **-h** option also halts and shuts down the system. Alternatively, **now** can be used instead of *minutes*, which forces an immediate reboot or halt of the system.

sleep *time*

Causes the command interpreter to pause for the specified number of seconds.

sort *files*

Sorts the specified files. The command has many useful arguments; see the online documentation.

split *file*

Splits a file into several smaller files. The command has many arguments; see the online documentation.

ssh *host* **-l** *userid*

Logs in to *host* via SSH, using the specified *userid*.

su

su *user*

su -

su - *user*

> Changes the current *userid* to *root* or to the specified *userid* (the latter requires *root* privileges). The - option establishes a default environment for the new *userid*.

swapoff *device*

> Disables use of the specified device for swapping (requires *root* privileges).

swapon *device*

> Enables use of the specified device for swapping (requires *root* privileges).

sync

> Completes all pending input/output operations (requires *root* privileges).

tail *file*

tail -f *file*

tail -n *file*

> Displays the last several lines of the specified files. The -**f** option causes the command to continuously print additional lines as they are written to the file. The -**n** option specifies the number of lines to be printed.

talk *user*

> Launches a program that allows a chatlike dialog with the specified user.

tar cvf *tar_file files*

tar zcvf *tar_file files*

> Creates a tar file with the specified name, containing the specified files and their subdirectories. The **z** option specifies that the tarfile will be compressed.

tar xvf *tar_file*

tar zxvf *tar_file*

> Extracts the contents of the specified tarfile. The **z** option specifies that the tarfile has been compressed.

telnet *host*

> Opens a login session on the specified host.

time

> Times the execution of a job.

top

> Displays a display of system processes that's continually updated until the user presses the **q** key.

touch *file*

> Changes *file* access time. If the specified file does not exist, the command creates an empty (new) file.

traceroute *host*

> Uses echo requests to determine and print a network path to the host.

umask *mask*

Specifies default permissions assigned to created directories and files.

umount *device*

Unmounts the specified filesystem (generally requires *root* privileges).

uname -a

Displays information about the system.

unzip *file*

Unzips a compressed file.

uptime

Displays the system uptime.

w

Displays the current system users.

wall

Displays a message to each user except those who've disabled message reception. Type **Ctrl-D** to end the message.

wc *files*

Displays the number of characters, words, and lines in the specified files.

who

Displays information about system users.

zip *file*

Compresses the specified file.

Table D-1 identifies Linux commands that perform functions similar to MS-DOS commands. The operation of the Linux command is not generally identical to that of the corresponding MS-DOS command. See the index to this book or the Linux online documentation for further information about Linux commands.

Table D-1. MS-DOS commands and related Linux commands

MS-DOS	Linux
ATTRIB	chmod
CD	cd
CHKDSK	df, du
DELTREE	rm -R
DIR	ls -l
DOSKEY	(built-in; no need to launch separately)
EDIT	pico, vi, and so on
EXTRACT	tar
FC	cmp, diff
FDISK	fdisk
FIND	grep

Table D-1. MS-DOS commands and related Linux commands (continued)

MS-DOS	Linux
FORMAT	fdformat
MORE	more
MOVE	mv
SORT	sort
START	at, bg
XCOPY, XCOPY32	cp

Index

We'd like to hear your suggestions for improving our indexes. Send email to *index@oreilly.com.*

I

i386, 13
i486, 13
if command, 268
ifconfig command, 273
Impress (OpenOffice.org), 108–110
info command, 300
init= boot argument, 288
init command, 257, 300
init.d, 191
initialization files, 279–281
initrd command (GRUB), 285
inittab file, 257
input focus, 77
input redirection, 259–261
input validation (Calc), 106
insmod command, 300
installing Red Hat Linux, 13–28, 29–67
    aborting the install, 56
    authentication, 51
    importance of backups, 30
    Boot Loader Configuration, 46
    boot partition requirements, 26
    booting the install, 30–32
        from CD-ROM, 30
        from floppy, 30
        PCMCIA and SCSI devices,
            complications associated with, 30
    CPUs, supported, 13
    custom installation, 21, 37
    default operating system, choosing, 47
    drives, requirements, 14
    emergency boot floppy, creating, 57
    hard disks, preparing, 21–26
        (see also hard disks)
    informational resources, 66
    installation types, 37
    installation user interface, 33–34
        graphical install, absence of, 35
    keyboard selection, 36
    language configuration, 50
    language selection, 36
    minimum hardware requirements, 13–14
    monitoring, 35
    motherboards, 14
    mouse configuration, 36
    MS Windows, collecting information
        from, 16
    network configuration, 47–50
    Online Help, 34
    packages, selection and
        installation, 53–56

    partition requirements, 25
    personal desktop installation, 20
    problems, 14
    required system configuration
        information, 15
    server installation, 21
    Setup Agent, 61–64
    step-by-step procedure, 29
    system clock, configuration, 51
    system information required for, 14–19
    text-based install, 35
    troubleshooting, 66
    types of installations, 19–21
    user accounts, configuration, 51
    video configuration, 57–60
    windows displayed during install, 33
    workstation, 21
Intel, supported and unsupported
    processors, 13
Interaction (Impress), 110
Internet
    accessing with Linux, 193–210
    security demands, 217
    setting up services, 232–250
iobase option, 290
IP addresses, 16
    masquerading, 245, 247
iptables service, 247
IRC (Internet Relay Chat), xii
irq option, 291
iso9660 filesystem, 70
is_pas_card option, 291
ispell command, 300

J

jobs command, 300

K

K5 and K6 processors, 13
KDE desktop, 8, 54, 93–101
    application links, 100
    configuring, 97
    Control Center, 98
    default desktop, chosing for, 182
    file manager, 95
    informational resources, 100
    Konqueror, 95
    Konsole, 97
    Panel, 97
    under Red Hat Linux 8.0, 81
    session, launching, 93

M

magic_number option, 291
mail command, 301
mailing lists, Red Hat Linux, 67
man command, 125–127, 301
manpages, 125–127
masquerading hosts, 245
MBR (Master Boot Record), 284
membase option, 291
metacharacters, 252–254
Microsoft
  operating systems, booting via
    GRUB, 286
  Windows
    applications, running in Linux, 12
    fdisk, 23–25
    filesystems, supported, 22
    installation information, collection
      from, 16
    Linux, compared to, 9
    Task manager, Linux equivalent
      to, 185
    Windows 2000/XP, Disk Management
      tool, 25
Microsoft Office
  Excel, compared to Calc, 105
  OpenOffice.org, compared to, 102
  PowerPoint, compared to Impress, 108
  Word, compared to Writer, 103
minimum hardware requirements, 13–14
Minix, 6
mkbootdisk command, 283
mkdir command, 131, 301
  in FTP, 235
mkfs command, 301
mkswap command, 302
modem configuration, 194–199
modes, 73
modprobe command, 294
modular drivers, 294–296
  dynamic loading, 294
modular kernels, 294
monitor configuration, 59
  risks, 60
monolithic kernels, 294
more command, 302
motherboards, 14
mount command, 140, 302
mount points, 41, 140
mounting filesystems, 74
mouse configuration, 36
mouse operations, 79

Mozilla web browser, 204–206
MS-DOS, 10
  commands and Linux equivalents, 305
  filesystem, 70
    loading onto floppy disks, 141
Multics (Multiplexed Information and
    Computing Service), 4
mv command, 133, 302

N

name daemon, 245
name servers, configuring, 244
named, 245
Nautilus, 85, 87–89
Navigator (Writer), 105
NetBIOS, 213
netmasks, 16
network adapter, information required for
    installing, 18
Network Administration Tool, 194
  host configuration using, 211
network clients, 193
network configuration, collecting
    information for, 18
networking, 193–204
  cable modems, 210
  configuration, 47–50
  DSL, 210
  LANs, setting up, 211–227
  Periscope script, 271–274
  Samba (see Samba)
  security, 250
  wireless adaptors, 201
newgroup command, 302
Nmap, 248–249
nmbd, 213
none option, 291
non-Intel processors, 13
noprobe option, 291
no_reset option, 291
nowerr option, 291
NTFS filesystem, 10, 70
  partitioning, 28
null device file, 260
numerical access mode values, 138

O

Online Help, 34
OpenOffice.org, 102–110
  Calc, 105–106
  Draw, 107

word processors (Writer), 103–105
working directory, 128
workstation installation, 21
Writer (OpenOffice.org), 103–105
wvdial, 193, 208–209
    default routes and, 272
wvdial.conf, 208

X

X Consortium, 8
X logins, 169
X Windows System, 7, 54, 74
    closing, 257
    configuring, 57–60
    failed login, 66

keyboard operations and, 77
    shell environment, starting from, 257
    terminating, 78
    troubleshooting, 55
XDMCP tabs, GDM Setup tool, 169
xDSL device type, 198
XFree86, 75
XFree86 Project, Inc., 8, 75
Ximian Evolution, 110
xinetd
    FTP clients and, 233
    Samba launch, configuring for, 214

Z

zip command, 136, 305

About the Author

Bill McCarty is associate professor of web and information technology in the School of Business and Management of Azusa Pacific University, Azusa, California, and was previously associate professor of computer science, in which capacity he taught for ten years in Azusa Pacific's Master of Applied Computer Science program.

Bill holds a Ph.D. in the management of information systems from the Claremont Graduate University, Claremont, California, and worked for 15 years as a software developer and manager.

Colophon

Our look is the result of reader comments, our own experimentation, and feedback from distribution channels. Distinctive covers complement our distinctive approach to technical topics, breathing personality and life into potentially dry subjects.

The cover image of a man wearing a wide-brimmed hat is a 19th-century engraving from *Marvels of the New West: A Vivid Portrayal of the Stupendous Marvels in the Vast Wonderland West of the Missouri River*, by William Thayer (The Henry Bill Publishing Co., 1888).

Jane Ellin was the production editor and proofreader for *Learning Red Hat Linux*, Third Edition. Jeff Holcomb, Andrew Savikas, Genevieve d'Entremont, Sarah Sherman, and Claire Cloutier provided quality control. Mary Brady, Darren Kelly, and Dave Read provided production support. John Bickelhaupt wrote the index.

Edie Freedman designed the cover of this book. Emma Colby produced the cover layout with QuarkXPress 4.1 using Adobe's ITC Garamond font. David Futato designed the CD labels.

Bret Kerr designed the interior layout, based on a series design by David Futato. The chapter opening images are from the Dover Pictorial Archive, *Marvels of the New West*, and *The Pioneer History of America: A Popular Account of the Heroes and Adventures*, by Augustus Lynch Mason, A.M. (The Jones Brothers Publishing Company, 1884). This book was converted by Joe Wizda to FrameMaker 5.5.6 with a format conversion tool created by Erik Ray, Jason McIntosh, Neil Walls, and Mike Sierra that uses Perl and XML technologies. The text font is Linotype Birka; the heading font is Adobe Myriad Condensed; and the code font is LucasFont's TheSans Mono Condensed. The illustrations that appear in the book were produced by Robert Romano and Jessamyn Read using Macromedia FreeHand 9 and Adobe Photoshop 6. The tip and warning icons were drawn by Christopher Bing.